*Us*
کے ساتھ

"Thrity Umrigar has created two wonderfully sympathetic characters who d... [Individual...] ...nsible.... This is ... Intimate... ...t the sensuous ... ...ife of the privileged is harshly in... ...erless, but empathy and compassion are evoked by both strong women, each of whom is forced to make a separate choice. Umrigar is a skilled storyteller, and her memorable characters will live on for a long time."

—*Washington Post Book World*

"Umrigar is a perceptive and often piercing writer.... Her portrait of Sera as a woman unable to transcend her middle-class skin feels bracingly honest." —*New York Times Book Review*

"Remarkable.... What makes *The Space Between Us* so engrossing is its ability to make readers feel empathy for its subjects.... To read Umrigar's novel is to catch a glimpse of a foreign culture, for better and for worse.... Class colors everything, but in the end, Umrigar shows, life's ups and downs are available to us all."

—*San Francisco Chronicle*

"[*The Space Between Us*] is a great book; I love it.... I couldn't stop reading until Bhima had her amazing epiphany of freedom at the edge of the sea. I am so happy for Thrity Umrigar! And proud of her as a woman, too.... It is so precious to have a book about a woman one rarely even 'sees' in society, whether Indian or American."

—Alice Walker

"[*The Space Between Us*] is provocative and disturbing."

—*Boston Globe*

"An eloquent tale, whose heart-stopping plot twists reveal the ferocity of fate."

—*Booklist* (starred review)

"Engaging. . . . Umrigar is an accomplished, natural storyteller."

—*Publishers Weekly*

"An affecting portrait of a woman and her maid, whose lives, despite class disparity, are equally heartbreaking. . . . A subtle, elegant analysis of class and power. Umrigar transcends the specifics of two Bombay women and creates a novel that quietly roars against tyranny."

—*Kirkus Reviews*

"Umrigar evocatively describes daily life in two very different households in modern-day Bombay, where the traditions that separate the classes and the sexes still persist. . . . Umrigar beautifully and movingly wends her way through the complexities and subtleties of these unequal but caring relationships."

—*Library Journal*

"With humanity and suspense, novelist Thrity Umrigar tackles love, loyalty, injustice—and survival."

—*Marie Claire*

"An intimate slice of Bombay . . . layered with keen, feminine insight into class and family, betrayal, guilt, and love. . . . Umrigar understands the way love mixes with cruelty and loneliness. She is a connoisseur of guilt—and knows how to describe it. . . . She is at her best, however, conveying the small moments that sustain or degrade the minuet of intimacy."

—*Cleveland Plain Dealer*

"Out of India's seething hotchpotch of humanity, Thrity Umrigar has created two vivid female characters, each representative of thousands of real-life Indian women. . . . This ultimately tragic story is told against the vibrant backdrop of modern Mumbai. . . . The book's pages glow with descriptions of the city. . . . [Umrigar] tackles, across the span of her characters' lives, many of the issues affecting India today: poverty engendering poverty, the power of privilege and wealth, domestic violence, class, education, women's rights, AIDS. This adds richness, making *The Space Between Us* far more than an analysis of fate and a portrait of the bonds of womanhood. It is also a powerful social commentary on the glorious and frustrating jigsaw puzzle that is modern India."                                    —*The Economist*

PRAISE FOR
## *If Today Be Sweet*

"Umrigar has undertaken to show us the cultural divide between Indian and American cultures. . . . She makes an interesting point, one she's mentioned in other works: We make up our own families wherever we are; we choose our circumstances; we are capable of being heroes anywhere."                                    —*Washington Post*

"A poignant story. . . . What might have been just another story about widowhood is, in Umrigar's hands, a canvas on which love, death, family, pain, and personal transformation are subtly painted. Readers see through Tammy's eyes as she struggles to understand her new role in life and the new definition of family. This novel transcends culture."                                    —*Library Journal* (starred review)

"Umrigar renders a sublime, cross-cultural tale about lives driven by tradition and transformed by love."                    —*Booklist*

"A tender portrait of a Bombay widow and her Americanized son, and the culture clash that ensues. . . . Umrigar's intimate portrayal of a mother and son divided by culture is a convincing testament to the enduring power of place."                    —*Kirkus Reviews*

"Both the opportunities—and costs—of forging a new life in America are thoughtfully explored. Ultimately, the novel reflects on what makes an individual part of a community and movingly depicts the heartaches, responsibilities, and rewards of family life—among one's own blood relatives as well as one's 'family of choice.' . . . A meditation on the complex process of building a new life."

—*Charlotte Observer*

"A tender fourth novel. . . . Umrigar shows the unseemly side of American excess and prejudice while gently reminding readers of opportunities sometimes taken for granted."    —*Publishers Weekly*

# first darling of the morning

**Also by Thrity Umrigar**

*Bombay Time*

*The Space Between Us*

*If Today Be Sweet*

# First darling of the morning

Selected Memories of an Indian Childhood

## THRITY UMRIGAR

HARPER PERENNIAL

NEW YORK • LONDON • TORONTO • SYDNEY • NEW DELHI • AUCKLAND

HARPER ● PERENNIAL

First published in India in 2004 by HarperCollins Publishers India, a joint venture with The India Today Group.

P.S.™ is a trademark of HarperCollins Publishers.

FIRST U.S. EDITION

Library of Congress Cataloging-in-Publication Data is available upon request.

ISBN 978-0-06-145161-4

08  09  10  11  12    RRD    10  9  8  7  6  5  4  3  2  1

To JBU, HJU and ETK

*With endless love
and infinite gratitude*

# Acknowledgements

I ONCE READ A LINE that said something to the effect of, 'Thank God we don't get what we deserve in life.' While writing the story of my childhood, I have on more than one occasion appreciated the wisdom of that saying.

I would like to thank all the people who populate the pages of this book. Each one of you has had an impact on my life and has given me gifts that I am grateful for. While telling this story was emotionally painful at times, it has also given me a renewed appreciation for the world I grew up in and for the love that saved me. Even when that love came with strings attached and conditions, it still made a big difference in my life.

I thank my immediate family – my parents, uncle, and two aunts – for encouraging me to follow my dreams even when they were struggling with fulfilling their own. Their example of selfless love and sacrifice is one that I will spend a lifetime learning how to emulate. I thank my cousin Gulshan for teaching this only child what it was to have a sister. I thank Mani aunty for teaching me to fight with the moon.

I am also grateful to Eustathea Kavouras and Sara Throop for their encouragement – and Sara's occasional scoldings – in getting me to finish this memoir.

# One

I AM OF THAT GENERATION of middle-class, westernized, citified
Indian kids who know the words to Do-Re-Me better than
the national anthem. *The Sound of Music* is our call to arms
and Julie Andrews our Pied Piper. It is 1967 – Hollywood
movies always come to India a year or two after their
American release – and the alleys and homes of Bombay are
suddenly alive with the sound of music. No matter that the
movie has reached us over a year after it is a hit all over
the Western world. All the piano teachers in Bombay are
teaching their beginner students how to plunk Do-Re-Me
until it seems as if every middle-class Parsi household with
a piano emits only one tune.

I am six years old and suffer from an only child's fantasy
of what life with siblings would be like. *The Sound of Music*
gives flight to that fantasy, provides it with shape and
colour. The laughter, the camaraderie, the teasing, the close-
knittedness of the Von Trapp family ensnares me, forever
setting my standard of what a perfect family should be. The
Von Trapps are as light and sunny as my family is dark; they
whistle and sing while the adults in my household are
moody and silent; the children are as shiny and healthy and
robust as I am puny and sickly and awkward. To see those
seven children up on that large screen, standing in descending
order of age and height, is to see heaven itself. My heart
bursts with joy and longing; I want to leave my seat and
crawl into the screen and into the warm, welcoming arms
of Maria. Take me in, I want to say, give me some time

and I will be as witty and playful and musical as the rest of you.

I have already seen the movie once but now I want to go again. Dad and his brother Pesi, whom I call Babu, decide that the entire family should go see the movie together. As always, my reclusive aunt, Mehroo, refuses to accompany us. 'Come on, Mehroo, it's a nice, wholesome family movie. You will enjoy it,' says my aunt Freny, Babu's wife, but to no avail. Pappaji, my grandfather, has recently had a heart attack and Mehroo refuses to leave him home alone even though he is perfectly mobile.

Mehroo is my dad's unmarried sister who lives with us. The oldest of my dad's two siblings, her childhood ended on the day her mother died. Mehroo was then eleven. Not only were there two younger brothers to raise (my dad, the youngest, was only four) but there was a father to protect from the razor's edge of his own grief. She took over the family duties as though she had been born for that role. Her father was a kindly man but he was so wrapped up in his own sorrow that he failed to notice the sad look come into his daughter's eyes, a sadness that would stalk her for the rest of her life. I suppose that from her father's lasting grief and devotion to his dead wife, from his endless mourning, Mehroo formed her own notions of what love should be. And what family became for her was a profession, a job, a hobby, an avocation. Family was all. Outside of its protective borders lay the troubled world, full of deceit and deceptions and broken promises and betrayals. It was an astonishingly limited worldview but it made her irreplaceable within our family structure.

Mehroo's love for me is legendary throughout the neighbourhood. So are her eccentricities.

She won't go to the movies – an amazing feat in a movie-crazy family.

She won't buy new clothes for herself. If someone in the family buys her material for a dress, she will save it for years before she will take it to the tailor.

She uses the same comb even after three of its teeth fall out, until my father finally throws it away in a pique of anger. But she frequently slips money to me when I leave for school.

She is a vegetarian in a household where chicken and meat, being as expensive as they are, are treats. If a spoon that's been in the chicken curry accidentally touches her potato curry, she will not eat it. And yet, she will cook meat for the rest of us.

She will eat food cold from the fridge without warming it up, although she will spend hours in the kitchen cooking for the family.

She refuses to pose for pictures, covering her face with her hands to avoid the camera. When she is compelled (by me, when I'm older) to be photographed, she refuses to smile. Every picture of her shows a serious, unsmiling woman. In some of them, her lips even curl downward.

She is miserly, cheap, teary, sentimental, thin-skinned, fiercely loyal, eccentric, indifferent to the world outside her family and devoted to her loved ones.

How do you solve a problem like Mehroo?

My cousin, Roshan, once mutters that if Mehroo was the next door neighbour, she wouldn't like her very much. The remark tears me up. I fancy that I understand Mehroo, in all of her contradictions, better than anyone else; that somehow I have X-ray vision that allows me access to the innermost chamber of her warm and soft heart. There is something elemental and primitive about my love for Mehroo and when I think of her, I think of her in animalistic terms – as a dog or a horse or a giraffe or a zebra, animals with sorrowful, kind eyes.

Now I decide that the movie situation calls for my brand of lethal, irresistible charm. 'Please, Mehroofui, please come,' I beg her. 'Just once, please, for my sake. I love this movie the best of all. You will, too, I promise.'

She shakes her head no, her brown eyes looking at me pleadingly. I sing a few lines from the movie, hoping to entice her that way. But she will not budge.

Pappaji finally erupts. 'Ja nee,' he says. 'Bachha ne dookhi karech. Making my little one unhappy like this. Nothing is going to happen to me in one evening. Treating me as if I'm a six-year-old schoolboy in half pants.'

It works. Mehroo comes and there we are on a Saturday evening, sitting in the comfortable seats at Regal Cinema, waiting for the red velvet curtain to rise and for Julie Andrews to burst forth onto the screen in full-throated glory. We sit in a long row: myself, Mehroo, Roshan and her parents, Freny and Babu, and my mom and dad. I can barely stay still on my seat because of my excitement. Even before the curtain has lifted, the magic, the promise of *The Sound of Music* has come true. Here I am with my own family, all of us looking as close and loving and happy as the Von Trapp family. For months now, I have had this recurrent fantasy of my entire family lying together on a big bed, all of us happy and cosy, and turning to each other for shelter and warmth, as if the bed was a ship tossing on tumultuous waters. All of us under the same roof, together. This is the closest I've come to duplicating that feeling outside of dreams and my heart throbs with love and happiness. I feel swollen and large, as if I could elongate my hands to touch the back of their seats and embrace the long row of family members.

At this moment, I have no prescience of how the currents of life will pull me away from that idealized dream of family; of how long and far I will travel and how my travels will put that dream forever out of my reach. No idea then of how I will unwittingly be yet another loss in my family's chronicle of losses. There is nothing in this carefree moment to tell me that I will someday trade love for freedom, that I will turn my back on Mehroo's example of self-sacrifice and devotion to family, and instead choose self-preservation and independence. That I will build my life and dreams on the back of their sacrifices.

Yes, I will return to them over and over again but it will never be the same. I will come as a visitor and a tourist, will return with stories to show Mehroo the stamps on my body from the different places I have travelled but she will not be impressed. For they will only serve to remind her of what is missing from my life – the rootedness of home. And Mehroo's questioning eyes will follow me and the bewilderment in them will never diminish, will forever be the lump in my throat.

But before there is all that, there is this heavenly night at Regal Cinema. For this glorious moment, here we all are at the movies, just like any normal family. Mehroo's warm hand is in my lap and when I sneak a peek at her in the dark, she is smiling. Everybody seems to realize that this is a special occasion, with Mehroo accompanying us, and I feel the unspoken admiration of all the adults for having been the catalyst for this outing. During the intermission, Dad is characteristically generous and comes back loaded with chicken rolls, Sindhi samosas and bottles of Gold Spot and Coke.

Munching my chicken roll, singing along to the songs as familiar to me as my name, I am struck by a beam of pure happiness, a drop of golden sun. When Christopher Plummer sings the line, 'Bless my homeland forever,' my hair stands up, as it always does. When Ralph betrays the Von Trapps in the abbey, I turn to assure Mehroo, 'Don't worry. Nothing bad happens.' She nods and squeezes my hand.

For one blissful evening, I am no longer envious of the Von Trapp family. I leave the theatre that evening, knowing my place in the world. I am a member of a family that is large and loving and goes to the movies together. I am loved by a sad-eyed woman who loves me above all else. I am the daughter of a father who buys everybody Gold Spot and chicken rolls and a mother who held my hand tight on our way to the movie theatre. I am the reason they are all here, I am the one who has drawn Mehroo out of the house, I am the one responsible for the smiles on their faces.

I step out of the theatre and into the world feeling fluid and grand and irresistible.

Dad has enjoyed the family outing to the movies so much that a few days later, he suggests a picnic. I am thrilled. I have never been on a family picnic before. But before he can announce his idea at dinner, mom pulls him into their room for a quick talk. He emerges a few minutes later and tells me that on second thoughts, he'd like it if just the three of us – mom, myself and he – went on the picnic together. I am surprised but am too excited at the prospect to disagree or complain.

We are to go to Hanging Gardens. We plan the picnic for days, with dad even promising to skip his usual practice of spending most of Sunday morning and afternoon at the factory. Either Babu or dad visit the factory everyday, even on the days the machines aren't humming. The ritual is as much a gesture of respect and superstition as it is demanded by necessity. At home, Mehroo chides me if I accidentally refer to the business as being closed for the day. 'The factory is never closed,' she says. 'Just say, "We're not there for one day."' But on the day of the picnic, dad leaves for the factory at eight a.m. and is back home by ten, to pick up me and my mom. He honks the horn but as always, mom is running late and I lean over the railing of the balcony to tell him that she needs another half hour. Even from two floors up, I can sense his irritation. 'Okay, I'll come up then,' he says.

By the time we leave, it's almost eleven and dad is in a bad mood. 'How much I told you yesterday about wanting to leave on time. Now what's the use of being out in the noonday sun,' he mutters. 'Our skins will be black as coal in an hour.' Like many light-skinned Parsis, my dad treasures and protects his lemon-coloured skin as if it is the Kohinoor diamond. While walking, he will instinctively duck for the shade and when driving with the windows rolled down, he puts a yellow duster cloth over his right hand as it rests on the window, to protect it from the sun's angry rays.

The tension in the car is palpable and instinctively I try to chisel away at it. 'Ae, daddy, want to hear a new joke I learned?' I say, leaning forward from my back seat. I tell him the one about the porcupine and the peacock and my reward is a faint smile in the rearview mirror. But his mood is still dark as he glances frequently at my mother, as if expecting her to do or say something that will relieve the tension. But my mother looks resolutely outside the window and it is clear that no apology for tardiness will be forthcoming.

This calls for more drastic action. I know that nothing improves my father's mood as quickly as spending money on his family, so out of the blue I say, 'Daddy, I want a chocolate.' Sure enough, he brightens up. 'Done,' he says and stops at the next convenience store we pass. He removes a ten-rupee note from the front pocket of his shirt. 'Now, go into the store and ask for the kind of chocolate you want,' he says. 'Make sure you get the change.' I walk into the store feeling tall and important, clutching my ten-rupee note. I stand before a glass cabinet, selecting the chocolate I want. A salesman hovers overhead. 'Who are you with, beta?' he says. 'Your mummy-daddy are with you?'

'My daddy is waiting in the car,' I say. 'He sent me in to buy a chocolate. I can count change,' I say proudly.

I leave the store with a large Cadbury's orange chocolate. Once in the car, I hand my dad the change. He lets me keep the chocolate but the ruse is up. I don't really want to eat it at this time. 'Mummy, I'm not hungry right now,' I say. 'Can you keep this for me?' My mother gives me a quizzical look but takes the chocolate from me and tosses it on the dashboard. We keep driving.

I can tell by the tight expression on both their faces that my parents have exchanged words while I was in the store. I want to help but suddenly, I feel overwhelmingly tired and sleepy. I curl up in the back seat and fall asleep. As I drift into sleep, I hear a steady murmur of words from the front seat. They are having another fight.

'Thrituma, ootho,' I hear my father say. We are at Hanging Gardens and I thrill at the thought of climbing inside the Old Woman's Shoe and the other structures based on children's nursery rhymes. I have been to Hanging Gardens only once before and am thrilled beyond belief about being back.

We have walked a few feet away from the car, carrying our little bag of chicken and chutney sandwiches, when I remember the chocolate. 'Daddy, my chocolate. I want to eat it after lunch.' He immediately turns back to the car but when he returns, he is empty-handed. 'Forget the chocolate,' he says with a grin. 'It has totally melted on the dashboard. Mistake leaving it there.'

I look at him open-mouthed. Suddenly, wanting that chocolate is the most important thing in the world. 'But I want it,' I say. 'I saved that chocolate for later.'

'I know, Thritu,' he says. 'Don't worry, I'll buy you another one at the restaurant here. It's no problem.'

I feel something akin to panic. He is totally misunderstanding what I'm saying. My heart feels wild and untamed, as if I've swallowed an ocean. 'No, no, no, I don't want another chocolate. I want *my* chocolate, the one that's in the car.'

He sighs impatiently. 'Don't be silly,' he says. 'I told you, the chocolate is all melted onto the dashboard. You will need a fork to eat it. It has dirtied the whole dashboard. Come on, let's eat our sandwiches and then I'll buy you another one.'

A wail starts somewhere so deep within me, it feels like it's originating from my knees and carrying upwards. 'I want my chocolate,' I say. 'The same one. I don't want another one.'

'This is exactly like what she did with the sara cake,' mummy says and I know immediately what she means. A few months earlier Mehroo had brought home a sara cake, a chocolate pastry, from the small bakery my family had opened as a side business a few years earlier. She had offered it to me after dinner but I had said I was too full. 'Okay,' Mehroo said. 'You'll be hungry in one or two hours. Eat it then. Nice and fresh it is.' But I refused, telling her I didn't want it. 'Are you sure, Thrituma?' Mehroo asked. 'Sure you won't change your mind later?' And I shook my head no.

Mehroo took the chocolate pastry out of its paper foil and held it between her thumb and index finger. She looked at it for a second and then popped it into her mouth. The instant the pastry entered her mouth, regret flooded my body. 'I want it,' I said. 'I want that sara cake now.'

Mehroo stared at me aghast. 'Shoo, now. Ten-ten times I asked you and ten-ten times you said no.'

'I don't care,' I wailed. 'I want my cake now.'

'It's seven o'clock,' Mehroo said helplessly. 'The shop is closed. I'll bring you another one tomorrow, I promise.'

'I don't want another one. I want the same piece now only. Give me my cake back.'

At that time, mummy had chuckled at Mehroo's distressed retelling of the story. Now, she is not amused. People are turning their heads to look at us and my parents are aware of this. Mummy grabs my arm as if she is lifting a chicken's wing and starts walking. 'Come on,' she says under her breath. 'Acting like a baby in public. Policeman will come arrest you if you keep this up.'

It is the wrong thing to say. I am out of control now, refusing to move, demanding the same chocolate. 'Make it whole again,' I tell my dad. 'I don't want it melted. I want it like it was before.'

He stares at me with horror. He has never seen me like this, so out of control, and he must realize that there are aspects to his daughter he knows nothing about. 'Thrituma, be reasonable,' he says but reasonableness has melted away, like chocolate in the sun. Mummy takes over. 'Keep quiet immediately or I'll give you one tight slap,' she says, her lips thin with anger. 'Spoiling everybody's day like this.'

I am sobbing now. 'I want to see my chocolate,' I say. 'I want to see it.' I am thinking I want to say goodbye to it, like saying goodbye to a friend whom I have insulted or hurt but it is impossible to convey all this to the adults who are looking at me as if I am a monster they have created. 'You can't eat that chocolate, I told you,' dad says, and for the first time there is real anger in his voice.

'I don't care,' I scream. 'I want to see my chocolate.'

He moves quickly then. He spins around on his heel and starts walking toward the car. 'Okay, come on then. Let's see your chocolate.'

Mummy and I walk behind him, trying to keep up with his long, angry strides. He flings open the car door and asks me to get into the front seat. 'There's your chocolate,' he says, pointing to the brown, gooey pile in the middle of the dashboard. The sight of the melted chocolate fills me with unbearable sadness and a sense of betrayal. I am unsure whether I am the betrayer or the betrayed but there is a sense of a promise broken. I want to explain all this to my dad but I can't. My grief is muddy and opaque and I can't talk through it. All I can do is wail and the nasal, high-pitched sound I make feels absurdly satisfying.

Dad slips into the seat beside me. Gesturing to mummy, he says, 'Get in.' She looks as if she is about to argue with him but something about the tightness of his face shuts her up. She gets into the front seat, so that I am sandwiched between the two of them.

My father puts the car in reverse and the uncharacteristic violence with which he shifts the gears stuns me into silence. 'Where are we going?' I ask.

'We're going home,' he answers. 'Turning back. The day's been ruined anyway. Satisfied now?'

I cannot speak. I dare not speak. This is worse than any punishment he could've thought of. The lump in my throat is so big that it hurts to swallow. Disappointment, guilt, shame, regret, all compete to occupy the innermost chambers of my cold heart. My eyes fill with tears but I blink them away, not wanting to draw any attention to myself. I want to fold up my body like the origami the older girls make at school, to make myself as small and invisible as possible. Over my head I can feel my parents glowering at each other and this only makes things worse. I want to take back every wail, every misguided shriek that emitted from my throat. The chocolate, sitting on the dashboard like mud, repulses me now. I do not feel any sense of kinship or responsibility toward it any more. I look at it as objectively as someone waking up from a dream. What had I gotten so hysterical about?

At home, I creep up the stairs and cringe as my dad rings the doorbell. Mehroo's surprised face makes my misery even sharper.

There will be other picnics over the years – field trips from school, outings with neighbours, days spent at the beach with friends and other family members. But never again will it be just the three of us spending a Sunday afternoon at Hanging Gardens. Like a candy bar in the sun, the days of summer will melt away and never again will it be just the three of us, a girl and her parents spending a Sunday afternoon at Hanging Gardens.

# Two

MEHROO IS DESCENDING THE STAIRS and already I am on the balcony to wave her goodbye. I wait with bated breath until she comes down the stone steps that lead from the lobby of our apartment building to the street. As soon as she reaches the street she looks up to where I am waiting on the second floor balcony and waves to me.

I blink back my tears and smile, a wide, clown-like smile that I hope my aunt can see from two storeys below.

I am seven years old and it is the second week of summer vacation. At ten a.m. the sun is already a snarling beast, raining its hot breath on the people below. I know that by the time Mehroo walks the short distance from our lane to the main street to catch her bus, she will already be covered in sweat, her soft, cream-coloured cheeks flushed bright red.

Despite the dazzling brightness of the day, inside the house it is dark. I know that as soon as I leave this balcony after my ritualistic waving goodbye, I will enter a dark and frightening and lonely world. I will spend the hours of the day waiting for Mehroo or my dad or some other adult to come home and rescue me from my mother's wrath. I don't know exactly what awaits me today but I know it won't be good. There will be some swearing, some threats, some accusations about spending all my time with my nose buried inside that damn book. There might be the familiar sound of the cane swooshing through the air before it lands on my bony body. The thought of that makes me wince.

Mehroo has barely left the house and already there is a lump in my throat the size of China. I had wanted to go to the factory with her today, maybe stopping at Jaffer's on the way to pick up a novel for me to devour, but mummy said there was homework to do. Mehroo had tried protesting that it is only the second week of vacation, that there would be plenty of time for schoolwork later in the summer but mummy told her that in that case she should take over my schoolwork too, since she'd already taken over everything else and stolen her only child away from her. Then they had their daily morning fight and were quiet only when dad raised his voice and said he was leaving for work without any breakfast because he craved peace more than eggs. 'Not even eight in the morning and already I'm tired,' he cried. 'Like a towel that's been wrung out dry, that's how I go to work everyday.' They were quiet as he got dressed hurriedly and raced down the stairs to his car, his face red and excited. As he got into his car, Mehroo yelled at her brother from the balcony, 'Please be careful. Calm down. Drive safely.' Mummy stayed in her room.

I feel miserable because I have caused this fight. If only I had not asked to go to the factory, none of this would've happened. So that when mummy accuses me of creating friction between her and her husband, I silently agree.

And now, my aunt has also left the house and there's only me and mummy at home. I pray that the doorbell will ring and some visitor – perhaps her brother, perhaps a neighbour – someone will arrive. Someone who will deliver me, save me from the long stretch of the day.

My aunt is now a quarter of the way down the lane and already she has turned back and waved to me three times. This is our daily ritual, but still I hold my breath in anticipation of every turn and wave. Turn and wave. Will she do it again? Will she wave now? Or will something, somebody, distract her? Will she run into one of the neighbours, will they walk part of the way together and will she forget to wave? Forget me? Or will she see the 64-number bus approach and will she run the rest of the way to catch it, in the process forgetting her niece, who is standing on this balcony believing that her very life depends on being waved to?

Everyday, my sentimental aunt faithfully, diligently, waves. Deep inside, I know that this ritual, this public display of our love, is every bit as important to her as it is to me. And yet, I'm always afraid. Everyday I trick myself; scare myself by creating more and more implausible scenarios of why she may not wave to me on that particular day. Each day, I hold my breath and feel my stomach muscles clench and relax to the rhythms of her waving. Daily, I dread the moment when she reaches the end of the lane and makes the left turn onto the main road. That is the moment of reckoning, when I have to return to the darkness of the apartment.

But not yet. Mehroo has reached the end of the lane. She stops, turns back and waves. She even blows me some flying kisses. I wave back frantically, standing on my toes to make sure she can see me. Then, she turns the corner and is gone. But my heart doesn't dip yet because I know what is coming. This, too, is part of the ritual. And yet, for all its familiarity, it still feels like a miracle when I spot Mehroo again. She has walked a few paces onto the main road and then returned to the corner. She waves some more. My heart singing, I wave back.

Three times. Four times. She disappears and returns. Is gone and comes back. My love feels so thick and heavy, it tastes like blood. Or grief. For the rest of my life, they will feel the same, this thick love, this thick grief.

I never know which will be the last time that Mehroo will come back and wave, before the adult in her remembers she has a bus to catch, that she's needed at the factory where she does the book-keeping for my dad. So I stand on the balcony and wait and with every passing second, the sting of her absence, of her really being gone, gets sharper. Somedays, I wait there an entire five minutes, hoping against hope for her return, scarcely believing that she has really left me. Somedays, I wait several full minutes and am on the verge of moving away from the balcony, when her familiar small figure appears in the distance, as miraculous as the sun on the horizon. That evening, she will tell me of how she was at the nearby bus-stop and when she was convinced the bus was nowhere close, she asked the next person to keep her place in line and darted to the corner to wave to me one last time. Because she knew that, like the dog on the recording label of His Master's Voice, I would be waiting.

This is how I come to know love, from my sad-eyed, excessively sentimental, self-sacrificing, hypersensitive, spinster aunt, who raises me as if I had been born of her small hips, as if I had fed on her tiny breasts. So that I never think of motherhood as a biological concept; so that I understand that the bonds of motherhood are formed daily, by acts of kindness and affection and devotion. This is Mehroo's legacy to me and despite her straight-arrowed, unwavering devotion, it is a mixed legacy, filled with yearning and ambiguity and loss and longing. In some ways, it would scar me for life, make me old at sixteen, unable to trust the simplistic declarations and easy, glib depictions of love that I saw all around me. No easy promises for me, because I had experienced a love as brilliant and pure and sharp as a diamond. Forever more, love would be something to be fought for and won, something exalted to reach for, something hard but promising, like religion, like talking to God.

❖

I head back into the house and a feeling of dread trails behind me. Mummy is in her room, going through things in her closet and I can tell by the way she mutters to herself that she is in a bad mood. I head directly for the bathroom, intending to stay in there for as long as I can. It is only when the latch clicks in place that I feel safe.

My respite is short-lived. Mummy bangs on the bathroom door and tells me to come out immediately. 'I know all your tricks, you lazy girl,' she says. 'Trying to avoid your studies at all costs. If you're not out in two minutes flat, you see what I'll do to you.' She hits the door with her switch for good effect.

My mother has long, thin, crooked fingers and most of the time they are curled around one of her many switches. Sometimes, after a cane has worn away, she makes me accompany her to the small shop where she buys her supply. I watch while she handles different canes, some long, thin and tapering, others that are shorter, thicker and blunter. I hold my breath while she picks them out, testing them with one hand on the open palm of the other. The longer ones make more of a swishing sound than the others.

My mother tutors many of the kids in the neighbourhood and most of them are older than me. During summer vacations, instead of going to the hill-stations or the beach, they gather at our house to study to get a jump-start on the following term. I love having them over because it takes the focus off me and because many of the savvy older kids kiss up to me because I am the teacher's daughter.

There is this one girl, Pervin, who is several years older than the others. She is a bit slow and it is rumoured that she has repeated several grades, which makes her an object of pity and silent derision. 'Stupid Pervin' I hear my mother call her behind her back. But she makes up for her slowness by her good-nature and perpetual cheerfulness. Pervin's face is covered with acne and it is my particular misfortune that Pervin has taken to making public displays of hugging and kissing me every chance she gets. Part of it is genuine affection but surely part of it is mere posturing, trying to get in the teacher's good books by sucking up to her only child. I run and hide from Pervin every chance I get because I am repulsed by her rough, acne-filled face as it brushes my smooth cheek. One day, I am eating porridge for breakfast when I glance in the bowl and realize that it looks and feels like Pervin's face. I stop eating porridge after that.

Most of the students my mother tutors are children of parents who are lower middle-class and who are grateful that my mother does not charge them much. Also, my mother is known throughout the neighbourhood for her dedication as a teacher. Unlike other tutors, she never looks at the clock while teaching, so that during the summer months, her students spend nearly the whole day at our place. The grateful parents never question my mother's teaching methods, just as they never question the red welts on their children's hands and legs when they return home. The smarter male students start wearing long pants to protect their legs from the sting of the cane but my mother complains about this lack of free access to their legs and their parents make them wear short pants again.

But today, it is just me and mummy at home. I want to ask where the others are but mummy has threatened to beat me if I look up from my textbook. I am sitting on the black velvet chair in her room with my left leg tied to the leg of the chair. She is forced to do this because I have a short attention span and get up too many times to go to the bathroom.

The day wears on. Finally, at one p.m., the doorbell rings. It is one of our neighbours, a woman who always moves at lightning speed and talks so fast I have trouble keeping up with her. Her son, Bomi, is with her. Bomi is a nervous looking boy who is one of my mother's students. He is short, chubby and he smells faintly of the coconut oil that his mother uses to slick down his black hair. The oil runs down his forehead, so that it is always shiny. He is just a little younger than me and my mother loves him because he is so obviously terrified of her. My mother claims to love children and she does because they don't fight back, because on their smooth, tender bodies she can leave her signature – the red welts that proclaim, 'I was here.' Because on their blank psyches she can leave her thumbprint, like black smudges that proclaim, 'I exist.' Unlike the adults in her life, the children she can control, manipulate and dominate. I can't articulate any of this but I know it somewhere deep down within me.

'I was wondering if I can drop Bomi off for the afternoon,' the neighbour is saying. 'My mother-in-law has taken ill and I just got a call asking if I can spend the day with her. He would just be in the way. Besides, he needs help with his schoolwork.'

'Oh sure, sure,' mummy replies. 'You go without a second thought. You know he will be safe here. We were just going to eat lunch. He can eat with us.'

The grateful woman gives mummy a quick hug and leaves.

After lunch, we sit down with our books again. Mummy begins to grill us on our spelling. We both do well until Bomi stumbles on a word. Mummy smiles benevolently and gives him a second chance. She throws him another word. But Bomi is now scared, and as often happens with him, his brain shuts down. He stares at my mother, a faint line of saliva trickling out of his open mouth.

There is a bathroom attached to my parents' bedroom and in a deceptively quiet voice, my mother asks Bomi to please step into it. His punishment is to stand in a corner of the bathroom on one leg.

Bomi tries but after a few minutes, begins to shift his weight from one stocky leg to another. My mother notices immediately. 'Do you have to do soo-soo?' she asks in a kindly way.

Bomi's eyes widen. 'No, aunty,' he says, the weight of his body frozen on one leg.

Her voice changes, becomes sharper. 'Because if you have to do soo-soo, do it in your pants. That's why you are in the bathroom. Otherwise, stand still.'

Several minutes pass. I sit on the black velvet chair in her bedroom and pretend to read my book. I want to leave the room but don't want to make any move that will draw attention to myself. I set my face in a sympathetic expression that I hope Bomi notices and my mother doesn't.

Finally, Bomi begins to cry softly to himself. I feel bad for him but another part of me is relieved that it is him and not me, who is the focus of this humiliation.

The crying upsets my mother who is sitting on her bed. 'Stop your crying,' she says, reaching for the ever-present cane and bringing it down on the bed for emphasis.

Bomi tries to swallow his sobs. 'Come out of the bathroom,' she orders him but Bomi is paralysed, his eyes wide with fear.

'Are you disobeying me? Chal, come out right now,' she repeats and this time there is a menace in her voice that I recognize.

As if in slow motion, Bomi lifts his leg over the threshold of the bathroom and walks around the bed to face her. I hold my breath.

Whoosh! The cane leaves an angry outline where it touches his bare leg. And another. For a moment, Bomi looks too stunned to cry. Then he bursts into tears, his chest moving up and down.

'No crying. *No crying*,' she orders and his lower lip moves like blubber as he tries to swallow his tears.

'Hold out your hand.'

I cannot watch. The cane to the legs I can handle but this voluntary holding out of an open palm, is the worst punishment. To do this you have to screw up all your courage, will your entire body into the gesture, enlist the help of every muscle, and then focus on the effort of not pulling your hand away at the last minute. Because it is understood that if she misses, if the cane hits open air instead of soft flesh, then there's more punishment. Then, the original crime may be forgotten and the crime of insubordination must first be dealt with.

If you do not pull your hand away, if you shut your eyes and hold your hand out steadily, if you prepare yourself for the current of pain that will run through your body at any second, still, the first whack comes as an insult, a shock to the system. Or worse, she will sometimes first tap the cane against your palm, as if to steady her hand, and just as you relax and let down your guard, the cane slices through the air and finds its deadly mark.

So I shut my eyes as poor Bomi stands there flinching, his open palm ready to meet the landing of the cane. Then, at the last minute, as if I cannot avert my eyes from the train wreck about to happen, my eyes fly open of their own volition and I am in time to see the cane make an arc in the air. I wince but at the last minute my mother pulls back, like a fisherman deciding to uncast a line, so that the cane gently grazes Bomi's fingertips.

'No punishment today,' my mother says but Bomi acts as if he has not heard her, his body still tense, his hand still outstretched.

'No punishment,' she repeats. 'Instead, we will just talk.'

She flashes me a quick look and her left eye closes in a half-wink.

'Tell me,' she says, in a pleasant voice, 'did you eat dinner yesterday?'

Bomi stares at her wordlessly, as surprised as I am by this sudden turn of events.

'Answer.'

'Y-yes, aunty.'

'What did you eat?'

Bomi thinks. 'Sali boti.' A meat dish.

My mother licks her lips quickly. 'Was the sali boti tasty? Did you like it?'

'Y-yes, aunty.' The voice is thin, as if he is about to faint.

'What kind of meat did your mummy use?'

Bomi looks at her inquiringly, confused. 'I don't know,' he mumbles at last.

'You don't know? I'll tell you. It was rat meat. Your mummy cooks dead rats for dinner.'

'No she doesn't.' Bomi's indignant voice is loud, as if parental loyalty has vanquished his fear.

My mother grins. 'Rat meat,' she repeats. 'Tell me, where does your mother catch the rats from?'

'We don't eat rat meat,' Bomi mumbles crossly.

Whoosh. The cane lands across his fleshy thighs. 'Tell me,' she says again. 'Where does your mother catch the rats?' And before he can answer, she hits him again.

Bomi suddenly starts wailing, a sound so loud and hair-raising, I can't believe that none of the neighbours ring the doorbell. I gaze desperately at the clock but I don't quite know how to tell the time. But I know it's too early for my aunt to be home from work. Nobody will come in time to rescue this boy.

Suddenly, he stops wailing, as if something inside him has abruptly pulled a plug. 'From the top of the water tank,' he blubbers. 'That's where the rats live, in a nest.'

My mother looks delighted at this unexpected bonanza. 'Top of the water tank? In the bathroom?'

He nods.

'And how does she get there?'

'A stool. She puts the stool in the bathroom and stands on it and catches the rats.'

'And then she feeds them to you for dinner?'

'Yes, yes. Feeds me rats for dinner. From the tank, yes.' And the chest heaves again.

My mother suddenly looks exhausted. She lifts the top end of the mattress and tucks the cane underneath it. Tenderly, she pulls Bomi toward her and kisses the top of his greasy head. 'Come here, you stupid boy. Now tomorrow, come here knowing all your spellings, understand? And if someone asks you what you ate for dinner, say you ate rat meat, okay?'

For the rest of the afternoon she is in a good mood, laughing even when Bomi makes a careless mistake in a math problem. When Bomi's dad comes to pick him up later in the day, she kisses the boy again. Bomi smiles his open smile. 'Thank you for the tuition lesson, aunty. Bye.'

That evening, as she is pulling me alongside her as we go on our daily visit to her mother's house, we run into Bomi's mother. As always, the woman looks haggard and rushed.

'Did some maja-maasti with your son today,' my mother says with a wink. 'He told me you force him to eat rat's meat for dinner every night. Said you catch the rats from the top of the water tank.'

The woman looks shocked and embarrassed. 'Such a dhaap-master he is becoming. God knows where he's learning such tall-tall stories. Probably at that school of his. I'll go home and give him a pasting for telling such lies.'

My mother looks solicitous. 'No, no, no beatings. Poor chap, I already gave him some caning today for not doing his homework. Besides, all children tell lies at this age. Look at this one here. Same problem.'

I look at my shoes while the woman pinches my cheeks and tells me I should be a good girl and make my mummy proud and didn't I know how much my mummy loves me?

✦

My mummy loves me, she loves me. Everybody tells me so.

I know about my mother's blinding, all-encompassing, all-sacrificing love because the neighbours tell me so. And all my mother's friends tell me so. And the grocer who owns the little shop down the street. And the old woman bent with osteoporosis who lives a few streets away and whose name I never learned. I know because everybody pulls me into private corners, because everybody's hands, bony or strong, pull at my shirt sleeves, everybody's eyes are sad and accusing, everybody's mouth opens to speak the same words: Why do you treat your mother so? Why are you just like your dad and the rest of them? Why don't you go out alone with your mummy the way you do with your aunts? Don't you know what a sad life she has, the poor thing?

All my life I have heard about my mother's sad life. All my life I have known that she is a Poor Thing, somebody to be pitied and felt sorry for. Everybody I know has told me so. Worse, I have seen it for myself, for haven't I witnessed that abrupt bursting into tears, the open-mouthed gasping for air, the terrible, gulping sobs? And haven't those sobs entered my heart like a needle, haven't they floated like black balloons, like poison gas, into the very inner-most chambers of my heart where they have settled like soot, darkening my days, blackening my own feeble stabs at happiness? Haven't I watched in wonder and dread as my all-powerful, strong mother with a tongue that can sting as hard as the cane she uses on me, haven't I watched her face crumple like paper under the force of her animal grief? Haven't the sounds of her unexpected and furious sobs made me want to slink away like a small animal, to lie down still and quiet and pretend to be dead? No, to crave death, oblivion, just to get away from the heart-breaking sound of her sobbing.

My mother has had a sad life and somehow, I'm to blame. My mother has a bad marriage and somehow, I'm to blame. She tells me so herself, in a tirade of words that I hear over and over again but still they do not lose their ugly power to destroy me. You are the reason for my bad marriage, she says, and I believe her. You can't stand to see me and him happy, she cries, and I believe her. I didn't give birth to a daughter, I gave birth to a snake, she says, and I imagine myself with scales and fangs. I should've had an abortion instead of having you, she swears, and I think she's right. All my life I will have a wish, bright and urgent as a freshly minted silver coin: that I had never been born. Not a death wish, not a suicidal wish but something lazier than that – just a desire to have never existed.

Sometimes I have a sense that my mother is wrong in blaming me for her bad marriage. I remember how, when I come home from school, Mehroo often opens the door with the words, 'Daddy is in a bad mood. Go cheer him up.' Still in my green uniform, I go into the bedroom and rub dad's head and kiss his broad forehead and tickle his ears and rack my brains to say something funny until he finally smiles. That small, faint smile is like a trickle of honey dripping from his lips and then I feel an insane, absurd sense of accomplishment. I want to tell my mother this, how I hate it when they have their silent fights, how hard I try to help them get along, but her assertion is stated so flatly it brooks no dissent. Also, I think, because she's older maybe she knows something about me, about my secret desires and weaknesses, that I don't. And so I say nothing.

When the neighbours, family friends, relatives, teachers and strangers – all the people that my mother complains to – give me advice and wise counsel, I never say a word. I look away, I shuffle my feet, I focus all my energy on swallowing the blood clot that forms in my throat. I use every ounce of self-discipline to not let the betraying tears spill like the monsoon rains. It is very very important for me not to cry in front of other people. It is very important to be a smart-aleck, a wise ass, a clown. It is essential to be praised by the adults for being sharp and witty, essential to be the first one among my peers with a pun or a quip. Otherwise, the whole thing crumbles and falls apart. Self control, perfecting the art of keeping a blank face, is very important when you are a spy in someone else's country. And I have secrets, oh yes, I have state secrets, I know things that could topple countries, that could destroy the established order. I play imaginary games, where I am a prisoner and bald-headed, faceless strangers are torturing me for what I know. And still I do not speak. To test my resolve, I pinch myself hard, bend my hand behind my back until it hurts, stand on one foot until it begins to ache. Finally, I am satisfied that I am up to the task of facing my adult interrogators.

The hardest is when they say untrue and awful things about my dad. Then, my silence doesn't feel brave and noble. Then, my throat gets red and raw from the lump that forms in it and I am ashamed of my silence, my cowardice. Then, I want to scream and claw at their pious, self-righteous faces because I know that an injustice is being done. I want to tell them the truth, about how I have seen my father cry silently, his shoulders shaking, after my mother has said something particularly cruel. I want to spill all the family secrets, but my spy's code of honour will not let me. On these occasions I feel a self-loathing so strong, it has a taste and smell to it.

'So will you be nicer to your mummy now, for my sake?' some well-meaning neighbour asks me, after lecturing me for a half-hour. 'Promise me you will side with your mummy against your daddy?'

Somedays, I nod. Somedays I pretend not to hear them. All days, I mutter dark things about them to myself.

# *Three*

After dinner, Mehroo and I often go for a walk. Around eight p.m. we leave the house and walk up to the main road. Then, instead of the usual left turn, we hang a right. Dressed in their sleeveless white jerseys and plaid lungis, the waiters at the old Muslim restaurant at the corner exhale their bidi smoke and greet us as we walk by. This is the restaurant from which we sometimes order mutton biryani (despite the rumour that they use beef instead of goat meat). 'Salaam wa'alaykum, memsahib,' they say to Mehroo. 'Hello, baby,' they smile at me. 'No biryani order in many-many days, what?'

Nodding our heads in greeting, we walk by wordlessly without making eye contact. We are never sure if the men are being polite or overly familiar. So we treat them the way we treat all working-class males – we acknowledge their presence and act as if they don't exist, in the same gesture. We show our indifference to them, we restrict our own greetings to a curt nod, lest they misunderstand our smiles or greetings.

I want to tell Mehroo about the cruel things mummy said to me today but I am too scared. Even if I make Mehroo promise not to tell, I am afraid it will slip out the next time she quarrels with mummy. And then mummy will turn on me with that wild look that she gets when she feels betrayed or hurt. Or worse yet, maybe Mehroo won't mention it to mummy at all but she will remember my story tomorrow morning when she gets ready to leave for the factory and just before leaving she will bend down to hug me and whisper, 'I hate leaving you all alone like this.' And then I will feel the sting of her abandonment even more deeply than I normally do. No, it is best not to 'tell.

Then I forget all about this because we are moments away from the textile mill and my heart races in anticipation. The mill is an old stone building broken up by the tall, arched iron gates. A narrow, slanting stone ledge runs under the dark, grated windows. I turn to Mehroo with beseeching eyes and wordlessly, she helps me climb onto the ledge and then keeps her hand on the small of my back to keep me from sliding backward. Holding onto the window grates, I peer in to see a sight that never fails to enthral me. Dark-limbed men, many with their shirts off and their skin gleaming with sweat, work in a huge cavernous room. They look tiny before the large, ancient machines that churn out brightly-coloured fabric. Sometimes, one of the men looks up and sees me and sends a quick smile my way. Protected by the grated windows, I smile back. But mostly, I take in the busy scene and the smell of the dye. The sight of people working as a team makes me feel absurdly happy for no reason I understand. All I know is that it is the same feeling I get when I watch the workers at my dad's wood factory lift the huge logs of timber and glide them through the various machines. Then, I breathe in the clean, scented smell of wood and sawdust (a smell I will forever associate with my dad) and feel the excitement of witnessing the birth of a product, something that will be of use in the world.

Years later, as a journalist in the U.S., I will walk down to the newspaper's press room and feel the same sense of joy – at breathing in the scent of printing ink, at watching a team of men working closely yet independently of each other, at seeing something being created – that I used to during my walks with Mehroo.

Mehroo tugs at me. 'Chalo, ma, time to go home. They will be worried.'

'Two more minutes,' I plead and invariably, she gives in.

On the way home, she lectures me: 'You're getting too big now, to be watching those people everyday. People begin to get the wrong idea...'

I'm unsure of what she means but her tone tells me that this is an embarrassing topic. Best not to ask too many questions. Besides, if I don't know what she means, then I can request her again to let me watch. As we walk home I savour every moment of walking in the cool, breezy night, slowing down as we get closer to the house to make the walk last longer. I like how the world looks when the sky goes dark, I decide. When I am older, I will go for a walk every single night, I resolve.

When we get home, I'm still wound up and not ready for bed. 'Play a game with me, Mehroofui,' I say.

'No. Everybody's getting ready to go to bed. Time to sleep.'

'Please. There's no school tomorrow. Just for five minutes, please.'

She relents. She always relents.

Ah, the sound of the small, pink, hard rubber ball rolling across the smooth stone hallway as we sit on our haunches and roll it back and forth. I want to throw it, want to throw as hard as the street urchins who play cricket on the main road during the city-wide strikes, but Mehroo won't let me. The thump of the ball may wake the other family members and anyway, the passageway is too narrow for rough play. I may break a light bulb or something. So I content myself with rolling the ball and soon I'm caught up in its mesmerizing rhythm. It rolls along the length of that long hallway, making a soft whirling sound. Given the repetitive, dull, singular nature of the game, I have to use my imagination to imbue it with whatever excitement or suspense I can. So I wait till the last possible moment before I let my hand touch the sweaty, sour-smelling rubber, trying to produce a fake lurch in my stomach by telling myself that it almost got away from me. Or I pretend that I am a prisoner and rolling this ball is a way to surreptitiously communicate with the prisoner in the adjoining cell, while all the guards stay sleeping.

Finally, my imagination fails me and I see the game for what it is. For a second, I gain a startlingly clear picture of myself – a bored, lonely, only child making up stories to bring some legitimacy to an embarrassingly tedious game. The minute I begin to think this, I yawn. Mehroo jumps on that yawn, taking full advantage of it. 'Let's get up, time for bed,' she whispers. 'Chalo, go do your business and let's go to sleep.' I grumble as any self-respecting child would but she can see my heart's not in it.

When I'm in bed, Mehroo comes and sits by the edge. She kisses my forehead, smoothens my brow, lightly runs her hand across my whole body. Then, she kisses me again. 'Good night,' she says. 'Say a quick Ashem Vahu and then go to bed. God bless you and sweet dreams.'

✧

I go to sleep. But not for long.

I feel Mehroo grabbing my shoulders and turning me around and I wake up for a few minutes before I fall back to sleep.

You see, I am a bed-wetter. I wet my bed every night, sometimes several times a night.

My family, in a desperate attempt to help me, has tried every cure anyone has suggested. There are ayurvedic powders to swallow and prayers to mumble. A few months ago, dad took me to Victoria Gardens, where he paid one of the zoo-keepers ten rupees for a tiny bit of camel's pee.

Dad looked grim-faced as the dark-brown urine was brought to me in a small paper cup. In a soft voice, he asked me to smell the hot liquid. I refused indignantly. My embarrassed father cajoled and begged and finally, I agreed.

I took a whiff and gagged immediately. 'Okay, okay, that's enough,' my father said quickly. 'Let's hope it works. Deshmukh told me it did wonders for his nephew.'

There was much anticipation when I went to bed that night and much disappointment the next morning when the brown outline on the bundled sheets confirmed my nocturnal failure. I, too, was crestfallen until dad gathered me to his side. 'It's okay,' he said. 'So sorry I made you go through that yesterday.'

I have been sleeping in Mehroo's room for years. When I was younger, I used to sleep in my parents' room but mummy was a heavy sleeper and resented having to wake up to the smell of urine and changing my soaking bedsheets in the middle of the night. Sometimes, she would sleep through the night and I would lie on the wet sheets all night long. On the nights that my mother did wake up, she'd grab my arm and yank me out of bed, her unspoken anger and resentment running like electricity through my arm. And if I refused to roll out of bed, she spoke harshly to me, thereby upsetting my father. All the anger in the room made me so nervous, I peed even more.

Finally, Mehroo intervened and I moved into her room. Every night, Mehroo places a rubber sheet – blue on one side, red on the other – on the bed under my waist and then covers the rubber with a horizontal cotton sheet. She also sets the alarm to awaken her three to four times a night. Crossing the tiled floor silently in her white-and-blue Bata rubber chappals, she bends at my bed and feels the sheets for wetness. If they are wet, she lifts my body, heavy with sleep, props me up in my bed so that I sleep standing, somehow undresses me, cleans me, dresses me in new pyjamas and then carries me to her bed while she changes the sheets on mine. I don't make this any easy for her, sleeping as I do through most of the exercise. When she does wake me up, I grumble and whine under my breath. A few hours later, the ritual starts again.

(Years later, when I am thirteen, a kindly neighbour whom my mother had complained to about my nauseating habit, pulls me aside one evening and asks me whether I know what auto-suggestion is. I have never heard the term. 'Before going to bed tonight, tell yourself over and over again, "I will not do soo-soo in bed tonight. I will get up when I feel the urge," ' he suggests. 'Just imagine yourself not wetting the bed.'

So I do. With more fervour than I've ever mustered, I tell myself: 'I will get up before I soil the bed.' There is a fierce desperation in me as I repeat the message to myself before drifting off to sleep.

It works. Since that night a problem which is the source of much friction in my house, which had left my family feeling helpless and ashamed and angry, for which my parents had tried to blame each other's side of the family – the problem simply vanishes. Vamoose. It is the triumph of mind over bladder.)

But that day is still many years away. Sometimes, Mehroo gets lucky because when she wakes up, the sheets are dry. Then, my aunt, who weighs less than hundred pounds, lifts my sleep-laden body and carries me down the long passageway that leads to the bathroom. I protest at being awakened but she shushes me into silence. 'Quiet, quiet. Others are sleeping,' she says. 'Go use the bathroom like a good girl and then you can go back to sleep. But sit for a minute after you think you're finished, samji ne? Empty your bladder fully.'

Ah, my Mehroo. What generosity of spirit, what irrational impulse made you love me so unconditionally? But wait, your love was not unconditional at all. I still recall my shock the day you candidly told me that if I wasn't your beloved brother's daughter, that if I had just been a girl who lived down the street, no telling if you would've still loved me. For a minute, I was mute with disappointment. We all flatter ourselves that we have earned our love, paid for it with our dazzling personalities, our irresistible charms and our noble characters. That love is more than an accident of biology and geography. And so, I was disappointed that the gift of your love had been bestowed because of chance and not because of the irrefutable logic of my magnetic personality. But then, I thought, Well, the fact is, I *am* her niece. Nothing can change that. Why worry about What Ifs and If Onlys?

And since we were linked by the ties of blood and destiny, you loved me as fiercely and fearlessly as a teenager in love for the first time. I can only imagine what needs taking care of a young child fulfilled in you. Perhaps it made up for the early death of your mother. Perhaps it helped take your mind off the joke life played on you a few years later.

This I know: You resisted my mother's constant complaint that you had stolen me away from her, that you had taken over her birthright, brainwashed me into loving you more than her. You withstood my father's daily beseeching that you concentrate more on the business than on me, that you leave me to the attentions of my mother. (No, no, no, Mehroofui, I would pray to myself. Don't do it. Don't do that.) You were an unwavering soldier, a straight line, the North star, your stout love as constant as the slow rotation of the earth around the sun, your devotion as reliable as the ebb and flow of the tides.

My earliest childhood memory: It is late at night and I am hot and restless from being unable to sleep. My four-year-old body is tired but I'm unable to relax, my body twitching and fluttering like a dying fish in Mehroo's arms. She carries me across her shoulder and walks the length of the long balcony. A cool breeze comes in from the open balcony and lands like kisses on our faces. Mehroo's hand is on my back, rubbing it and thumping it in a rhythmic motion. Thump, thump, thump goes her hand, light but firm against my hollow back. The rhythm is strangely elemental and comforting, like the purring of a cat. It soothes me, makes me languid and sleepy. A great sense of peace, different from the fevered restlessness of a few moments ago, descends on me. I know that this light woman with the brown, wavy hair who is pacing the balcony while she is holding me, I know that this woman loves me. That she is sacrificing her sleep, letting her arms go tired under my weight, stopping only occasionally to look at the half-moon, because she loves me. Her hand on me, thumping my back, begins to feel like a hum. Or maybe it is my body that's humming, that's vibrating with joy and peace. I fall asleep, knowing that I am loved.

## four

ALTHOUGH I GET TEASED BY the other girls and despite the fact that Olga D'Mello is the bane of my life, school is my escape from home. Although all my grade cards say that I am fidgety and that I daydream too much and have a hard time sitting still, I like the sense of order and lack of chaos at school. Here, the adults do not fight with each other every morning and Mother Superior does not storm out of morning assembly, the way dad leaves the house at least once a week.

But tomorrow, mummy is coming to school and I sense that my two worlds are about to collide. On my way home from school I plan when to give mummy the note that says Miss Bharucha wants to see her tomorrow, just how much I'm going to tell her about what happened earlier today and whether to explain how and why things spiralled downward so fast. Or will trying to defend myself make mummy even more angry? How can I possibly explain to her the absolute terror that I feel around Miss Damania and how it was that terror that made me do what I did?

I'm in third-grade and the gym teacher, Miss Damania, is a tall, bony, ostrich-like woman with a beaked nose and long, thin, claw-like fingers. I live in mortal fear of her. I am a dismally poor athlete, an ungraceful, sickly child and unforgivingly absent-minded. Miss Damania's mode of punishment is particularly cruel and psychologically terrifying in a way that punishment from the other teachers is not. Miss Davidson, the Anglo-Indian piano teacher, for instance, throws us across her knee, lifts our green uniforms so that it exposes our underwear and then smacks our buttocks with a ruler. The nuns use the ruler to rap us on our knuckles and arms and occasionally, they slap us. But Miss Damania's punishment is different and I'm her favourite target. She comes at me with her claws outstretched, like a witch from a bad theatre production. The time that it takes for her hand to shape itself into a claw and grab hold of the fleshy part of my throat, lasts an eternity. She then shakes my flesh, so that my head moves slightly from side to side. It is the most peculiar pain, being clawed at the throat, but what's worse is the sensation it arouses. It feels like drowning, I think, but am not sure why. Perhaps it is that feeling of being tossed around by a force stronger and more powerful than you. But even weeks after the last shaking, I find it hard to swallow and can feel the imprint of Miss Damania's fingernails on my throat. The other beatings I can laugh off, boast about even, but this one feels dirty and humiliating to me. I can get off Miss Davidson's lap with a swagger, can take a blow across the arm without flinching and without tearing up, but being shaken like a rat makes my eyes well up no matter how hard I try. The shaking does exactly what it is intended to do – it makes me feel small and powerless and rodent-like. I want to hide from the flashlight gaze of Miss Damania's eyes; want to burrow deep into the safety of the rows of girls in their green uniforms ('Green parrots,' the kids from the nearby school tease us) who stand around me. And I hate her with an intensity, a rage that only the powerless and voiceless can muster. Because by coming for my throat, she is literally rendering me voiceless, is freezing the explanations, the excuses in my mouth before I can voice them. 'But . . . but . . .' I begin, ready to give her what seems to me a perfectly reasonable explanation for whatever crime I'm guilty of but I can never get past this single word before I am being clawed. And I know, sure as I know anything, that she is enjoying this. Miss Davidson spanks with a certain gusto but there is always a wink behind her actions, a sense that she is playing a role – of the bullying, loud-voiced teacher who nevertheless has a heart of gold. Mother Superior hits and slaps wearily, sighing as she does, shaking her head at our unfathomable behaviour. She hits with a sense of obligation, as if she is burdened with the duty and responsibility of turning a bunch of wild, untamed, Indian hooligans into polite, smart, obedient girls. But Miss Damania loves terrorizing us. She salivates at the sight of a cringing girl, she licks her lips with the anticipation of tears rolling down a cheek, she enjoys towering over us, thin and distant as a skyscraper, as we whimper and plead and try to squirm out of her grasp. It is not enough to punish us for our sins; we have to be broken first. So I am panic-stricken when I realize in the second period that I have forgotten to pack my gym shoes. I have on my black patent leather school shoes but where are the white keds that I have to wear to gym class? I look in my blue school-bag two times, three, as if looking will magically produce the shoes. Just two weeks ago Miss Damania had warned me about not forgetting my shoes any more. She had warned me in front of the whole class and I have now disobeyed her. That is how she will see it. I know better than to even try to explain the situation to her and to ask for her understanding. My throat constricts at the thought of the torture to come.

Then, a thought so perfect that it feels like a gift. Only last week, I had mastered the art of writing my 'r's like my mother does, rolling them instead of having them stand alone. It had felt like a rite of passage, an entry into the guarded fortress of adulthood. Practising her 'r' repeatedly and finally getting it made me feel adult and accomplished. Now, it suddenly occurs to me that I can disguise my handwriting to make it look exactly like my mother's. My grammar is good and I know I can imitate my mother's phrases perfectly. For instance, my mom begins her sentences with Kindly instead of Please. 'Kindly excuse Thrity from ...' I can write a note to be kindly excused from carrying my keds and can sign it as my mother. The idea feels like inspired genius, a divine inspiration. Excitement replaces terror.

During lunch recess, I sit alone and painstakingly write the note. I have to make sure none of the teachers see me at work. I put the torn sheet of paper in between the pages of a textbook, to make sure nobody sees what I am doing. When I am finished, I am pleased with my first work of fiction. Gym class is the second-to-last class of the day and the rest of the afternoon flies quickly.

Miss Damania looks up from reading the note. 'Who wrote this note?' she says immediately.

I am speechless at the question.

The dark eyes narrow. 'Who?' she repeats. 'Answer quickly.'

'My mummy did. I swear, miss, she did.'

'Bad girl,' she spits. 'Lying while standing under this picture of Jesus.'

I am trapped in my own lie. Wretchedly, I realize there is no place to go but deeper. 'I swear on God, miss,' I say, pinching myself on the throat the way we do when swearing.

Pinching myself was a mistake. Miss Damania's eyes narrow as they focus on my throat. My eyes are already filling with tears as I watch her claw-like hands move in the direction of my throat. I feel her nails dig into my flesh. My head moves from side to side as she shakes me like a rat. 'No, no, no, miss,' I whimper. 'Please, miss, please.'

'Who wrote the note?'

Terror engulfs me. 'I did, miss, I'm sorry. I did. Please forgive me, miss.'

'Dirty girl,' Miss Damania spits. 'Incorrigible liar. Plague of Egypt.' With each word, she shakes my throat for emphasis.

When the other girls tell the kindly classroom teacher, Miss Bharucha, what happened in gym class, her face pales. 'This is a note for your mummy,' she says to me. 'Tell her to come see me tomorrow.'

Mummy comes to school the next day anxious to apologize for my lying and cheating and ready to commiserate with my teachers. But to my amazement, Miss Bharucha barely mentions the incident. Instead, she is sympathetic and solicitous and says that she has an idea: I should leave my gym shoes in the classroom closet at the end of gym class. That way, I don't have to worry about remembering to pack them. I begin to breathe easier. But just as my mother is getting up to leave, Miss Bharucha says the dreaded word. 'Your daughter is very sensitive,' she says gravely. 'She will have to learn to be a little tougher.'

I want to bury my head in shame. For years I believe that being sensitive is a bad thing, another black mark like the others that follow me throughout my school years: Talks and fidgets in class. Does not live up to her potential. Makes careless mistakes. Daydreams. To which, my mother lends her own complaints: Reads too many novels. Is forgetful and absent-minded. Is a poor eater. Will not drink her milk.

Most of these labels I can shrug off. But being called sensitive dooms me, marks me as an easy target for bold, brash girls like Olga D'Mello. But it would be too much to expect a grown-up to understand this.

They are everywhere and they haunt me. They are on the streets, they appear quietly as shadows when we stop at a traffic-light, they gaze at us hungrily when we eat pani puri at Chowpatty Beach. Worse, they infiltrate my dreams at night.

Still, the dreams are not unpleasant. Mostly, it is the same dream over and over again with some variation on the theme: It is thundering and raining heavily outside and I am herding them in, loading the city's destitute and homeless and poor into school-buses and transporting them to the basement of my school. What we refer to as the basement is actually a large, open-air room that is located on the ground floor and overlooks the playground. During morning recess, we buy battatawadas and Cokes in the tiny cafeteria located in one corner of this room. Elsewhere, there are the long wooden benches where we eat our hot lunches everyday.

But in the dream, the room is empty. Or rather, it is bare of furniture but filled to the point of bursting with Bombay's unwanted humanity. Unshaven men with tangled hair, scrawny children with dirt-streaked faces, painfully thin women with large eyes, are huddled together, some sitting on their haunches, some standing, others laying down on thin but warm brown blankets. The slanted rain is coming in, wetting those on the edge of the basement so that they try to inch their way toward the warm middle. Their neighbours good-naturedly try to help them, so that there is no cussing or shoving, even when the food trucks arrive with milk and sandwiches. Instead, there is a constant hum of excitement and the tight quarters feel cosy, rather than stifling. Outside, there is rain and thunder; here, there is a warm, snug feeling, like sitting before a fireplace on a cold winter's night except that we are generating heat from each other's bodies rather than an external fire.

The other variation on the dream is that we are on a ship rather than in my school's basement. This time, the solid concrete reality of the basement gives way to the tossing and turning of the ship on the turbulent waves. But in the dream, nobody gets sick, nobody has to lean across the railing of the ship and lose their dinner. Rather, everyone is eating well, ignoring the heaving waves and the whipping wind and taking comfort in the safety of numbers. All of us in this together. Every inch of space on the ship is taken, with bodies tightly packed in but nobody seems to care as we bump up against each other. Again, the swell and thrust of humanity, again, dampness and cold on the outside, and the powerful 'warmth of human connection on the inside.

I invariably wake up from these dreams with an amazing sense of exhilaration because I believe that I have found the solution to India's most intractable problem – poverty. Every one of my civics textbooks starts with the line, 'India is a rich country with poor people.' Well, that has to be true no more. All one has to do is gather in all the street people every night and feed them milk and chicken sandwiches and Coke. I don't understand why the adults always shake their heads grimly and declare that the poor will always be with us.

I once try telling Miss Carlson about my dream, try describing to her how I fall asleep in the warmth of its glow and how happy I feel when I wake up from it. I guess I am hoping she'll help me write a letter to the Prime Minister or something but Miss Carlson only hears me for a few minutes and then kisses me on the forehead and says I am a good girl and isn't it a shame that I wasn't born Catholic. Then, as always, I give her ten paise from my lunch money and she sells me a picture of one of the saints. But on this day I refuse the card that she hands me. 'No, Miss Carlson, it's okay,' I say. 'You keep the picture today. You can sell it to another girl instead.'

Miss Carlson's blue eyes grow misty. Her pink face, which is as creased as a crumpled sheet of paper, grows red. 'What a good child of God you are, my dear,' she says. 'Not like those other heathen girls, those plagues of Egypt. Perhaps you will join the convent someday.'

Although Miss Carlson is not an ordained nun, she lives with the nuns at the convent for reasons that are unclear to me. I realize that she has just paid me the highest compliment and her words make me feel guilty. I have not refused Miss Carlson's offering for reasons of piety or charity but because mummy has made me promise not to bring home any more pictures of saints. Since I give Miss Carlson ten paise everyday in exchange for a card, the card collection is getting unmanageable. And mummy is too superstitious to throw away any of the religious cards once I hand them to her. 'Bloodsuckers, that's what these nuns are – yes, even your beloved Miss Carlson, even if she's not really a nun,' mummy mutters ... 'Taking lunch money from a child, as if they don't charge enough tuition fees. But okay, baba, even if you give them the money, at least don't accept another picture. Tell her to sell it to another unsuspecting bakra. More profit for them, that way.'

If even Miss Carlson does not understand my dream then I know it is hopeless trying to talk to any other adult. With her pure white hair, which she wears in a page boy cut, her short, tiny, pixyish body and her kind, soft heart, Miss Carlson is a cross between an innocent child and a saint. If she doesn't understand, nobody else will.

Besides, I still cringe when I remember the episode from a few months ago.

Roshan had left school on a Friday with six of her friends and stopped by Dipeta, the bakery that my family had opened a few years ago. Mehroo had fed the girls chicken patties and chocolate cake and given them Cokes to drink. They had left that evening with full stomachs and in good spirits. I was on my best behaviour while the older girls were there. But as soon as they left, I began whining. 'My turn,' I said, tugging at Mehroo's fingers. 'When can I bring my friends to the shop?'

Mehroo was distracted, waiting on a customer. 'Next week,' she said as she was wrapping up some bread rolls. 'If you want, we can have a small party for a few friends at Dipeta next Friday. But don't invite more than three or four girls, okay?'

I'd rather invite my school friends to Dipeta than to my house for one of our parties. For my birthday, I got intolerable birthday parties to which all the silly, well-behaved, soft-spoken neighbourhood girls were invited. I had to cut my specialty cake with a knife that was decorated with a pink satin bow. Then, there was the excruciating moment when the adults asked the girls with the good singing voices to sing a song. The girls giggled and squealed and squirmed and blushed. They were shy and had to be coaxed to sing. I did not join the chorus of voices asking them to sing. I knew that they would invariably have high, airy voices and that they would invariably sing some bullshit song like *Strangers in the Night*. These were good girls and I wanted nothing to do with them. They were not my people.

I spent most of the following week trying to decide who to invite but the thought of having to leave any of my friends out, was too depressing. Besides, something else was nagging at me. Friday came around without my having invited a single classmate. Instead, I went up to the street urchins who invariably gathered around the shop. 'See this eating-drinking shop? It belongs to my father,' I said to dirty-faced children my own age. 'You all go tell your friends to gather here in five-ten minutes. There will be lots to eat and drink.' They stared at me dumbfounded for a few seconds and then they ran, whooping all the way.

Within minutes, they were back. Mehroo, and my dad, who had stopped at the shop on his way from the factory, looked up to see a group of twelve children standing outside the shop, some of them giggling in excitement, others shoving and pushing each other, a few of them hopping on one foot. 'What the hell?' dad said, as he made to shoo the group away. The urchins looked ready to scatter like pigeons if my dad took another step towards them.

I stood in front of dad to block his path. 'These are my friends,' I said quickly. 'Mehroo said I could invite my friends for a small party today. Roshan had her turn last week. So instead of my school friends, I decided to invite my Dipeta friends. Now you have to feed them.'

Mehroo started to say something to claim her innocence but I was looking up at my father. I watched several expressions flit across his face – annoyance, surprise, confusion, and finally, a bemused resignation. 'Okay, Thrituma,' he said. 'You win. But just this time, okay? We cannot do this often.'

I skipped to where the children were waiting patiently. 'Come in, come in,' I said but the children hesitated, waiting for my father to give them a command. Dad pulled me aside. 'We cannot have them all the way inside the shop, you understand?' he whispered. 'Their hands and feet are too dirty – it will chase our regular customers away. Just tell them to come to the front of the store and wait there. And I cannot afford to give away bottles of Coca-Cola. They can have ice candies instead.'

'Okay, daddy,' I agreed, not wanting to push my luck.

The group gathered in the small foyer that led to the store. Mehroo took out the red-and-white paper plates that said Dipeta on them and filled each of them with small cakes, and chicken patties. She took a few daar-ni-poris and cut them into equal-sized pieces, and then placed the individual pieces on each plate. In the meantime, dad was reaching into the deep freezer to take out the ice candies. 'What flavour, what flavour?' I asked the group but most of them were too shy and tongue-tied to speak. One of the bolder kids from behind the group finally shouted out 'Orange' but the rest of them just looked at me with their big eyes.

Mehroo began distributing the plates and the children took them from her eagerly. But once they held the plates in their hands, they were unsure of what to do next. They stood silently, waiting for some command or signal. I took one of the plates from Mehroo and bit into a chicken patty. 'Eat,' I said and they did, their eyes never leaving my face as we munched on the goodies, staring at each other.

Several months after the incident, the adults are still talking about it, repeating it each time they want to impress a family acquaintance. They place both hands on my shoulders and brag about how warm-hearted and sensitive I am. But each retelling of the story makes me cringe because they are taking an absent-minded, spontaneous gesture and turning it into something different. Part of the reason I had approached the street kids was because I was bewitched by their horseplay and games and wanted to be included in them. It was my need that had drawn me to the urchins but in the retelling of the story, they had become the needy ones. Also, Roshan glares at me each time the story is told because she picks up on the unspoken critique – while Roshan invited her school friends, Thrity sought out the poor, the marginalized. Can't the adults see that they are unwittingly pitting me and Roshan against each other? I marvel again at the insensitivity of grown-ups.

And I do not want any more of their praise. So I do not share my solution to the poverty problem with anyone. I feel as if I'm sitting on an important state secret but that can't be helped. Perhaps one day I'll have a chance to share my plans with the Prime Minister herself. And then India will be poor no more.

FOR YEARS, THE OVALTINE LADY has been my real mother. Nobody knows that this is so.

The Ovaltine woman has long, straight black hair and a round, dimpled face. She has two children, a boy and girl, who look nothing like me. These children are shiny, happy, and bright as young pups. They bound in every afternoon after school, drop their satchels and head into the kitchen, where their mother has two steaming cups of Ovaltine waiting for them. I imagine that it is dark and raining outside, that it begins to thunder even as the children sit in the warm, safe kitchen sharing the treasures of their day with their beautiful, soft-spoken mother.

But what I most love about the Ovaltine woman are her hands. As she shuts tight the metal lid on the big, brown can of Ovaltine, the camera zooms to a close-up of her long, slender, well-groomed fingers. It is hard to describe the wistfulness and longing I feel as I sit in a darkened movie theatre and watch those graceful hands. To me, those hands say motherhood. I imagine that those hands are capable of smoothing out all my rough, jagged, splintered edges; hands that can take the rawness of my life and turn it into something round and wholesome. Hands that can save me, that can pull me back from the edge I'm about to step off – from the world of gloom and desperation and rootlessness that I am about to enter. I imagine that those hands have healing powers, that they can comfort, nurture, restore, rebuild. I am unsure of what is broken in me, what needs rebuilding, but I long for deliverance just the same.

But the Ovaltine woman stays on the silver screen. She has two celluloid children of her own and does not come to rescue me. Like them, I too, drink milk – sometimes with Ovaltine, sometimes with Horlicks, sometimes with raspberry syrup but unlike them, I do not smack my lips after I have gulped down the very last drop. Unlike them, I am allergic to milk but nobody seems to notice. My mother takes my dislike for milk as a personal affront to her parenting skills. She pushes milk on me with a kind of religious fervour. But I refuse this conversion by sword. Every chance I get, I pour my glass of milk down the kitchen sink. Once, Mehroo catches me red-handed. With tears in her eyes she says, 'There are children starving down the street from us. And here you are, wasting precious milk. Shame on you.'

I have heard this line many times but still its logic eludes me. All the more reason not to drink the milk I think, so that those poor starving babies can have my share. I have pondered this paradox for several months, convinced that only my young age keeps me from solving the riddle at its core.

My mother also insists that I swallow a raw egg every morning, faithfully following the instructions of the alcoholic family doctor who had treated me for a serious lung problem when I was six. No adult will tell me what the matter is with my lungs. (Years later, when I ask one of them whether I had TB there is a lot of shuffling of the feet, and clicking of the fingers to ward off evil but no direct answer. 'Not quite,' is the closest to a direct answer I would ever get.)

I stare at the yellow yolk swimming in its transparent sea and imagine an eye following my every move. The eye is watching me watch it. The eye is watching me grimace. Now, the eye watches me tilt the stainless steel cup as I put it up to my mouth. Gulp. The eye is now floating somewhere inside me. Sometimes when I swallow, I feel the egg as a dull ache in my back as it makes its way down. When I complain to my mother she says, 'See? It's a sure sign of weakness. You need to increase your intake.'

I know that food is my mother's shorthand for love. I know it is one of the few ways she knows how to express her feelings about me. From my grandmother's stories about the hard times that followed her husband's sudden and premature death, I have learned that my mom and her siblings grew up in poverty. I have heard about how, once the steady pay cheques stopped, the family lived on the money from his meagre pension and whatever they could get from Parsi charities. I know the premium my mother's family puts on food and feeding others. I once caught her sister licking a packet of Polson's butter with her tongue and was horrified and embarrassed. In my house, Mehroo would not even let us lick our fingers after a good meal. I also know that compared to my family, with its spartan eating habits, my mother's family is a family of enthusiastic meat and fish-eaters.

But try as I might, this emphasis on food repels me. There is something oddly animalistic and savage about my mother's desire to feed me. I think if she could chew my food for me, she gladly would. She reminds me of a female lion, especially in the way she steals pieces of mutton and chicken out of the family meals that Mehroo cooks before she leaves for the workshop, and forces them into my mouth. Sometimes, she has to pry my jaws open because I hate the taste of hunks of meat. I chew and chew until the meat is dry and yucky in my mouth and then, sometimes, I gag on it and spit it out. Her wrath descends on me then, her eyes dark with fury and powerlessness. I think in those moments she must know how different we are from each other and hate me for growing away from her. I don't care. I hate her too during those moments, hate and fear the mad fury that makes her shove food into my mouth, hate the humiliation and powerlessness of having to chew and swallow food that I despise.

There is also something else: I am excruciatingly aware that this is stolen food, am ashamed of the furtive movements my mother makes as she runs in the kitchen, fishes out the pieces of mutton from the daal or the white sauce that Mehroo has cooked and hurriedly pushes them into my mouth. My father's business is not doing well, I know, and meat is a luxury. Beside, what's in the dish is meant to serve the entire family and I know what will inevitably follow: Mehroo will come home in the evening, get ready to warm the evening meal and immediately spot the missing pieces. She will accuse my mother who will swear on her mother's head that she knows nothing about this. She may also burst into tears and accuse Mehroo of deliberately making her use her mother's name in vain. And I will choke on my secret, much as I have choked earlier on the piece of meat. My Catholic school education – with the nuns telling us daily that lying is a sin – will collide with my mother's strict instructions to never tell the others about the missing pieces of meat. As usual, I will fall between the gap of what I learn daily during Moral Science and what I must do at home to keep the peace. It never occurs to me to defy my mother and speak the truth and my role in this drama makes me feel complicit, dirty and shameful.

Indeed, food complicates every aspect of my life. Sometimes, if my mother is still sleeping when I dress to go to school, I manage to escape out the front door without drinking my milk before any adult can nab me. But my road to freedom is short and ends two flights down in the building's lobby. I pray desperately for the rickety old school-bus to arrive when I hear my mother's footsteps coming down the stairs. My stomach heaves. There she is, in her long nightgown, carrying the glass of milk, a piece of cardboard or newspaper covering it from dust and flies.

I open my mouth to protest when the ground-floor apartment door opens and the old, white-haired lady who lives there comes out. 'Drink your milk, deekra,' she says in a kindly fashion. 'So many children not so lucky, to have a mother who loves them so much.' I drink the milk, praying that the school-bus does not arrive until after I am done. Immediately, I feel the familiar, bloated sensation. I promise myself that when I'm older and living on my own, I will never ever drink milk again.

It is eleven o'clock at night but still sleep won't come. The fever courses through my weak body like lava, sending lightning-like chills up my whole body. I am half delirious with fever but I can still feel the anxiety that scuttles like tall shadows in this room. Every so often, Mehroo pokes her head through the doorway of my mother's bedroom and I can feel my worried mother shake her head no, to Mehroo's unspoken question: Has the fever come down yet? Babu comes in the room and stands silently gazing at me, his hands crossed behind his back, leaning against my mother's wardrobe, made of teak wood. I want to open my mouth and assure them all that I'm all right but my mouth is dry and hot and I worry that talking will unleash a coughing spell. Also, even in the throes of delirium, some part of me is enjoying the attention.

'Go to sleep,' mummy finally tells the others. 'I'm here with her. I'll wake you up if there's any need.' One by one the adults all extract promises from her that she'll be sure to wake him or her first, at once only, if there's anything wrong at all. As always, they all bend down and kiss my hot forehead, or rather they kiss my hair because my forehead is covered with a wet rag dipped in a mixture of water and eau-de-Cologne. The higher the fever, the less diluted this mixture becomes, with my mother liberally pouring the eau-de-Cologne into the dented aluminium bowl she keeps specifically for this use. 'Sweet dreams, Thrituma,' Mehroo whispers. 'Try to go to sleep like a good girl.'

Daddy kisses me last. His eyes are red with disturbed sleep. An hour ago, tired from the long day at the factory and overcome by the drowsiness that he can never fight, he had tried falling asleep on his side of the bed but the noise generated by the tiptoeing adults had woken him up. Also, there is this unspoken bitterness between him and my mother whenever I am fighting a high fever like this. She wants him to stay up with me along with her, but when he tries, she resents the intrusion. So he gives up in frustration but she misreads that frustration as indifference. I know all this because they both tell me their 'side' of the story after I recover from each episode of sickness. Telling one's side of the story is very important in my family. Mostly, I try to assure both of them that I feel very cared for when I'm sick and am never bothered by who specifically does what. This reassures my father but offends my mother, who always concludes that, by not appreciating how much more she has done for me while I'm sick, I've taken my dad's side against her.

But all this will happen days later when I am well. For now, I relish the sweetness of the cold rag against my hot forehead, float in the glory of my mother's gentle stroking of my hair. The fever is so high that even my hair aches and the rhythmic stroking is strangely comforting. This is the only time when my mother touches me in affection, when I'm this sick, and I bask in the feeling of her tenderness. My own heart feels liquidy with love and gratitude. It is almost worth being this sick, just to see this other side of my mother – gentle, compassionate, soft-spoken – come out of the hard, brittle shell she usually is covered in, her love for me oozing like yolk from a shell. My mamma loves me, she loves me and this time I don't find out from the baker or the neighbours, this time she telegraphs this knowledge to me from the soft brushing of her own wise and slender fingers against my hair. This is the Ovaltine woman come to life.

I know that all of this care has been brought on by fear, her fear of losing me. No matter how often I get sick, she is still haunted by the memory of the lung ailment I had when I was six and had to get a shot every second day for a full year.

I have unpleasant memories of that year – the long, crowded bus ride to the doctor's dispensary after being at school all day; doing my homework while sitting in the drab, crowded waiting-room filled with sad-looking people; standing half-naked behind a huge, cold machine in a pitch-black room as the doctor screened my lungs; the hot, acrid smell as the doctor's assistant boiled the needle on a kerosene stove; the sharp prick of the needle on my skinny, fleshless thighs; the recurrent nightmares about my white underwear being soaked in blood from a puncture caused by an errant needle.

Often, my mom took me to a nearby Irani restaurant for a treat after our visit to the clinic. There was a waiter there who I loved, and he, a shy, working-class Muslim man, was so tickled at the idea of a middle-class six-year-old calling him her friend, that he invariably slipped me a treat – a jelly roll, a mava cake – along with our order. I usually sipped a Fanta or a Mangola and munched on an order of potato chips that I dipped in pumpkin ketchup. Depending on her finances, my mother would sometimes order herself a drink; often she just sat there, urging me to hurry up so that we could start the ordeal of the bus ride home.

However, even this simple pleasure – which I knew was my mother's way of loving me, of letting me know she felt bad that I have to go through this torture at the doctor's office – came with a price tag. It was well known that my mother demanded her monthly allowance from my dad regardless of the state of his finances. Money was often tight at home but my mother would scream and fight with dad to make sure she got her money, which she insisted was for basic provisions. For this reason, my mother felt it necessary to keep our restaurant visits a secret from the rest of the family, especially from Mehroo, who, she told me, would consider this to be a frivolous expense. I found it hard to believe that Mehroo would begrudge me a snack in a restaurant but I was not up to challenging my mother. So I promised her not to reveal these outings but somehow, the secrecy took the joy out of them.

The legacy of that year lingers. It has made my mother think of me as a frail and sickly child and I have obliged her by regularly falling ill ever since. As I am now.

I know that the instant I am better – the day the fever does not spike after sundown, as it usually does; as soon as I can sleep through the night without coughing – all this tenderness and demonstrated affection will vanish, will be pulled away from me like a retractable arm. In fact, that is how I will actually know for sure that I have indeed recovered, by the first harsh word that my mother will say to me. Usually, it plays out like this: her relief at my recovery takes the form of berating me for getting sick in the first place (by not swallowing my daily egg/by walking slowly in the rain without a raincoat/by not eating well/by eating an orange or sweet lime despite doctor's orders to the contrary/ by not having any stamina). Knowing that things have gone back to normal, I further aggravate the situation by asking to be moved back to my bed in Mehroo's room. My mom calls me ungrateful, matlabi, a snake, reminds me how she hasn't slept in four whole nights while attending to my fever and implies that my father and Mehroo are only available during the good times while she has sacrificed sleep and rest for my sake. 'We all know how much he is around when you're sick,' she says. 'He's so worried about you, ask him why he didn't even come home till nine o'clock day before yesterday.'

My father overhears this and feels compelled to point out that one, she has only done what every mother in the history of the world has done for her child and two, he was in a business meeting and someone has to work to keep the house running. My mother waits for my dad to rush out of the room after his little speech and then she looks at me. 'It's all your fault,' she says bitterly. 'Always coming in the way, between the two of us.'

Two days after I've recovered, Babu comes home from the factory with a gift for Roshan and me. It is a little baby bunny.

A few months ago, one of the timber merchants had presented Babu with two female rabbits, one black and one white. My soft-hearted uncle had taken one look at the creatures and fallen in love with them. He would raise them at the factory, he decided. The next day, dad drove the entire family to see them. Growing up in Bombay, I had never seen a real rabbit. At the factory, the foreman, who for some mysterious reason was resentful of the animals, declared that Roshan and I should not stand too close to the rabbits because everybody knew that if a rabbit blew into your eyes, you'd go blind. We ignored him. Babu put an arm around Roshan and me and told us that we could each name and adopt one of the two. Everybody went gaga over the white one, which prompted me to declare that I wanted to adopt the black one. I was the one who ended up giving them their brilliantly creative names – Blackey and Whitey.

I was utterly in love with my new pets. 'Happy?' Babu asked me and I nodded vigorously. The rabbits were the first pets I'd ever had and I went to school the next day with stories about how Blackey and Whitey had eaten lettuce out of my hands and how they'd slept in the wooden cage my dad had built for them. Even Mehnaz, whose brother used to pick her up from school in his Jeep with his pet monkey sitting on his shoulder, was quiet and looked suitably envious.

Babu, too, established an immediate bond with the animals. Even the foreman marvelled at how they soon recognized his footsteps so that they came racing to the door as soon as Babu walked into the factory each morning. 'Hello, hello, my babies,' he'd coo and head straight for the lettuce to feed them.

'Dammit, Pesi, at least get settled at your desk first,' dad grinned but Babu just fixed a stern look at his younger brother and told him that these poor creatures had been waiting all night for him to feed them.

Then, a surprise. The merchant had lied to Babu. It turned out that Blackey was a male and one day, as sudden as a meteor shower, there was a litter of baby rabbits. 'Saala liar,' Babu yelled at the merchant but the man simply grinned and shrugged and said who knew with rabbits? But the baby rabbits were too cute for Babu to stay angry for long. He decided to raise them until they were old enough to be adopted out. He even made the merchant promise to take one. 'After all, you are the bloody grandfather, head of the household,' he said and the man acquiesced.

I was in ecstasy. I went to the factory as often as I could and if the thought occurred to me that one of these days these babies would be gone, I didn't linger on it. I was just happy to stroke and play with the tiny creatures while their parents hovered nearby and kept an eye on things.

In our excitement, none of us had thought about the stray cats that roamed around the timber market. But one day a subdued foreman met Babu at the entrance of the factory and said he had some bad news. A cat had killed several of the babies. Babu let out a cry of pain and indignation. When Blackey and Whitey came up to greet him that day, he imagined that they moved slower and heavier than usual and that Whitey looked grief-stricken. Babu could not look her in the eye.

A few days later, despite everybody's best efforts, the cat struck again. As it turned out, only the runt of the litter had been spared. The baby rabbit was almost all white with a big patch of black on its back. To Babu, its colouring was a sign that this rabbit, the only one that survived, was destined to carry on the family line. This baby rabbit bore the mark of both its parents and it was Babu's duty to see that it lived. So he brought it home with him that evening. He presented the rabbit to Roshan and me and told us how the cat had struck again killing all of the little baby's brothers and sisters and that it was up to us to take perfect care of this little one.

We put the rabbit on the dining room table and crowd around him. Mummy has the brilliant idea of telling our neighbours and soon the doorbell is ringing and different people come in to coo at the rabbit and stroke its little head. I am bursting with pride and happiness. I can't wait to go to school the next day and tell my friends that we now have a pet *at home.* I am even allowed to carry him but knowing my reputation for clumsiness, all the adults are tense while I have him in my arms. 'Careful, careful,' Mehroo murmurs. But I am as tender as Mother Mary with Jesus. After a few minutes, Babu takes him from my hands and sets him on the table. 'He must be tired. They need a lot of sleep,' he says. 'We should let him rest.'

'But we haven't named him yet,' I exclaim. It seems preposterous to have a pet retire for the night without naming him first. But when Babu asks me to come up with a name, my mind goes blank. 'Blackey-Whitey?' I say but even to my ears, it sounds so lame that I don't wait for the adults to respond.

'Come on, the name-fame can wait until tomorrow morning,' Mehroo says. 'The poor thing will be sleeping tonight anyway, so he doesn't need a name. Now, let's let him rest.'

We set the nameless, siblingless baby rabbit into a small cardboard box that Freny has lined with rags. He falls asleep almost immediately. I feel something move in my chest, a feeling of such tenderness that it is a physical sensation. Perhaps I will name him Angel. All of us take turns wishing him good night. 'Good night, God Bless You and welcome to your home sweet home,' Mehroo says when it is her turn.

I wake up early the next morning and my first thought is for the rabbit. Everybody else is still asleep, the sound of their breathing and snoring filling the house. I head directly for the cardboard box and peer in, hoping that the rabbit is awake.

I look and all I see are the covers. I lift the corners, even while I realize the impossibility of the rabbit having slipped between them. My hands grow more impatient as I run them all across the box. The rabbit is not in there.

I head toward Babu's room and wake him up. He gazes at me sleepily. 'The rabbit,' I say urgently. 'He's not in his box.'

Babu leaps out of bed. 'Did you disturb him during the night?' he asks me sternly.

'No, I swear. I went to see him two minutes ago, only.'

Babu checks the box, too. No rabbit.

By now, the entire household is awake. Lights go on in each room as we rub our eyes sleepily and begin searching for the missing rabbit.

'Let's check under the beds,' dad says. 'He's probably

hiding. We should've not allowed so many people to visit last night. Probably scared the poor fellow.'

Since I am the youngest member of the family and the most agile, I volunteer to slip under each bed to look. Freny gives me a flashlight so that I can see better. No rabbit.

I am in the living room when I hear Babu let out a cry. He is on the balcony and is half-leaning over the railing. He has just spotted something white and black on the street, looking like a ball of crumpled paper. I begin to rush toward the balcony but Babu stops me. 'No,' he says. 'Don't come here. Just ... stay in, that's all.' I halt in my tracks. A feeling of dread is climbing up my limbs and my heart suddenly feels as heavy as cement. Babu does not wait to put on his shirt. He goes down the stairs and into the street in his sadra and pyjamas. Minutes pass. Dad goes to the balcony and when he returns he flashes a quick, warning look at Mehroo that I know I'm not supposed to see but I do. Everybody has fallen quiet and the frenzied activity of the last few minutes has ceased completely as we wait for Babu to return.

We hear his heavy footsteps climbing the stairs. When he walks in, his eyes are bloodshot and his shoulders sag. 'It's him,' he says. 'God knows how but he climbed out of the box and made his way to the balcony. In a million years, I didn't think ...' He stops and shudders and we all know what he's thinking, about the poor creature's sickening flight down two storeys and the dreadful thud with which his flight had ended.

I want to wail, to throw up, to beat on something until my hands bleed, to hurt myself in some way. I can still feel the rabbit's softness under my fingers. Perhaps I had frightened him by carrying him, scared him so much that he looked to escape from my clutches by hurling his soft body into the untrustworthy air. Perhaps it was my vanity,

my plans to brag about him at school that had caused this
to happen.

As if reading my mind, Freny says, 'It's my fault. I
should've picked a deeper box. If only he'd not been able
to get out none of this would've happened.'

'It's nobody's fault,' dad says. 'It just happened.' But we
can all tell his heart isn't in it.

Babu leaves the room and heads for his shower. When
the garbage woman rings the doorbell, he gives her an extra
five rupees for picking up the rabbit's battered body from
the street. 'Pick it up gently,' he tells her. 'He was our pet.
Treat him with dignity, understand?' The woman nods,
amazed at getting paid for something she would've done
for free.

Dad and Babu leave for the factory without breakfast.
I am not so lucky. I am still made to swallow my eye and
glass of milk before I head downstairs for the school-bus.
I decide not to mention to my friends what has happened.
I cannot risk one of them saying something mean or smart-
alecky. If Olga or one of the others were to make a joke of
it, I don't know if I'd be able to control myself. Best not
to say anything.

When Babu gets to the factory, Blackey and Whitey do
not rush up to greet him. Blackey makes his way toward
Babu a little later but Whitey does not come even when
he calls her to come get her lettuce. When he goes up to
her, she stares at him for a moment and then closes her
eyes. Babu is devastated. 'She knows,' he whispers to dad,
who dismisses the notion and tells Babu to use his
commonsense.

'How could she know?' he reasons. 'She's a *rabbit*, for
God's sake. And anyway, it was an accident. You had the
best of intentions.'

But Babu is inconsolable. And the fact is indisputable –
this is the first day that Whitey has not come up to the

entrance to greet Babu. Her rejection cuts like a knife, making his guilt ten times stronger.

By the afternoon, Babu has made up his mind. He calls Shantilal, another timber merchant whose ten-year-old son adores Blackey and Whitey, and makes a deal. If Shantilal wants the rabbits, he can have them. There are just two conditions. One, he would have to take them home, not raise them in the market. And two, he'd have to come for them right away.

I am dumbfounded when Babu comes home that night and says he has given the rabbits away. 'But they belonged to Roshan and me,' I want to scream. 'Whitey and Blackey were our pets, not yours. You should've asked us first.'

But there are many reasons I can't say any of this. First, I am excruciatingly aware of how much pain Babu is in. I know how responsible he feels for the baby rabbit's death and how deeply Whitey's rejection has hurt him. I know that even the act of giving the two rabbits away is actually an act of love, although I'd be hard-pressed to untangle the whole messy web of betrayal and sacrifice and guilt that makes it so.

Second, I know that Whitey and Blackey did not really belong to Roshan and me, that Babu was being generous when he allowed us to claim ownership to two creatures who depended on him for their survival. For the first time, I dimly understand the link between love and responsibility. We are responsible for those we love, I realize, and if we abdicate that responsibility, then we cannot lay a claim to love.

And finally, I know that the world still belongs to the adults and although, in their kindness and mercy they may pretend to share it with us, ultimately it is still their world. It is they who decide when we are old enough to stop playing with dolls, when we should give away toys that they've decided we've outgrown, and when they should get rid of pets that we believed belonged to us.

So I join the rest of the family in consoling Babu and agreeing that he did the best thing under the circumstances and that the rabbits are better off living in Shantilal's home than at the factory where they always had to worry about stray cats.

And I join the family in our conspiracy of silence. We never mention Blackey and Whitey again, though sometimes I see Babu standing at the balcony and staring at the spot that I imagine is where the baby rabbit landed. The next time I visit the factory, I notice that the pen has been dismantled. It is as if Blackey and Whitey never existed.

# Six

IT IS A NIGHT IN May and the excitement in the house is fever-pitched. I am running around the house like a fire engine, knowing I'm making a nuisance of myself but unable to stop. Part of my excitement is pure performance, something to make Mehroo happy, to validate her own feelings of anticipation. Also, isn't this what daughters are supposed to do when their fathers return after two months abroad? Isn't this what the Von Trapp children were like, didn't they burst into the room happily when their father returned from a trip?

For some reason, we don't go to the airport to pick up my father as he returns home after spending two months in Japan touring Expo '70. I have fallen into an exhausted sleep when the doorbell finally rings at three a.m. but am awake and flying out of bed before it can ring a second time. So that I am by the door when someone opens it to reveal a tall, slim, serious-looking man in a dark brown suit and narrow tie. But as his eyes focus on the smiling faces of his relatives – Babu in his sadra and striped pyjama bottoms, my mom and my aunts in their cotton duster coats, my cousin Roshan in her sleeveless pyjamas and me in my blue satin ones – his face lights up. For a second, he looks disoriented, not knowing whom to kiss and hug first but then we are all on him and spare him the decision, a multi-headed army of puckered lips and engulfing arms. 'Bhai, family kem che? How is everyone?' he manages to splutter out to his brother.

I am sitting on my haunches and hugging his legs, waiting for him to acknowledge me when the lights in the adjacent apartment are turned on and the neighbour's door flies open. Perviz aunty, the older lady who lives next door, swiftly crosses the common passageway and stands at the threshold of our apartment. 'Come, come, Burjor,' she says, 'too many months you have been away. Welcome back to your loving family and your good home.' Dad feels compelled to disentangle himself from our arms and briefly put his arm around Perviz, in acknowledgment of her greeting. I feel the adults around me tense at this intrusion into our ranks, at this aborted homecoming, even while their minds tell them to appreciate the fact that Perviz stayed awake long enough to greet my father upon his return.

I am the lucky beneficiary of Perviz's intrusion because the wave of adults has parted and finally dad can spot me. He drops on his haunches, so that his warm, sparkling eyes are level with mine. 'Hello, Thrituma,' he says to me softly. 'I have missed you so much.' I am suddenly filled with a terrible shyness, as if he is a stranger to me, so that when he pulls me closer to his chest, I feel my body getting stiff and I must resist the urge to pull away. But before he or any of the adults can notice, we hear the heaving sounds of the men who are carrying my dad's heavy suitcases up the two flights of wooden stairs. The men are workers from my dad's factory and Babu had asked them to come over for precisely this reason. The arrival of the two large suitcases creates another round of excitement. I disentangle myself from my father's embrace and follow the bags. The two grunting men have hoisted the suitcases on their shoulders and Babu hurriedly directs them into the living room, where they look as if they are about to drop them on the floor with a thud. 'Saala, idiots,' Babu scolds. 'Bricks instead of brains. What do you think is inside these bags, gold bars, that you can just drop? Lower them gently, gently.' The two men grin, familiar with my uncle's quick anger but also with his soft heart. Pesi reaches into his pyjama pocket to retrieve two notes, which he presses into the palms of each man. 'Okay, go,' he says. 'Buy yourself some mithai tomorrow, to celebrate my brother's safe return.' The two men leave, touching their foreheads in appreciation, nodding shyly to my dad on their way out. 'Factory all okay?' he says in response and I am disappointed that this is all he has to say to them.

At the front door, there is some movement. Mehroo, noticing that Perviz is about to enter the apartment and make herself at home, thinks quickly on her feet. Yawning in an exaggerated way, she says, 'Chalo, it's getting late. We can do the opening-fopening of the bags tomorrow. My bhai is tired right now. We should all go to bed.' I find my toes curling in embarrassment over Mehroo's obvious ploy but if she notices, Perviz aunty does not say. In response, she stretches her arms and pretends to be sleepy herself. 'Good idea,' she says. 'Bas, I wanted to stay up to look at my Burjor one time only. Now I can sleep peacefully, knowing he is home safe and sound.'

Once inside, my uncle performs the nightly ritual of applying the stopper and locking the front door. The adults look as if they are about to act on Mehroo's words and leave the suitcases unmolested until the next day. But I am sick with a feeling of letdown because I had asked my dad for a walking-talking Japanese doll and I want to know if he has remembered. None of his letters home had mentioned the purchase of a doll. I know that I will never fall asleep without knowing for sure.

I tug at his sleeve. 'Please, daddy,' I say. 'I want to open the bags now only. Please. I cannot wait till morning.'

When he first looks at me, his eyes seem tired and sleepy. But then he shakes his head once, as if to shake off the cobwebs of sleep and he grins. 'I also cannot wait till morning,' he says, pulling a set of keys out of his suit pocket. 'You open the first bag.'

Carefully, proudly, as if I am carrying the flame at the Olympics, I take the key and fumble with the small lock on the largest suitcase. 'To the right,' Babu advises. 'Turn the key to the right.' I tug the lock open, praying that this is the bag that carries my doll.

At first, I do not see the doll because my dad's shirts are neatly folded on top of the box. Also, there are scores of gold coins the size of a man's fist, strewn all over the top of the suitcase. 'Oh, God,' dad mutters. 'They must have fallen out.' He picks up one coin and hands it to me and I realize it is chocolate wrapped in gold foil. The chocolate coin feels soft and mushy in my hand. 'It's all melted,' I say and my mom bends to scoop them out one by one, before the chocolate leaks into the suitcase.

I can barely contain my excitement now, hopping from foot to foot. As always, the adults laugh and as always, I ham it up even more to keep their laughter coming. I am almost nine years old and already I am cast in the role of the family clown, the comic relief. Getting carried away, I start pulling out dad's neatly pressed shirts, tossing them out of the suitcase as if I am tossing out dirt from a cave that I'm excavating, until Mehroo puts a firm hand on me and stops me. 'Behave yourself,' she says to me firmly. 'Act ladylike, now. Two more minutes will not hurt you.'

But they do, they do. The minutes feel excruciatingly long until we reach the bottom of the suitcase and there, lying in a large pink and white box wrapped in transparent cellophane paper, is my Japanese doll. I let out a yelp. He'd remembered.

Somebody lifts the box gently and opens it. A large, pinkish doll with an unblinking gaze is put in my hands. I am disappointed that the doll is not wearing a kimono but my disappointment vanishes when my dad pulls a round, white pendant at the nape of the doll's neck and out pours a flurry of high-pitched Japanese words, which my dad translates for me. I tug at the string myself but impatience makes me pull too hard and the string simply boomerangs back and my doll makes a choking sound. 'No, pull slowly, like this and release gently,' my dad coaches. A torrent of words escape the doll's mouth again. I am totally enamoured.

Somebody opens the second suitcase but I am no longer interested. I keep pulling at the string, savouring the sound of the incomprehensible words. A few other gifts land my way and I give them a cursory glance. I notice the yards of dress material he has brought for all the women, hear them fawning over them, but I am not interested. But then, a kind of hush falls over the room, followed by a rapid gasp from my mother and my aunts and this gets my attention. Sitting cross-legged on the floor, my father pulls out a large blue box from the second suitcase. 'This is my pride and joy,' he says. 'It's the finest bone china, a complete teaset.' He glances quickly at my mother and aunts and continues: 'Unfortunately, the set is not for the house. It's a business gift for Thakoor. He's helped us a lot during the bad times, as you all know.' My mother looks as if she is about to argue but both my aunts are nodding in assent, swallowing their obvious disappointment, and she feels compelled to nod too. Dad smiles, a sudden, happy smile. 'But if my collaboration with the Japanese goes as planned, there will be many such sets for the house, God willing.' The other adults smile their assent, used as they are to making all kinds of sacrifices for the family business. But I can hear the sighs that they are willing themselves not to breathe. They are disappointed and trying their best not to show it. My dad must've heard something too because he stares at the box sadly for a minute and then sits upright as if he's made a decision. 'You should at least look at the pieces before I give them away,' he says. 'Mehroo can pack it all back later.'

He opens the box as carefully as if it contains a soufflé. Each cup and saucer is individually wrapped in soft, white tissue paper and he uses his handkerchief to touch them and set them carefully on the newspaper that Mehroo has spread on the floor. Bewildered and excited by the reverent way in which the adults are admiring the set, I put my doll down and rush to where my dad is sitting. 'Let me see, let me see,' I say, grabbing one of the cups.

'Careful, darling,' he says, his eyebrows shooting up. 'It's very delicate...'

I'm not exactly sure what happens next. I try to set the cup down and somehow it lands on the stone floor harder than I'd anticipated and somehow it lands on its side, so that I'm suddenly holding only the cup handle in my hand. I stare at the handle in horror and my eyes are already welling up as I see that horror mirrored on the faces of the adults around me. I force myself to meet my father's gaze but his face is a mask. Only the slightly parted lips convey his disappointment.

I want to wail, sob, say I'm sorry, curse myself for my ancient clumsiness, want to curl inside myself and disappear but to do any of these things would be to shatter the silence that has descended upon the room. It has all happened so fast – the pride in my father's voice, his regret at having to give the teaset away, his careful handling of his treasure and my impulsive, thoughtless destruction of it – that no one quite knows how to react. Finally, I see Mehroo and my mom both simultaneously reach for my shoulders, as if to yank me up before I do more damage. I tense up, waiting for the recriminations and lamentations about my clumsiness and my impulsiveness that I know must follow, when I hear my father speak.

'It's okay,' he says. 'It's just a cup after all. Tomorrow, at the factory, I'll glue the handle back in such a way that Thakoor will never even know it was broken.'

All of us remain unconvinced. I still want to die. Seeing this, he cups my face. 'It's all right,' he repeats, smiling this time. 'Don't worry. I know you didn't do it purposely. Now, come on, we have other gifts to open.'

I have already spent eight years of my life living with my father. Although he has mostly been a shadowy presence in my life, has not quite played the influential role that Mehroo has, has not quite stood in sharp relief to the others in my life, I have known for a long, long time that I love him. But today, for the first time, hearing him say those words, watching him struggle to make the lump in his throat disappear, I make an exciting and new discovery: I *like* my dad. I like this tall, serious, kind man sitting in front of me. I'd have liked him even if he didn't belong to me.

✧

A few weeks after my father returns from Japan, he takes me to the Parsi-owned Paradise Café for lunch. The Paradise, with its funky paintings of a naked Adam and Eve in the Garden of Eden, is one of my favourite restaurants. We each order our favourite dish – chicken steak for me; chicken lollys for him. As we eat, dad tells me about Japan, the elegant restaurants that he dined in, the grand reception he got from his Japanese hosts. I listen for a while but then my mind wanders. Suddenly, I shush him into silence. 'Daddy, please. Just be quiet for a moment.' He looks at me quizzically but obliges. I close my eyes and bow my head. After a few seconds, I look up again. 'Okay,' I say. 'Now you can talk again.'

'What were you doing, Thrituma? Why did you tell me to be quiet?'

'I was just imagining that I was having lunch with the Emperor of Japan.'

My dad tilts back his head and laughs, a laugh that climbs up and down an entire octave scale. Overhearing my dad's laughter, Jimmy, the restaurant owner, looks over from his place behind the cash register and beams. Every time we leave Paradise together, Jimmy always tells me how happy it makes him to see the closeness between me and my daddy.

Now, dad takes my hand in his and kisses it. 'God Bless. May all your dreams come true. May you someday really have lunch with the Emperor of Japan and other important people.'

I beam. I love that I can make my father laugh. I love that he revels in my flights of fancy, love the boyishness in him that makes him share my appetite for large dreams.

✧

Much like a Polaroid photo, my dad has come into focus for me since his trip to Japan. Before that, he was an elusive figure in my life, someone who flitted in and out of my life, the dual pressures of a demanding business and a fraying marriage conspiring to drive him out of the house. Occasionally, he would play 'Driver, Driver' with me, where we would each take turns sitting behind the other on the raised threshold to his bedroom and pretend to drive a bus. But the picnics and summer vacations and swimming lessons that my classmates took for granted, had eluded us.

Still, he was immensely popular with my friends, this madcap man who once drove through a park with me and two other friends riding on the hood of his car. After one of my birthday parties, he took all my friends downstairs to feed milk to every stray dog in the vicinity.

But what most charmed – and bewildered – my friends about my dad was his insistence that he was my older brother and not my father.

'This is my dad,' I'd begin on those occasions when he'd drop me off at school after I missed the school-bus.

'No,' he would say in a loud voice, frowning a bit. 'I'm not her dad. I'm her older brother.'

My classmates would stare at me and then at the dark-haired, youthful man who had just bounded up the stairs two at a time. 'Uncle, please, tell the truth, no,' someone would finally plead and then he'd give in with a grin. Drawing me close to his side, he'd say, 'Yes, I'm her daddy but she's also my best friend.' I'd squirm in his grasp, embarrassed and proud at the same time. And the other girls, remembering their aging, grim-faced, stern fathers, would sigh.

For my seventh birthday, my father had declared that rather than trouble my friends' parents, he would drop each one of them off to their homes. We piled on top of each other, eight or nine giggling girls in his old black Hillman. 'Okay,' he had asked. 'Who wants to be dropped off first?' But there were no takers. Nobody wanted to go home yet. 'Drop her off first, uncle,' Anita said, pointing to Roxanne.

'No, not me first,' Roxanne squealed. 'Pick someone else.'

Dad caught my eye in the rearview mirror and raised his eyebrows slightly to alert me to what was coming. Whistling tunelessly, he headed for the nearest traffic circle and drove around it once. 'Okay, we'll keep going round and round the island until someone volunteers to be dropped off first,' he said. The carload of girls giggled when he went around it a second time. By the fourth round, they were looking at each other uncertainly, glancing at me for direction. But I looked resolutely ahead. By the sixth round, there was much shuffling and whispering, broken by an occasional tentative giggle. By this time, dad was singing, 'It's a hap, hap, happy day,' and somehow, this broke the ice, convinced them that they were in the company of a madman, albeit a funny madman. 'Okay, uncle, me first,' someone said. 'You can drop me off first.'

'Done,' dad replied. 'Now, who's next?'

The next day at school, the classroom teacher stopped me in the hallway. 'Sounds like the girls had a good time at your house. But tell me, is it true that your dad drove around the same traffic island fourteen times before he dropped the first girl home?'

'Nobody wanted to be the first to be dropped off,' I explained. 'And anyway, he only went round a few times.'

The teacher shook her head. 'I see. Maybe I should call your dad and get some tips from him about how to discipline my class.'

Like me, my dad doesn't have a practical bone in his body. This trait distinguishes us from the rest of the family. If we bring home flowers, Mehroo lectures dad on wasting money. 'Bring home some fruit or vegetables, something we can use,' she says. 'What good are these flowers that'll die in two days? I can't feed the children flowers.'

The same ethic governs the gifts I receive from my family. For my birthday, I get polyester blouses and gabardine pants. I only want to wear jeans. Nobody buys me any. I long for a pair of suede shoes but the adults tell me they will get dirty in the Bombay dust. So I get yet another pair of black patent leather shoes. I have such a hard time finding shoes that fit my requirement for comfort and my family's requirement of elegance, that every shoe salesman at Metro Shoes in Colaba hates my guts. I am convinced of this.

Everybody knows that I devour books like chocolate cake, that I love music with a passion. Yet, no adult ever buys me a book or a record as a gift. Besides, it's probably just as well that they don't buy me the kind of gifts I want. Seeing how little they know my taste in books or music, I'll probably end up with polyester books and gabardine records.

✧

My father broods.

It is an old family curse, this brooding. My grandfather was a brooder also. That's how my dad refers to himself, as a brooder. He ruminates and worries and thinks obsessively about the past. He remembers slights and insults and embarrassments, collects them the way other people collect seashells. He is what the nuns in school have labelled me – hypersensitive. He considers himself an unlucky man, a man whose achievements have not measured up to his talents. He works harder than anyone I know and yet the family business is like the old B.E.S.T buses that ply the streets of Bombay – spluttering, working in fits and starts, running well on some days and breaking down on others.

We are alike, my dad and I. I have known this since his return from Japan because after the incident with the teaset, we have been spending a lot of time together. We have taken to going to the seaside at least once a week. Sometimes mummy accompanies us and those times are different than when it is just dad and me. Mummy complains continually about dad's driving, asks him to slow down and nags at him until I feel myself stretched as tight and taut as a guitar string.

I may look like a younger version of my mother but under the skin I resemble my father. We are alike in all the important ways. I see his face on gloomy, rain-heavy days, see how the wind and the rain makes him melancholy-happy, how it propels him, this kind of subdued weather, and I see my own soul reflected in him. I, too, love weather like this when the skies are grey and heavy with rain. Like him, I love the sea more when it is rough and in turmoil, than when it is calm and orderly. I, too, understand well that complicated melancholy feeling, because that's when I write my poems and my stories. It's a feeling I dread and welcome, at the same time. Bad weather frees something within me, makes me feel large and grand and as big as the world itself, ready to take on the roaring ocean with a roar of my own. I despise the ordinary, cloudless, sunny Bombay sky because it makes me feel small and ordinary and just – me. It doesn't take me outside of myself, doesn't make me feel powerful and capable of anything, the way a tumultuous day does.

We never discuss any of this, my dad and I. In fact, I'm not even sure that he knows how I feel, only that I 'like' rainy days, also. But I sense all this in him and it makes me feel close to him. I already have a well-honed radar for spotting loneliness in others, or so I fancy. I figure I can recognize them anywhere, that something about the way their faces search the skies or that hollow look in their eyes, tells me who my people are.

My father happens to be one of my people, even if our mode of expressing ourselves is different. My father is dually cursed – although he feels the same lonely-crazy feelings that I do, he is not a writer. So the outlet that lets me express myself on paper, that keeps me from going insane, is unavailable to him. Instead of writing, my dad hums. On wet twilit evenings when the city streets are bathed in gold and orange light, when the Bombay sky bleeds red and purple blood, my father hums.

We are driving down Marine Drive, on our way to Nariman Point, and my father is humming a mournful, sad song. Next, he starts singing although he inevitably does not know more than six lines to any song. His voice is slightly nasal and rich and deep. It is a beautiful voice although he is totally unaware of the fact for the simple reason that no one has ever told him so. Because my father mainly sings in the car, as if he needs movement in order to free his voice. He never asks me to join him in the singing and even if he had, I wouldn't. I have a terrible voice and am deeply ashamed of the fact. Also, I am too shy to sing out loud. This is one of the things that amazes me about him – how easily and unselfconsciously he sings, as if it is merely an extension of speech. I am used to school outings and birthday parties where the girls who are good singers have to be coaxed and cajoled into singing. Even then, there is much squirming and giggling and general embarrassment.

'I, I, I, I love you very much … I, I, I, I think you are grand,' my father now sings. It is one of two cheerful songs that he sings. The other is, 'It's a hap, hap, happy day.' But I am not satisfied until he sings my favourite, a slow, soft lullaby in Hindi, a song in which the singer asks sleep to come gently. When I was younger, my dad used to sing the lullaby to me on nights when I'd lie awake soaked in sweat, running a high fever. Invariably, he would run his hands through my hair when he sang and the rhythmic stroking and the timbre of his voice would create a nest in which I could sleep. Now, I beg him to sing that song and he readily obliges. As always when he sings this song, he pulls me closer to him, so that one of his hands rests on the steering wheel while the other cradles me in the crook of his arm. His voice gets more nasal and plaintive and he stretches out each note to give it even more of its sad power. I feel the inevitable goosebumps on my arm. If he notices, he doesn't say.

Luckily, this lullaby does not affect me as strangely as the other songs do. From the time I was an infant, I have reacted violently to certain songs and sounds. There was an old woman who used to wander through our neighbourhood each morning with her emaciated cow and a bag of hay. Passers-by and folks from the nearby apartment buildings gave her coins for feeding the cow. That was how she earned a meagre living. But it was not the appearance of the rail-thin woman or her bony animal that aroused my pity. As an infant, I saw neither. Rather, it was the long, lingering, trembling wail with which she asked folks to feed her cow, that upset me dreadfully. Every morning she passed from under our balcony, her thin voice floating two storeys upward. Every morning, I lay in my crib and burst into tears when I heard that voice. This continued for months until Mehroo hit upon an idea. She approached the cow-owner and promised her a fixed monthly sum of money in exchange for her not wailing under our window.

The cow-woman's wail is just the first of a series of sounds that fill me with dread and sadness. Certain songs that everyone else thinks are happy and cheerful elicit the same response in me because of a certain minor key. My response to them is so strong that listening to those songs becomes unbearable. 'Turn off the radio,' I beg my cousin Roshan but she just looks at me strangely. 'It's a hit song,' she says. 'It's my favourite. Leave the radio alone.'

Sometimes, I leave the room in tears. Other times, I grit my teeth and try and get through the song. Occasionally, I try to explain my feelings to Roshan or one of my mother's students, who are listening to the radio during lunch. 'It makes me feel all bad, this song,' I say. Almost all of them are older than me and already, they have that uncomprehending look that adults get on their faces when you're trying to tell them something really important. 'If you don't like the song, just leave the room,' one of them says. Mostly, they just laugh. 'Mad, che mad,' I once overhear one of them say to the other. And they turn the volume up.

My dad and I reach Nariman Point and he finds a small spot into which he confidently backs the car. This is one of the rare occasions when we have not stopped on our way to pick up a chicken roll or a tandoori chicken to eat in the car while we stare at the water. I am old enough to realize that my father is a spendthrift and that this habit causes problems at home. Mehroo often bemoans the fact that there is not even enough money at home to pay the butcher, who keeps a daily tab. Dad promises her household expenses as soon as he receives a certain cheque. If Mehroo complains to Babu, he will tell her to speak to my dad. But then Babu approachs his wife, Freny, who is the only family member who has a job outside of the family business. Usually, Freny will help out.

Regardless of his financial situation, my father finds it hard to refuse me anything. Often, as we head for the seaside, I see him remove the last notes from his pocket to buy me a treat. But I am too old now to be able to enjoy the treat without realizing its cost to the other family members.

Tonight, unhappy that I've refused his offers to buy me dinner, he coaxes me to buy something from the various seaside vendors who approach our car. I refuse and begin to lecture him about the value of saving money, in much the same way that I have heard Mehroo do. He listens silently.

'Daddy,' I say. 'Save just two rupees a day. Remember that piggy bank I bought you for your birthday? It was so you could save a little bit everyday. Please. Two rupees only. That's what the nuns at school also say – doesn't matter how much you save, just save a little.'

He shakes his head then. 'No, Thritu, don't ask me for that. I'm not the kind of man who can save a little-little everyday. When I save, it will be phaat! – all in one stroke.'

# Seven

THE BELL RINGS, SIGNALLING IT'S time for composition class – my favourite class of the day. My classroom teacher, Miss D'Silva, walks in with today's assignment. Just last week Miss D'Silva had read my essay out loud to the whole class. I had sat in my seat, my head bobbing with pride while Miss D'Silva drew the class's attention to certain lines in my essay. She was particularly enamoured by the one that read, 'Mr Brown stood in the middle of the room disguised as Santa Claus.' My teacher claimed that that sentence revealed a sophistication beyond my years. 'This is the result of reading voraciously,' she said and then asked if we knew what voracious meant. All heads turned to look at me but my hand stayed where it was on top of my desk and I kept my eyes cast downward, afraid to reveal that I had no idea what the word meant and hoping that everyone would mistake my downcast gaze for modesty.

But now it is time to shine again. I am ungainly, unathletic, uncoordinated, lousy at math and mediocre at almost everything else. Writing is one of the few areas where I am indisputably good and so I look forward to the two hours of composition class each week the way most kids look forward to chocolate. Before Miss D'Silva has finished writing today's topic on the blackboard I am already holding my pencil tightly in my hand, raring to go. But just before the lead in my pencil kisses the blank white sheet of paper in front of me, Miss D'Silva says something that turns my world upside down. 'Now listen girls,' she says. 'For once in your life, do not make your characters blond and blue-eyed. And for heaven's sake give them real names, that is, Indian names, not names like Mr Jones and Mr Henderson.'

I freeze. My mind goes blank. The pencil in my hands, so charged with possibility a minute ago, suddenly feels limp and heavy. For the first time in my young life, I am experiencing something akin to writer's block. I have no idea how to create characters who look and talk in ways other than the ones in the books I have grown up reading. I try to give my characters an Indian name, but all I can think of is Colin and Jack and Susan. I try to imagine what an Indian character might look like but I don't know how to create someone who doesn't have curly red hair or straight, sandy-brown hair. As for making up a character who talks the way we do – who says, 'yaar' and 'men' instead of 'I say, old chap' and 'Jolly good, old man' – I don't have a clue where to start. Until now, my characters have eaten scones and blueberry tarts instead of chutney sandwiches and bhel puri, and to make that culinary and cultural leap seems impossible and daunting and upsetting of the world order.

For even more than I am the child of my parents, I am the child of Enid Blyton.

Like all my peers, I have grown up reading Enid Blyton's books, memorized entire passages from them, escaped in them. I have solved mysteries with the Secret Seven, I have had great adventures with the Famous Five. I have outwitted bumbling British Bobbies with the Five Find-Outers. I have travelled to boarding school with the girls at Malory Towers as they've snuck into each other's dorm rooms for midnight snacks and tromps through the British countryside. I have had crushes on both, the silent, curly-haired Colin and the extrovertish tomboy Georgina. I have lived vicariously in the world of secret passwords and fraternal clubs, in the world of childhood camaraderie and adventure and mystery.

I have shed hot tears yearning for a golden spaniel like Scamper, who is Peter's dog in the Secret Seven.

My obsession with Enid Blyton started a few years ago. Up to that point I was reading the Archie and Richie Rich comic books that my cousin Roshan brought home from Jaffer's Lending Library. But one day, my aunt Freny came home with a Secret Seven book and told me she thought I was old enough to read real books now. I was petrified. I was convinced that I was not old enough to read novels, that I needed to stick to books with pictures as well as words. 'Just try it,' Freny said. 'If you don't like it, I'll take it back.' And so, with great trepidation, I flipped open the book. And found to my great surprise that the words were no more difficult than what I was used to. And that I was lost in the book by page four. And that reading a full story was infinitely more satisfying than reading a comic book. I finished the book the next evening and begged for more. That Saturday, Freny took me to Jaffer's and got me my own membership. And so, at a humble lending library in the middle of a busy Bombay street, my love affair with books began.

Indeed, I have lived so intensely in the fictional world of small-town England, that I know more about this world than the hot, crowded, equatorial city of dark-haired men and women that I dwell in. Nothing that I am reading either at school or at home reflects this world. At home, I read one Enid Blyton novel a day. In my English-medium school, Hindi is taught like a foreign language. My literature textbooks carry poems by Wordsworth and stories by Dickens. Nothing by an Indian writer. Except occasional passages from one of the Hindu epics, either the Mahabharata or the Ramayana. But these seem like ancient history and after all, both narratives are mythologies and it is hard to see how to adapt these tales with their inflated, dramatic language, to my own life. In some ways, the adventures of

Enid Blyton's blue-eyed, freckled young heroes in pastoral England seem more relevant to my life than the pursuits of the Mahabharata's dark-skinned heroes who may look like me but whose world of chariots and archery and old-world chivalry means nothing to a city kid growing up in the Bombay of the early 1970s.

My teacher seems oblivious to the semantic earthquake she has set off in my life with her words. But for the first time in my life, I am sweating a story, staring into space as I chew on my pencil, making a few feeble starts and then erasing them with my scented eraser, the one with the picture of Fred Flintstone on it. I rack my brains to think of some male Indian names. Raj? Ram? Even to my young ears, they sound prosaic and dull. I look around the room. Many of the girls in this class are Catholic with names like Susan and Brenda and Carol, so they're no help. As for the ones who're not Catholic, I'm suddenly confused about who has an 'Indian' name and who doesn't. After all, haven't I heard my family say that my name is a Persian one? Does that qualify as Indian? Is a 'real' Indian name only a Hindu name?

That evening, at home, I want to ask my mother these questions but am at a loss as to how to frame them. And this leaves me feeling inadequate and uneasy. For the first time in my life, I realize that writing is not the easy, almost absent-minded outpouring of emotions that I had always thought it was. That there's more to writing than making up a birthday poem you know your mother will like. Miss D'Silva's words have unleashed something even though I don't know what to call that something. But I dimly recognize that writing is – can be – a complicated and important thing. And that it is tied to other things, things like culture and nationality and history and where you live. This is a brand-new thought: that all writing is not the same and that where you live can define who you are and so change the way you write. I am both excited and confused by how a simple request to change the physical description of our characters is taking me down a new path, making me think about things that I had never thought of before. But I'm also achingly aware of how inadequate my thinking is, how, after a while, my brain simply stops skipping down this new path because I do not have the tools with which to navigate it. And in a flash, I understand something new: That just as reading and writing are linked, so are questions and answers. You have to know how to phrase a question in order to get the right answer. This insight dazzles me and I flip it around in my mind the rest of the evening.

Dad and Mehroo come home from the factory that night and I can tell he is in a good mood.

Over dinner, he tells us a story. 'I got shouted at the factory by the kamdar today,' he says with a grin. 'All of it was Mehroo's fault.'

The kamdar was a tall, grey-bearded, distinguished-looking Muslim who had been my dad's foreman for years. Always dressed in a white kurta-pyjama that stayed spotlessly clean even while my dad's starched white shirts came home covered with grease and sawdust, the kamdar was a soft-spoken but stern-faced man who never hesitated to speak his mind before my father, whom he treated like a brilliant but not very worldly younger brother. Mostly, my father was amused by his foreman's treatment of him. Occasionally, he would mutter about the kamdar getting too big for his breeches and forgetting who was boss. But he also appreciated the fierce, almost familial loyalty the foreman showed toward the business. The kamdar ran the workshop with a kind of patriarchal, proprietary air. He referred to the factory in terms that made you believe that it was his grandfather who had started it. It was he who scolded and kept an eye on the younger, unworldly workers who had left their Northern villages and moved to Bombay and had ended up at my father's factory. The timber market in which the factory was located became more than a place of employment for these men; it became home. They slept under the stars on their narrow rope cots; they cooked their aromatic evening meals on tiny kerosene stoves that glowed in the dying light of the day; they bathed outside the factory before my dad showed up in the morning; they procured water for drinking and toiletries from God knows where.

The kamdar was especially fond of Mehroo. He kept a paternal, protective eye on her because she was the only woman who showed up to work daily in a place that was exclusively male. Most of the timber merchants in the market were old-fashioned Muslims, who went home to wives who covered their faces in purdah when they left their homes. As the only female – and single, to boot – Mehroo should have been the object of much gossip and derision but she wasn't. The flip side of Muslim conservatism is a kind of quintessentially Indian chivalry and respect toward women. Perhaps it was some notion of gallantry that sheltered her. Or perhaps it was the openly protective stance both of her brothers took toward her that deflected any attempt at flirting or innuendo. Certainly, Mehroo herself, with her serious face, her obvious devotion to her two brothers, her doggedness and hard work, did not invite any sexual advances. Anyway, by the time I was old enough to be awed at the fact that my domestic, mild aunt was a pioneer when it came to infiltrating an all-male industry, Mehroo had been my father's business partner for so long that most of the other merchants had long since accepted her.

My dad was still grinning. 'Saala, what curses that kamdar was directing at me. All because of your Mehroofui.'

'What happened?'

The kamdar had stood outside the door of my dad's air-conditioned office and eavesdropped on my father yelling

at my aunt. 'New clothes,' he heard my dad yell. He leaned
closer to the door to hear more snippets of their conversation,
'Nice, expensive clothes ... Spending money,' he heard my
dad say. 'Please, Burjor,' he heard my aunt reply. 'This time,
just forgive me. Just ignore it...'

The kamdar was livid. He paced on the dirt floor until
my father left his office. Then, he lit into him. 'Burjor seth,
God forgive you for what I heard today,' he cried. 'All these
years I am working for you and never thought this day
would come. Arré, seth, this woman has been like a mother
to you. Raised you the way a cow raises a calf. And this
is how you repay her? Shame, shame, even Allah would find
this hard to pardon.'

My father looked confused. 'What did I do wrong? I
was only trying...'

'Wrong, seth? What you did wrong? Yelling at your poor
sister because she bought some expensive clothes? I say, sir,
what's wrong if she spent some money on herself? Womenfolk,
they have their shauk and desires. Business is going good,
Inshallah. And all because she keeps the books for you. And
you yell at her for spending some of her own money...'

My father began to laugh. 'Saala, bevakoof,' he said. 'I
was yelling at her to go buy some new clothes, idiot, not
because she went shopping. See the same rags she wears
everyday? I was angry because she refuses to take some
money to go shopping. I was telling her the same thing you
are saying, that this is her money too and she must spend
some. You don't believe me, go back in and ask her.'

The kamdar looked mortified. 'Praise be to Allah and
please to forgive, seth. All these years I've known your
family, I should've known. Mehroobai is lucky to have a
brother like you. God Bless all three of you. Your old father
will be proud of you even in Heaven.'

We are all chuckling as my father finishes telling this
story. 'Shame on you, Mehroo,' mummy says. 'Getting my

poor husband in trouble like that.' I tense for a moment, waiting to detect an edge in mummy's tone but there is none. Mehroo smiles self-consciously and offers a light shrug.

I relax and allow myself to enjoy the moment. If only every family meal could be like this.

✧

It happens.

I haven't tasted a scone yet and I know now that my many neuroses, my fear of heights, will never allow me to be a carefree tomboy like Georgina, but at least one of my Enid Blyton dreams has come true.

I am now the proud companion of a golden cocker spaniel who looks exactly like Scamper from the Secret Seven.

I come home from a party one evening and our street is shrouded in darkness. The power is out in the entire neighbourhood. Dad meets me at the bottom of the stairs with a flashlight in his hand. When we arrive at our apartment, the entire family is waiting for me at the front door. There are candles in the passageway in the apartment. 'Come,' dad says. 'There's somebody waiting for you in the living room.'

So my first look at my puppy is in the glow of a flashlight. He is curled up and lying in a lined box, his eyes shut tight. His golden ears are almost as big as his body, his tail is absurdly short and his cute-as-a-button nose shines like black leather. He is fat and tiny enough that dad can hold him in one hand.

There is a kind of happiness so strong, a gratitude so profound, that there are no words for it. I look at dad and then at the puppy, who is now awake. Although it is dark, I take in the expectant look on the faces of all the adults. They are all waiting for me to say something but there are no words to express what I feel. No, nothing will do except this whoop of joy and this mad dance that I am performing, hopping from foot to foot. The adults are grinning now and I go on dancing my happiness until the puppy gets scared by all the noise I'm making and begins to whimper. I stop immediately.

I have waited so many years for this dog, have shed so many tears for him while I pleaded and begged for a pet, have seen him in my dreams so often, that it does not occur to me that he will be named anything other than Scamper. From the first moment that I hold this wriggling, sniffing, squirming piece of golden fur in my hands, I think of him as Scamper. 'Hello, Scamp' I whisper. 'Hello, boy.'

But the next morning, Mehroo pulls me aside. 'You have to think of a different name for the puppy,' she says.

I am aghast. 'But why? I have always wanted to name a dog Scamper. Everybody knows that.'

'Well, there is a problem. You know, the servants won't be able to pronounce his name. Better think of a less complicated name.'

In the end, we name him Ronnie. So much for East meets West. The gap between the life I lead in my head and the life I actually live, yawns wide. The Enid Blyton dream lies forgotten in the pages of a Secret Seven book.

# *Eight*

TWO EARTH-SHATTERING REVELATIONS IN two days. This is almost more than I can bear.

The first revelation involves Mehroo. Dad and I are on our way to Crawford Market to buy some fruit when he lets slip about Mehroo's dead fiancé. The world stops for a moment. I had not even known that Mehroo had ever been in love, much less that she was once engaged to be married. I am twelve years old, I want to say to dad. How come nobody ever told me about this until now? But instead, I simply listen as he relates the whole sad story.

A few years after her mother's death from TB, Mehroo herself contracted the dreaded – and often fatal – disease. After her recovery, my distraught grandfather sent her away to a sanitarium in the hill-station resort of Panchgani to recuperate. My dad was heart-broken. Since their mother's death, Mehroo had become both mother and sister to him. And more – often, she was the only one who could reach their father, whose grief had made him as distant as a star. My grandfather, a gentle, scholarly man, found his boisterous, active sons too much to take. Without knowing it, he grew resentful of their loudness, their jokes, their laughter, because it felt like a disturbance, a violation of the silent world he had built for himself. And so, dreading the long silences of the house, my father didn't want his sister to leave.

In all the years that I knew Mehroo, she never once talked about the months in Panchgani. But my father recalled not recognizing his sister when the family went to visit her a few months later. Looking at the young woman with thick brown, braided hair, with cheeks red as strawberries and smooth as cream, he mistook her for an Englishwoman. So he watched with astonishment when my grandfather enveloped this stranger in a hug. 'Hello, pappaji,' she said. Oh my God, it's Mehroo, my father thought.

The glow on her cheeks was from more than the good food and the clean hillside air, the family soon found out. Mehroo was in love. At the sanitarium, she had met and fallen in love with another TB patient. His name was Rumi and he was twenty-five and an engineer in the airforce. He lived in Karachi, hundreds of miles north of Bombay. Decades later, I saw an old Technicolor photograph of the two of them together. Rumi is tall and slender and has a lush dark moustache over full lips. He is wearing a dark suit. Mehroo is shorter but her eyes are ablaze with youthfulness. Neither one is smiling in the picture but despite the formality of the studio portrait, there is a closeness between the couple that is palpable. They look very much in love.

For the first few days that Mehroo was home, my father felt shy and awkward around his sister. The familiar older sister who, after their mother died, had bathed him, cooked for him, later, dressed him for school before she herself got ready for school, had been replaced by this serene, slightly mystical stranger. Mehroo herself marvelled at the change in her brothers. 'Look how big you two got while I was gone,' she'd say almost to herself. But after a few days, as Mehroo took over the household responsibilities again, after she resumed care of him from the older aunts who'd been keeping an eye on the boys, it was as if she had never left.

But the three males in the house felt another loss approaching and feared that this time it would be permanent. 'I don't want you to go,' my dad said fiercely after Mehroo had explained the situation to him. 'If your Rumi is so great, he can move to Bombay and live with us.'

'Try to understand, brother,' Mehroo said mildly. But he was inconsolable.

My grandfather was equally adamant. He feared for his daughter's health and the separation from her family. His mind was made up by the time Rumi's maternal aunt, Perin, came to press Rumi's case for marriage. 'A good boy from a good family, he is, Hormazdji,' Perin said. 'Your Mehroo will be like a queen in our family, I tell you.'

But Hormazd was not convinced. 'Two TB patients marrying each other,' he demurred. 'Any doctor would advise against it. What if there are problems later on, God forbid?'

'Nonsense, nonsense, Hormazdji. Both children are healthy now, by the grace of God. I have faith Ahura Mazda will keep them safe and sound.'

Hormazd tried a different track. 'Mehroo has run this family since my dear wife's demise. I am a widower, with two young sons to raise. With my bank job, how will I manage on my own? Karachi is so far away, the other end of the country. Who knows when I'll see my Mehroo again?'

Perin was ready for him this time. 'Rumi has told me to inform you that he personally will bring Mehroo to Bombay at least once a year. He is having a large family in Bombay; they can stay with us – or with you,' she added hastily.

But the fear of tuberculosis haunted my grandfather. It was bad enough that his only daughter had come down with the same disease that had killed his young wife. He couldn't allow her to marry a man who carried the same dreaded germs. He refused to allow Mehroo to marry Rumi. Mehroo was heart-broken but marrying against her father's wishes did not occur to her.

But for two years, she corresponded secretly with Rumi. Letters addressed to her from Karachi would arrive at her best friend's home and be delivered to her at college. She would reply to the letters before she got home from college that evening. Her brothers knew about this exchange and conspired to keep the secret from their father.

I am not sure how my grandfather ultimately found out about the letters. But that night, father and daughter talked. Nobody knows what they said to each other. But after two years of breaking his daughter's heart, Hormazd suddenly caved. Mehroo was free to marry Rumi.

The preparations for the wedding, which was to be held in Bombay, began immediately. Perin aunty helped Mehroo pick out saris for her wedding and her engagement. Clothes were purchased for the groom's family. My dad and uncle also got into the act, almost delirious with excitement at the thought of a wedding in the family. Despite the shadow of the imminent separation, a rare sense of joy and fun engulfed them all.

My dad still remembers the day the bad news came. It was exactly two months before the wedding. The doorbell rang and Rumi's aunt – the same woman who had a few weeks ago helped Mehroo pick out her wedding sari – came in hurriedly. 'Where's Mehroo?' she asked my father. Then, before he could answer, she lurched toward the kitchen.

Mehroo looked up from the kitchen counter, where she was chopping onions. Her eyes were red from the onions and her face flushed in the Bombay heat. 'Su che, Perin aunty?' she asked. 'What is the matter?'

The woman took a step toward her niece. 'Mehroo, Rumi's dead,' she blurted. 'He had pneumonia for two days only...'

The rest, I have to imagine. Dad does not recall what followed after the awful moment when grief and death walked into their lives a second time. Scenario #1: For a second, Mehroo keeps chopping the onions, mechanically, much like those bodies that twitch and move even after they've been beheaded. Scenario #2: the knife falls from her shaking hands, so that she has to jump back to avoid its sharp descent. Then, she starts screaming, so that for a moment, Perin thinks that the knife has struck her foot. Scenario #3: Mehroo stares at Perin in mute horror. Her eyes widen as the words seep their poison through her body. Then, she drops wordlessly to the floor.

Dad finishes telling the story. I'm not sure if he has any idea about how it affects me because I do what I always do when my heart is breaking: I rearrange my face to make it go blank. I don't let the pain that I feel show in my eyes. I ask careful questions that show no hint of the turmoil and confusion I feel. I tell dad I'm going to wait in the car while he shops at Crawford Market. After he leaves, I allow my jaw to sag in disbelief, let my eyes well with unshed tears, permit myself to feel the sting of betrayal and shock

Confession: At first, I mostly feel sorry for myself. As the youngest member of the family, as someone Mehroo has cared for from my days in the cradle, I had simply accepted as fact that Mehroo loved me more than anyone else in the world, that her life had basically started after my birth. Oh, I knew she doted on her brothers, knew how much she had adored her father, but that was different. Those people had always been part of my life, were known entities and therefore no threat to me. They were not competitors; they were family. Therefore, they didn't count.

But this strange man who has stepped from the mists of the past into the fields of reality, what am I to do with him? This man who has been created by my dad's storytelling, this dead man who has been made alive again by the power of words, where do I bury him now? This man whom Mehroo had loved before I was even born, why do I think of him as a rival? Why do I feel as if Mehroo has cheated on me, betrayed me somehow? How am I now supposed to think of my small, spinster aunt, this one-dimensional, black-and-white figure I had believed existed only to love me? Now that she is suddenly restored to full colour, now that I have to recognize her full humanity, her right to love whoever she chooses without asking my permission, what am I to do with the cardboard image of her that lies tattered at my feet? And why am I jealous of a man who died years before I was even born? After all, he is dead and I am alive. Isn't that revenge enough?

And suddenly, I hear myself and my self-absorption dissolves and then I feel a pain so sharp, so piercing, it takes my breath away. Mehroo had suffered this magnificent wound and I had known nothing about it. I am living in the same home as a woman who has been felled twice by the death of love and yet she is the one tending to me, nurturing me. I am twelve and old enough to know what the end of love feels like, how it rises before you like a brick wall, cutting off all visions of the future.

When we get home, I want to ask Mehroo questions about Rumi, want to tell her how sorry I am, want to at least tell her I know about Rumi. And that I understand. But I remain silent. I'm not sure why. There are no explanations for my silence. Except for maybe this self-serving explanation: For whatever reason, I had learned at a very young age to protect a certain deep part of myself, to not reveal even to those who loved me, a certain core, a certain nerve that was too raw and too vulnerable. The deeper and more intensely I felt things, the more guarded I became. The more silent and introspective I grew from the inside, the more smart-alecky and verbal I felt compelled to be. There was a white space inside me that I was too scared to share with anybody. The irony was that my wretched hypersensitivity, my thin skin, my terrifying capacity to be easily hurt, I knew I had inherited from Mehroo. I knew in the instinctive way that children know things that Mehroo's eyes hid a raw sadness that echoed mine.

And so, I go up to her that night while she sleeps on her single bed and kiss her forehead. She opens her liquidy, brown eyes. 'What is it, Thrituma?' she asks.

I shake my head, trying to keep the lump in my throat at bay. 'Nothing.' But that doesn't feel enough. So I pay her the highest compliment I know. 'Your eyes remind me of an old horse. Kindest eyes I know.'

She smiles.

✧

The second revelation comes the next day when dad and I take Ronnie, my golden cocker spaniel, to the vet. We pull into the large, spacious grounds of the animal hospital and despite my worry about Ronnie, I find myself breathing easier in this tranquil, beautiful place. But Vishnu, the assistant, informs us that our regular vet is away for a month and another vet is taking his place. We are a little annoyed by this but take our place on the hard wooden bench and await our turn.

The door opens and the new vet introduces herself. My jaw drops. It is the Ovaltine lady come to life. The vet's dark hair is tied in a bun and her cheeks are not dimpled but her gentleness, her soft, low voice, her graceful hands as she scratches Ronnie's head, tell me it's the Ovaltine lady just the same. She wears a light pink chiffon sari with silver earrings and she smiles at me tenderly, pats my head and tells me not to worry so much, my dog will be all right. I am enthralled. I want to tell her that she is my real, long-lost mother, I want to tell her that I am adopted and had been raised by wolves and had been awaiting her arrival all my life. But then I suddenly remember Mehroo and her devotion to me and the sad story I had heard yesterday, and I am confused. It occurs to me that I already have too many mothers and that one more, no matter how pretty and graceful and loving, will only complicate matters. I think of all the mothers I have and I know I should feel grateful and sated but I can't shake this broken, empty, bereft feeling I have inside me.

There is something else that's confusing me and that's the way the Ovaltine lady is talking to my dad. There is a searching, speculative look in her eyes that I recognize but do not yet understand. They are talking softly and she is patting my dog all the time that she is chatting with my dad. I hear him say, 'Not his usual appetite,' and 'Did potty inside the house,' but I am barely listening to him. Because what grabs my attention, what transfixes me, is the look on my dad's face. He looks smitten and lonely and wistful and it takes me a minute to recognize his expression as mirroring my own. It takes me a full minute to realize that my dad and I are hungry for the same things – kindness and love and beauty and grace – and that neither of us has found these things in my mother. It makes my eyes sting with tears, this realization, so that I turn away and mumble something about going outside to play with the other animals.

I don't know how much time goes by but then dad is outside with Ronnie straining at the leash as usual. The Ovaltine lady is by his side and when she sees me, she smiles. Half crouching toward me so that our eyes are level, she tells me that Ronnie will be fine and not to worry at all. My dad smiles in gratitude and extends his hand toward her. 'Thank you,' he says softly. 'No problem,' she replies. 'It was nice to meet both of you.'

Dad puts his hand around my shoulder as we walk toward the car. As we pull away, the Ovaltine lady is walking back toward the clinic. Her pink sari glistens like a halo in the mid-morning sun.

We are both quiet on the way home, lost in our own

thoughts. Then, I hear my dad sigh, a long, heavy sigh and I feel compelled to say, 'She was nice, wasn't she? Actually, I liked her a lot better than our usual vet.'

'Yes,' he says, 'she was very nice.' Then, as if he cannot keep the words to himself any longer, he adds, 'This is how I'd always dreamed it would be – that the woman I would marry would be like that, soft-spoken and caring.' I wait for him to say more but he falls silent.

I want to tell my father that I understand him – understand both, the dream and the betrayal of that dream. I want to tell him about my Ovaltine lady fantasy and how, today, for the first time, I saw the fantasy made flesh. I want to tell him that we want the same things, him and I, and that I understand how the not having it has left a hollow, numb spot in each of us. I want to tell him what mummy does and says to me when he is not around, how scared and alone I feel, I want him to turn around and drive back to the animal hospital and ask the Ovaltine lady to run away with us and I want the three of us to drive somewhere, drive far far away, away from the edge of our lives and into a freefall of dreams and possibilities.

I say nothing.

I watch Ronnie, his head hanging from the window, his golden ears flapping in the breeze and I remain silent. I swallow the lump that forms in my throat, I look out the window and blink my eyes until the tears disappear.

But from this day on, I will carry another's grief and longing along with my own, so that my sorrows will no longer be just my own. I will be connected to my father in ways deeper than the accidental geography of birth and blood. From now on, I will see my dad as a fellow traveller, a comrade scarred and betrayed by the same unattainable ideal. My father, I will realize, had his own Ovaltine woman.

For years we will talk about that day at the vet's, talk

about it casually at times, wistfully at others. It will become our own private shorthand for what is missing in our lives, for the incomplete parts of us.

And it will mark us, this unfulfilled desire, so that we will recognize each other in the dark, so that we will be more than father and daughter. We will be confidants; I will console him, bear his cross, spend decades seeking permission from the universe to be happy in my own life, in the face of the knowledge of his grief.

And we will both forever be seeking our way out of the greyness of drab reality – he out of the cobwebs of a ruined marriage, I out of the entrapment of the mythologies of motherhood – and we will spend our lives looking for our way back to the shining celluloid fantasy of the Ovaltine lady.

# Nine

MAD PARSI. The nickname is given to me by a fourth-grade teacher and it sticks, follows me like a shadow through school.

It is a formidable reputation to live up to. Fuelled by the caricatures of Parsis in Hindi movies, the Mad Parsi tries her best to live up to her billing. No stunt is too outrageous, no feat is too daring. Suddenly, she is the custodian of the reputation of an entire group of people whose eccentricities are already the stuff of legend. It is up to her to carry on this proud tradition.

Her reputation is sealed in sixth grade when she comes to school on a Monday and tells her friends she has discovered a new hobby – smashing windowpanes with her bare fists. (Let the record show that she has done this only once, and that too, on a pane that was already cracked, thereby escaping any injury. These details, needless to say, are left out of the retelling of the story.)

But by sixth grade, there is another contender for the title of Mad Parsi. Anita Khalsa is a tall, gangly girl with a wide, infectious grin straight out of a Billy Bunter novel. Her mother is a mild-mannered, stately woman whose characteristic response to her daughter is a bemused shaking of the head, as if she still can't believe she has given birth to this funny, giraffe-like girl.

For a while, Anita and I run neck to neck but on the Day of the Blue Tongue, she inches past me and she is now the maddest of the mad Parsis. What happens is this: in

biology class we learn that writing ink is made from fish
oil. The next day, Anita arrives at school with a brand new
bottle of Parker's blue ink. Since we are allowed to use only
fountain pens in school, we carry at all times, a fountain pen,
a bottle of ink, and sheets of pink blotting paper. And so,
Anita's bringing a bottle of ink to school arouses no suspicion.
At my school, the nuns looked at ballpoints with the same
suspicion and contempt they reserved for condoms.
'Disgusting contraptions,' Sister Hillary would say if one of
us was caught with a pagan ballpoint pen. 'Ruins people's
handwriting. Girls from good families use fountain pens.'

Shortly before lunchbreak, Anita makes a dramatic
announcement. After lunch, she will drink the ink.

We hurry through the hot lunches that are delivered to
us by the tiffin-carriers. The carriers are thin but muscular
men who every morning pick up hundreds of hot lunches
packed in three-piece metal containers from individual homes
and then deliver them to schools and offices all across the
city. My particular tiffin-carrier appears at school balancing
a long wooden box the size of a small boat, on his head.
I often fantasize about skipping school and following him
as he navigates his way into a crowded train with this
wooden plank on his head.

After lunch, we make our way back to our classroom
on the second-floor as discreetly as we can. If the teachers
get wind of Anita's scheduled performance, they will stop
it. This is the first year that we have a classroom with a door
and we make the most of the privacy this affords us. A
month ago, there was the infamous shoe fight, where for
some mysterious reason none of us could later remember,
we removed our shoes and threw them at each other. Outside,
it had been raining hard, turning the grounds into a soggy,
mucky, mud field. At one point, as the fight grew more
boisterous, somebody's shoe went sailing out the open
window and landed in the mud two storeys below. We

cheered the shoe's landing until Zenobia, a fair-skinned, placid girl with a sweet nature, offered to go rescue it. We watched from the window and clapped as she retrieved the mud-covered shoe, holding it up triumphantly for us to see. But just as she was about to return to class, somebody had a brilliant idea. As long as Zenobia was down there, we may as well throw more shoes into the mud. And so we did.

When Mrs Pereira walked into class that afternoon, she was greeted by forty giggling girls sitting at their desks with wet, mud-caked shoes. But we had Mrs Pereira well-trained and she never engaged in conversation with us if it could be avoided. Who knew what could happen? A question about wet shoes could produce an answer about a tunnel to China, if she wasn't careful. So she ignored the puddles of mud on the floor, flipped opened her book and began to read to the class.

Indeed, we had turned Mrs Pereira into a master of avoidance, an accomplishment that we were proud of. Day by day, week after week, we had systematically broken Mrs Pereira's spirit so that she now jumped each time one of us spoke and winced when one of us raised our hands.

'Miss, miss, miss,' Roxanne would say, waving her raised hand frantically.

Mrs Pereira would look up from her copy of *David Copperfield* warily. 'What is it, Roxanne?'

'Please miss, something you just said that I don't understand. Please miss, what is a rubber band? Can you explain?'

'A band of rubber. Now be quiet.'

The rest of us were delighted at this interruption and Mrs Pereira's obvious irritation. 'That was brilliant, yaar,' someone whispered to Roxanne.

Two minutes went by. Henrietta raised her hand. 'Excuse me, miss. Miss?'

Mrs Pereira looked distressed. 'Yes?'

'I just wanted to know, miss. Can I eat this apple in class?' The rest of us gasped. Eating in class was taboo, a sin along the lines of writing with a ballpoint.

But Mrs Pereira was flustered. 'No. Yes. I mean, do what you want. Just be quiet, all of you. No more questions, now.'

'Yes, Mrs Pereira. Thank you Mrs Pereira,' the entire class said, in that sing-song way that we knew drove her crazy.

Henrietta took a loud, crunchy bite from her apple and then passed it on to the girl sitting next to her. We passed the apple around as if it were a joint, timing our bites to when Mrs Pereira started a new sentence.

When the bell rang to mark the end of the class, the befuddled teacher shut her book and fled the room before we could even rise to wish her good day. We looked at each other and nodded with satisfaction. Another successful class.

Two days later, we had another surprise waiting for Mrs Pereira. She opened the classroom door to walk into a room that had been mysteriously rearranged. We had moved the long, vertical rows of desks to the back of the classroom and reconfigured them so that all our desks were lined up horizontally in three long rows. The ceiling fan spun madly over a room that was three-fourths empty. And here was our tour de force – we had attached three cloth sling bags to the ceiling fan, so that when it was on maximum speed, as it was then, the bags whirled around like demons, the mirror work on the green bag flashing in the noonday sun.

Mrs Pereira took in the rearranged furniture, the almost empty classroom, with a deadpan expression on her face. But she flinched involuntarily at the dangerously spinning bags, as if they were a guillotine that would behead her. We giggled, and poked each other in the ribs waiting for her to acknowledge our handiwork or at least, to turn off the fan.

Instead, she moved her desk a few inches so that it was away from the flapping schoolbags, flipped open the textbook and buried her head in it. Chapter five, she intoned in a flat voice.

Anita and I looked at each other, crushed. The moving of the desks was her idea, while the ceiling fan was mine. But given Mrs Pereira's deflating reaction, neither idea seemed particularly brilliant. I felt an involuntary, grudging admiration for our teacher. And immediately vowed to come up with a trick for the next day that would elicit more of a reaction.

Now, someone shuts the door to the classroom, while another girl volunteers to stand guard to make sure there are no teachers nearby. The rest of us stand in a circle around Anita, who unscrews the cap on the ink bottle with a flourish and holds the bottle up to her lips. The rest of us wince. 'Anita, don't, men,' someone says. 'What if it's poisonous or something?'

But Anita's cheeks are flushed and she has that telltale gleam in her eye that tells us her mind is made up. 'Didn't you pay attention in class today, girls?' she says in a high-pitched, prim voice, wagging her finger at us just like Mrs Pinto does. 'Ink is made out of fish oil. And that is good for you.' And before we can stop her, she tips back her head and downs a third of the ink. She gags a bit but keeps drinking.

Watching her, I am caught between two contradictory thoughts. On the one hand, I am seized with admiration for Anita. On the other, I know that I will have to figure out a way to outdo her to seize back the title of Mad Parsi.

But the thing that seals my admiration and affection for Anita is what she does next. She tips her head again and drinks some more. And then, she smacks her lips. That smacking of the lips is what makes us break the dumbfounded, worried silence that has gripped us and burst into cheers.

Anita grins. Her teeth are blue.

✧

I am at a birthday party for my friend Diana, one of the most popular girls in school. Bone-thin but wiry, she is, in my mother's admiring phrase, an 'all-rounder' – a good student and a competitive athlete. The nuns and teachers adore Diana because not only is she bright and intelligent, she is polite and well-mannered. Also, she comes from Parsi royalty – her father is a prominent doctor and hails from a family known for their sophistication and cultured ways. So I know it is a privilege to be invited to a birthday party for Diana.

The house is large with high ceilings and cream-coloured walls. It is the kind of house that makes me want to lower my voice when I speak. This house, these people are different from my house and my family in ways that I can sense but not articulate. Diana's mother is a soft-spoken, cultured woman who is doing her best to entertain the boisterous group of sixth-graders at her home. We play a variety of games like Charades and then it is time to eat. Diana's mom turns to us. 'Will some of you go into the next room and carry out a few chairs? We need some extra ones.' I immediately volunteer to help and follow two other girls into the next room where Diana's older sister is sitting cross-legged on the floor with some of her friends. As always, they ignore us. A record is spinning on the player. I listen to the song but it sounds totally unmusical to me and I don't understand any of the words. I have lifted a chair and am carrying it out of the room when I hear Diana's sister say, 'I can't get over this song even though I've heard it a million times. Just listen to the lyrics. They're like a poem. I tell you, this is the song by which the 'sixties will be remembered.'

'What's it called?' one of the older girls asks.

Diana's sister sounds incredulous. 'You mean you don't know *The Boxer*?' she cries. 'But this song is going to be a rock classic, I tell you.'

I have no idea what they're talking about. But the hair on my arm stands up and I am filled with a rush of excitement. Where I come from, nobody ever talks this way about music. Where I come from, a song is something to be whistled along with and music is an impractical luxury, like flowers and art and museums. Nobody I know has ever asked me to listen to the words of a song. I love what Diana's sister has said, the self-importance in her voice, the confidence in her tone, the way the others nod solemnly, as if they're all part of a secret tribe. Suddenly, I want nothing to do with the silly, childish girls who are wolfing down chicken sandwiches all around me. I want to let myself back into the other room and join the holy circle of the older girls, I want to listen again to that song as intently as they are, want to understand what the mumbling voice of the singer is saying, want to be grown up enough and smart enough to say wonderful, inexplicable, glamorous lines like, 'This is the song by which the 'sixties will be remembered.'

But I am stuck with the chicken sandwiches girls. I do not have the confidence to rise from the table and ask to be let into another circle. Also, I know that like most older sisters, Diana's older sister won't give me the time of the day. A slow, sad feeling sweeps over me. Just as Miss D'Silva's words had parted the curtains for me for an instant and provided me with the glimpse of some other, wondrously complicated world, so have Diana's sister's words. But then the curtain has closed again, banishing me as always to the world of giggling schoolgirls who sang *Born Free* and *A Spoonful of Sugar*, who said inane, predictable things instead of inexplicable, outrageous declarations that made my hair stand up in excitement. A sour feeling of longing and loss lodges in my stomach, so that I turn away from my half-eaten sandwich. 'Are you all right, Thrity?' Diana's mother asks and I nod my head mutely, trying to not let my misery show.

I am different from these giggling girls at the table. I

know this now. There is another world out there, a world where perhaps there's a corner for misfits like me. But how to gain entry into that world is a mystery bigger than any that the Secret Seven ever solved.

My Enid Blyton obsession has finally melted away into adulthood but not without a last hurrah. It happens the day Freny tells me gently that she thinks I've outgrown my beloved author, and yes, even the Billy Bunter and Nancy Drew novels I've been reading and that it was time I read something more appropriate to my age, such as Mills and Boon romance novels.

I am appalled. What, give up my beloved childhood friends whose lives I was more familiar with than the lives of the kids I went to school ? Peter, Georgina, Colin, Scamper, and Billy and Bessie Bunter had kept me company while the adults were too busy for me, running around as they were in their own private circles of misery. To deliberately give up such loyal friends would be a dastardly act of betrayal. I remember the countless hours I had spent reading these novels to the point where I could recite entire pages by heart – a feat that I used to perform regularly until the evening my mother slapped me in the presence of the old woman who lived on the ground floor. We had just returned from a parent-teacher conference where Mrs Patel had complained about my habit of repeating the very last thing that she said. 'It makes the other girls think she's making fun of me,' she'd said. 'I can't tell if she's trying to be a smarty-pants or not.' And although I vigorously shook my head no, mummy decided that the teacher's complaint was genuine and somehow linked to my ability to memorize entire passages from books. During the bus ride home she'd told me that both irritating habits had to stop immediately and I had promised and so both of us were equally stunned when I began to recite lines from *Last Term at Malory Towers* as we ascended the building steps. The door to the ground floor apartment had flown open just as mummy's hand flew across my mouth and for a moment I was too ashamed and appalled to cry. It was the first time mummy had ever struck me in front of a stranger. She began stuttering an explanation to the old woman on the ground floor but I was running up the stairs, two steps at a time. But the slap worked. From that day on, I lost my ability to memorize passages. Most days, I didn't care. But some days, it felt like a loss, like forgetting a card trick you had known all your life.

So when Freny asks me to give up Enid Blyton, it feels like another loss. We are in her and Babu's room during this conversation and a garlanded picture of the prophet Zoroaster hangs on the lemon-coloured wall. With a dramatic flourish, I walk over to it, stand on my toes and touch the bottom of the photo frame. 'I swear to God I will never stop reading Enid Blyton,' I say. 'These are the only books I want to read my whole life.'

Freny suppresses a smile. 'Okay,' she says. 'But if you ever want to read anything else, just let me know.'

Two weeks after this declaration of undying devotion to Ms Blyton, I casually pick up one of Roshan's romance novels. On the cover, a tall man with thick dark hair wearing a loose white billowy shirt and tight black pants is sweeping a slim-waisted girl with long red hair off her feet. Making sure that Roshan is not around, I flip through the pages, stopping when I come across a passage of what appears to be torrid love-making.

I am hooked. Hello, Brad and Luther and Hal. Goodbye, Fatty and Peter and Colin. Goodbye, Georgina the tomboy. Hello, Daphne the virgin.

# Ten

J ESSE HAS THICK BUSHY EYEBROWS that she hand-plucks fiercely
when she is trying to concentrate, a mop of wild hair and
a pair of pink denim jeans.

It is the pink jeans that makes us friends.

For some reason, the adults hate Jesse's jeans, are
offended by them, read into them things about the wildness
of her spirit and her untamed nature. The jeans make them
think Jesse is an unpredictable nonconformist who looks
down her long Parsi nose at their simple, middle-class ways,
and since this is mostly true, it makes them hate her. Nobody
in our neighbourhood – where we all lived and died by the
all-pervasive code of, 'What will people think?' – dares to
wear pink jeans. Also, it is unheard of for a teenage girl to
care so little about her personal appearance, to wear sneakers
instead of high heels, to care more about books than
jewellery, to prefer silver to gold, to run her hands impatiently
through her short hair, instead of combing her long tresses.
And to make matters worse, Jesse talks openly of her many
platonic relationships with the boys she'd gone to school
with, talks about them with an easy casualness that has none
of the simpering coyness that usually defines the way girls
are supposed to talk about boys. Rumour has it that Jesse
had been in love with a Muslim classmate and her scandalized
parents had packed her off to her grandmother's house in
Bombay but if Jesse knows about the rumours floating
around her like a dark horde of bees, she does nothing to
refute them.

Instead, she speaks with great affection about the small town that she grew up in and the liberal, progressive co-ed school that she had attended. And in doing so, she pisses off the folks in the neighbourhood even more. Most of the Parsi families who can afford it send their children to Catholic schools, where we flatter ourselves that we are receiving a great education at the hands of the Irish and British nuns. But Jesse pokes fun at our arcane, private school ways – how we are divided into different 'houses' or groups named after different saints, how we fight so zealously at the annual inter-school athletic meets, as if winning medals for our school is the ultimate expression of our purpose on earth. At her school, she tells us, her frumpy but brilliant principal gave a prize to every student who participated in a sport. And the prize itself was revealing – instead of the militaristic gold and silver medals that we receive, the kids at Jesse's school each received a ribbon. While we pay lip service to homilies like, 'It's not what you win, it's how you win,' Jesse's school puts that in action.

But the greatest insult is that Jesse doesn't seem as fawningly grateful about being in Bombay as we want her to be. After all, we are Bombayites, residents of the greatest city in India. In our pride in our city, in our pity for anybody who is not from it, we are as arrogant and insular as New Yorkers. We want all newcomers to be cognizant of their good fortune at being in Bombay, want them to pay homage to that fact. But Jesse insists on continuing to talk about her sleepy little hometown – as we see her small but bustling city – as if it was something to be proud of.

I am thirteen when Jesse comes to live with her grandmother in the apartment next door to ours. But we have known each other for years before Jesse moved permanently to Bombay because she and her younger sister had spent every summer with their grandmother. Our apartment and her grandmother's flat shared a connecting door at the balcony. Jesse's sister, Perin, was only two years older than me and we spent most of our summer holidays being shunted from one apartment to another while the older girls – Jesse, Roshan and the third floor neighbours – ganged up against the two of us and avoided us as if we had leprosy.

It is Lust for Life that makes us friends.

A few months after she has moved to Bombay, I run into Jesse at the bakery across the street from our apartment building. She waits until I purchase the bread and we stroll home together. It has rained earlier and the streets are slick and orange from the twilight evening. 'It's a beautiful evening,' I say, almost under my breath.

'Yes it is. Reminds me of that Moody Blues song, *Voices in the Sky*. Do you know it?'

I shake my head no and Jesse begins to sing softly, in a beautiful, wistful voice that runs through me like a chill.

*Bluebird, flying high*
*Tell me what you sing*
*If you could talk to me*
*What news would you bring?*

I suddenly feel absurdly, insanely happy. The song and Jesse's sorrow-tinged voice echo perfectly the liquidy, lone-wolf feeling that has gripped me at dusk for as long as I can remember.

We have reached the front entrance to my side of the building. Jesse stops singing and stares at me for a second. Then she says, 'I notice when I come home from college each evening, you're usually on that rocking chair on the balcony. What do you do? Homework or something?'

'I write,' I mumble.

'Beg pardon?' she says, with her fake South Indian accent.

'I write ... poetry,' I say, feeling my face flush.

But Jesse doesn't do anything cringe-making, like calling me a poet or asking me to show her some of my poems. Instead, she says, 'I just bought a 45 that I think you may like. Would you like to stop by after dinner this evening and listen to it?'

There are some raised eyebrows at home when I say I am going over to Jesse's apartment for a few minutes. I notice that Roshan looks startled, as if the closeness in their age makes it much more logical that she should be the one invited over. I pretend not to notice the hurt and embarrassment on her face.

The song is Don McLean's *Vincent*. I know who he is because *American Pie* is one of Sister Hillary's favourite songs but I've never heard *Vincent*. From the first, 'Starry, starry night,' I am hooked, mesmerized by Don McLean's clean, silky voice, the stark melody and the impressionistic, powerful lyrics. *Frameless heads on nameless walls* ... how can someone come up with a line like that? In that moment, my own pathetic poems shrivel and die anonymous deaths, buried in the notebooks they have been born in.

The record ends. 'Again,' I say in a choked voice. 'Can you play it again?' It is my intention to memorize the lyrics before I leave this evening. Despite the dark – Jesse has turned off all the lights in the living room, so that we can listen to the record in total peace – I think I see a look of approval on Jesse's face.

We play the song seven times in a row. When the last note dies away, I say in my usual, overly dramatic way, 'I pray to God that someday before I die I write a poem half as good as this song.'

To my surprise, Jesse snickers. 'Don't pray to God about it. If you want to write a good poem, read some great poets. What's God going to do, write the poem for you?'

'Don't you ... believe in God?' I ask, not wanting to hear the answer.

'No,' Jesse answeres shortly. 'And I don't believe in all the Lord Zoroaster this and Jesus Christ that, mumbo-jumbo either.'

I gulp hard. The pink jeans I can defend Jesse for. Not believing in God is a different story.

But then I think of how Jesse had sung *Voices In the Sky* earlier in the evening, purely, achingly, and how she has sat with her eyes closed while Don McLean sang *Vincent*, an expression on her face like she was in church, and I know that although she is an atheist, Jesse still believes in something large and beautiful. I realize for the first time that it is possible to pray without believing in God, that it is possible to be so in love with the heartbreaking beauty of the world that that alone becomes some kind of a religion.

'You know, Van Gogh didn't believe in God either,' Jesse is saying and I make my way back to the present.

'Van who? Who's that?'

'Van Gogh? He's the painter that he's singing about in *Vincent*. Haven't you heard of the Impressionists?'

I shake my head mutely, despair climbing up my limbs like a fever. I had never realized how much there is to know in the world and how little I knew of it. I had not even considered that Don McLean was singing about a real person. I am sure Jesse will now turn away from me in disgust.

Instead, she goes leaping out of the room and returns with a heavy, glossy book. It is a book of paintings titled *Vincent*. She hands it to me and I turn the pages as reverently as any Pope ever handled a Bible.

These are the paintings of a madman. This much is obvious to me as soon as I start turning the pages. A laugh of shocked delight escapes my lips. I gasp in pleasure as I turn each page, feeling a whirling, crazy joy as I take in the enormous, fiery suns, the swirling skies, the crazy crooked lines, the mad, passionate brush strokes.

Jesse sits next to me while I look, pulling on her eyebrows.

Her face is expectant as she searches mine and it occurs to me that she is willing me to love this book as much as she does, that she is seeking me out, just as I am seeking out her friendship. The thought surprises, scares and delights me.

'The mark of Cain,' she murmurs, after she has stopped scanning my face.

'What?'

'Oh, sorry. Nothing. Just a line from a book I love, called *Damien*. It's by a German writer called Hermann Hesse.'

I nod. I have given up trying to keep up with this strange, brilliant girl, who is this unexpected blend of loud-mouthed confidence and vulnerable sensitivity.

The next evening, I am sitting on my rocking chair on the balcony, trying to write a poem that will capture the gold of the evening sky, when Jesse pounds on the connecting door. 'Open up,' she yells, when I look up from my notebook.

She has two gifts for me, the first in a long row of gifts. The first is a copy of the art book I had looked at yesterday. The second is a book called *Lust for Life*. It is a thick book, serious looking, the kind of book a grown-up would read and Jesse explains that it is a biography of Van Gogh. My heart drops at the word 'biography'. I am mostly reading Mills and Boon romance novels. I am not sure that I can handle a book like this. But after making the usual protestations that nice Parsi girls from good families make each time someone gives them a gift, ('Oh, you shouldn't have wasted your hard-earned money on me, really') I accept the two books.

Later, it hits me that I have never before received a book as a gift. I am used to getting gifts of clothes and shoes from my family.

Equally unfamiliar is the fact that Jesse has written an inscription inside the book. I know that if I were ever to give a friend a book, mummy or Mehroo would ask me to leave it blank, in case my friend wanted to return the book. The fact that Jesse has written in the book and made it unreturnable, is an act of such bold self-confidence that it adds to the novelty of the whole experience.

I read the inscription: *To Thrity*, it says. *For the love of colour and light.*

So the game is up. This strange, brash, eccentric girl knows me better than my own parents. We are going to be friends, after all. I am doomed to defend her, protect her, fight for her right to wear pink jeans. I know this friendship will exact a price, that I will no longer be able to pretend to be the nice, quiet good girl whom all the neighbours love. Jesse will require me to choose sides.

*For the love of colour and light.* But there is no real choice, is there? Jesse has seen through me, seen through my humble, goody-two-shoes act, to a soul that is as restless and defiant as her own. For years now, I have secretly divided all the people I knew into two camps – the earth-dwellers and the sky-dwellers. Jesse is definitely a sky-dweller.

Lust for Life. That's what I suddenly have, all right.

✧

I read Van Gogh's biography in two days.

And learn more about the mysteries of my own life than about his. All the things that have never made sense to me before – why I never feel comfortable when I'm with the 'in' crowd, why I always stick up for the underdog, why I don't lust after the things that make most of my friends happy, why the evening sky has made me feel melancholy and lonely for as long as I can remember, why certain songs have a heart-tearing effect on me – all of these suddenly become clearer.

I have been a misfit for a long time. Now I have a companion in a crazy Dutch painter who was dead long before I was born. *Lust for Life* affects me in peculiar ways. I suddenly develop a slight stutter when I speak and tear my hands through my hair in what I imagine is an eccentric, erratic gesture. I begin to eye family functions and glittery events like weddings with great suspicion, holding myself apart from the gaiety and superficiality that such occasions demand. For a brief while, I carry a notebook at all times, pretending to write poems even when no poem suggests itself. I refuse to accept rides to school from my father, preferring to walk or ride the bus, trying to reject the small privileges of affluence, in much the same way the young Vincent turned his back on his wealthy family of art dealers.

If Jesse notices these changes, she does not say. Instead, she plies me with other books, until the words, Monet, Dali, Turner and Degas roll off my tongue as effortlessly as the names of classmates. On weekends, we visit the booksellers who have set up shop on the pavement at Flora Fountain and I dig into my own pockets to buy art books. Someday, I hope to have a collection to rival Jesse's.

These books give way to other books. Jesse introduces me to Shaw, Dostoevsky, Hesse, Chekov, Steinbeck. I lose myself in the world of books, revel in Shaw's biting wit, the morality of the Russians, the brash confidence of the Americans. I read so much that at times I have a hard time concentrating on and remembering my own life. My head swims with words and dialogues and the names of characters. At night, I dream strange dreams in which waterfalls of words pour out of me, an endless, easy stream of beautiful language, held together like beads on a string. I get up the next day and I write. I write poems, stories, essays. At times I feel as if I have no body, no knit of flesh and bones that holds me together. Instead, I am held together by words, a phantom body that will disappear if the words do, like a line drawing that can be erased.

I give up wearing pink, printed blouses for white kurtas

and refuse to smile in photographs, assuming instead a serious, studious look. But some of my posturing is genuine – Jesse has unleashed in me a desire for knowledge that no teacher, nun or textbook was ever able to do. For the first time in my life, I don't want to take the easy, lazy way out.

Every evening Jesse and I stand on our respective apartments, lean on the railing of the balcony and talk until the sky turns orange and then indigo and then black. We talk about music and art and books and comment often on the changing light of the day. I feel completely fulfilled and energized by these conversations, as if they fill a void that I hadn't even known existed. I hunger after every morsel of knowledge that Jesse drops, storing it away like a dog his bone. Mehroo comes out repeatedly and calls me to dinner but I ignore her calls. The hunger for the world is bigger than the world itself and no dinner of mutton cutlets and okra is going to feed it. Often times, I wonder where my life would've led if Jesse hadn't moved next door to me when she did and then I could weep with gratitude at this twist of fate. I ask myself if I would've ended up being one of the countless bland, docile, conventional girls that the neighbourhood is filled with and once I even suggest this to Jesse but she shakes her head impatiently. 'What bloody rot,' she says. 'You would've discovered all this whether I was here or not. You have too much intelligence to have ended up like Dolly Dollhouse or Polly Pollyanna.'

I laugh at that but I'm not so sure.

Things have been different for me at school since the last few years. Now, I am one of the undisputed group leaders, known for my outrageous stunts, defiance of authority and general extrovertishness.

It was not always so.

Years ago, I was the kid who was the butt of other

children's jokes, the silly, amiable, star-struck kid who tagged along behind the other, more popular girls, who were faster, louder, bolder. Handicapped by my wretched sensitivity, I would pretend to laugh at jokes that had me as the punch line even while I was dying from inside. I would read the Charles Atlas ads on the back pages of the Archie comic books, would identify with the ninety-nine-pound weakling who had sand thrown in his face, and would fantasize about the day when I would turn into somebody confident and assertive. But in the meantime, I laughed as loudly as the rest of them when somebody cracked a joke at my expense.

'Hey, girlie,' Olga would say. 'How come your one eye is smaller than the other? It makes you look like a cockeyed crow or something.'

'A cockeyed crow?' someone else would repeat. 'Olga, men, you are too much sometimes.' And I would swallow the hatred for Olga that lodged like a pebble in my throat and smile appreciatively at Olga's wit.

And then one day, I decided to change. I stood before the bathroom sink at home and decided it was time to put an end to the jokes. I wasn't exactly sure how to shatter this mould, this role of the good-natured buffoon that I was getting typecast as, but I knew that if I were to maintain a shred of self-respect it had to end.

So I did a revolutionary thing. The next time Olga made a wisecrack about my legs being so short that God should've thrown in a ladder for free, here's what I did: Nothing. I did not join the others in their laughter. I did not join in the chorus of praise of how clever and funny Olga was. Instead, I simply stood there looking at her unsmilingly, my face as blank as chalkboard.

And Olga panicked. The ground beneath her feet had shifted, some small, as yet invisible, cracks had appeared where she stood, but she could not detect what had changed. She knew that something was different, that the balance of power had somehow seesawed away from her but she could not put a finger on it. She looked at me uneasily, as if it was dawning on her for the first time that she needed my complicity, my fawning affability, for her to hold on to her position of power. Actually, watching the various emotions – unease, distrust, embarrassment, fear – flit across Olga's round face, it dawned on me for the first time how much Olga needed me to build her up. I felt something akin to the heroin rush of power.

'What's up, men?' Olga said, in a desperate attempt to stop the transfer of this invisible force from her to me. 'Why are you scowling like some dirty fisherwoman?'

I felt a second's panic at this open challenge. But then, I remembered my resolution from a few days ago and when I spoke my voice was even and thankfully free of the emotional tremor that it usually carried. 'Oh sorry,' I said. 'I just didn't think what you said was funny, that's all.'

Olga spat out a comeback and spent the next few days trying desperately to recapture her old glory, but the tide had changed. And I had had my first lesson in the power of transformative change.

By eighth grade, I am one of the most popular kids in the class. The nuns love me because I come up with original songs to celebrate all their feasts and saint's days, the teachers are fond of me because I spend the afternoon recess coaching the 'slow' girls in history and English and my friends show a bemused admiration for my willingness to never refuse a dare.

And then Jenny arrives from New York.

# Eleven

JENNY IS ACTUALLY THREE YEARS older than most of us but she has been placed in the eighth grade because everybody knows that the education she received in America is far inferior to ours. There are rumours that her brother in New York shipped her back to Bombay after finding her half-naked with her boyfriend, a rumour that immediately makes her seem like a goddess from a different planet. We all marvel at the incongruity of Jenny's New York sophistication and her simple, elderly parents whom we see occasionally at school. Jenny's parents are Catholics from Kerala and her mother is a shy, introvertish woman who barely speaks a word of English.

Jenny is anything but simple or shy. With her American accent, her constant gum chewing and her casual slang, she is a colourful burst of glamour in the school where most of us have known each other for years. She is also very beautiful, with dark chocolate skin and thick jet-black hair that rests in bangs that come up to the edge of her large, black eyes. Unlike the rest of us, she is always popping candies and chocolates in her mouth but the sugar has not eaten into her large, white, perfect teeth. She talks differently than us, referring to the loo as the 'restroom' and ordering a 'pop' instead of a soft drink. She also drives the nuns crazy with her insistence on wearing her uniform short enough to display her muscular thighs. While the rest of us wear our white socks up to our calves, Jenny comes to school wearing ankle socks. Within weeks, we are all folding our socks at the ankle.

Our first conversation is about music. In a fortunate happenstance Jenny and I ride the same school-bus, she getting on about twenty minutes before I do. 'Hey girl, I liked that crack you made in Mr Singh's class yesterday,' Jenny says to me one day, rolling her 'r' as she says 'girl', just like they do in Hollywood movies. 'Say, somebody mentioned to me that you're into rock-and-roll. What kind of bands do you like?'

But when I say the Beatles, Jenny seems disappointed. 'Oh yeah, they're all right. But what about newer stuff, like, for instance, do you like Deep Purple?'

'Yeah, I like him a lot,' I lie.

Jenny looks embarrassed. 'Um, actually, it's a group.'

I feel my ears turning red. I am convinced that this glamorous American girl who is three years older than I am, will have nothing to do with me after this, having seen me for the impostor, for the wannabe hipster that I am. So I'm pleasantly surprised when I board the school-bus the following morning and Jenny hands me a copy of Deep Purple's *Burn*. 'Here,' she says lightly. 'I brought this in for you to borrow. Check it out and tell me if you like it.'

I check it out. I like it. I ask her if she'd like to borrow some of my albums and she offhandedly says she'll get off the school-bus with me one evening and check out my collection. I am charmed by this casual informality that does not wait to be invited. It is so different from the stifling, rule-bound society that I am used to.

But when Jenny accompanies me home one evening, I can tell immediately that the adults don't like her. My mother seems taken aback by how much more mature and physically developed she is compared to most of my gawky friends. Mehroo seems perturbed by Jenny's apparent lack of manners. Unlike the fawning, nauseatingly polite stance that my friends and I adopt when we visit each other's homes, Jenny is polite but reserved. She does not spend much time chatting with the adults, wanting instead to go into the living room and start spinning some records. And when we get there, she turns up the stereo to as loud as it will go. My stomach muscles clench as I brace for what's coming. And sure enough, Mehroo is in the room a few minutes later, covering her ears with her hands, and shouting to be heard over the music. 'It's too loud,' she shouts. 'I'm sure the neighbours on the ground floor can hear it also. I cannot do any work in the other room. Turn the volume down.'

But instead of apologizing profusely Jenny merely fixes her dark eyes on Mehroo. 'That's all right , aunty,' she says. 'We'll just shut the door.'

Mehroo looks as startled as I feel. Ours is not a family where individual privacy is valued enough that we can go around shutting doors on each other. Indeed, the only time we shut doors is when we are in the bathroom. But Jenny looks blissfully unaware of how revolutionary her words are and after giving me a, 'What kind of creature have you dragged home?' look, Mehroo leaves the room.

Jenny immediately gets up and shuts both doors to the living room. I keep my face deadpan and my manner as casual as hers but from the inside, I'm a mess of emotions – aware that Mehroo will be hurt by this gesture and that mummy will use it to bolster her instinctive dislike for Jenny but also feeling the kind of triumphant freedom and carefreeness I have never experienced before.

It is the first of many such experiences. Two things are clear to me soon after I meet Jenny: One, most of the adults I know do not like her and are made uneasy by her presence. Two, they are unaware of the opposite effect their advice of my not getting too close to Jenny is having on me. Their dislike of her makes me seek her out even more because I can finally experience the dual pleasures of pissing off the adults and the heady feeling of defiant freedom that being with Jenny gives me. My friendship with Jenny makes me feel connected to America, pulls me out of the narrow pathways of my own life and transports me to a distant, almost fictitious, land of youthful energy where the idols of authority are being toppled everyday.

But first, Jenny and I have to grow in size. The two of us alone cannot take on all the forces against us – the nuns and the teachers at school, my family, even my schoolmates who are scandalized by her frank stories about her steady boyfriend in America with whom she 'did things' and stories about how a classmate at her New York high school had thrown a bottle of ink at the teacher he had been annoyed with. I think the ink story scandalizes us more, growing up as we are in a society where teachers are revered as mini-gods. Anyway, we are soon joined by two other friends – Patty, a Catholic girl whose brothers had settled in Australia and Yasmin, a girl from a progressive Muslim family. Now, we are a band of four and ready to take on the world.

The school has a sickroom – a small room with a single cot where we could go and nap for a few minutes if we were feeling unwell. The room has a stairwell leading up to a door and one day Jenny decides to push open the door to see what lies behind it. She discovers an attic where the nuns store their belongings. But there is enough floor space for three or four girls to sit quietly and talk in hushed whispers (through the walls we can hear the low murmur of the nuns' voices as they moved around in the nunnery) while they pass around a cigarette. Patty also makes a discovery that convinces us that we were destined to discover this room for our clandestine meetings – lying on the floor next to the neatly packed cardboard boxes is half of a coconut shell, which made for the perfect ashtray for the ashes from our cigarettes. The dry shell is our talisman against getting caught, our good luck charm. And indeed, we would never be caught red-handed although Mr Narayan, the math teacher, often flashes me his alert, eagle-eyed look when I traipse into his class after one of our sessions.

There are a few narrow escapes. One evening after school has ended for the day, Jenny has a brainwave – instead of walking all the way to the girls' restroom to light a cigarette, perhaps we can sit on the floor in the back of the classroom and smoke there. I have the good sense to suggest that perhaps we should light only one cigarette at a time, to keep the smoke down. For a few minutes we smoke in peace. Then, we see Sister Hillary walk by the classroom and duck down, hoping she hasn't seen us. But Sister Hillary, a quiet, slow-moving nun who, rumour has it, is mildly retarded, has spotted me and is making her way toward us. The burning cigarette is in my hand and it is too late to stub it out. I jump to my feet and rush to the front of the classroom, trying to keep Sister Hillary away from the others. I hold the cigarette behind my back as I face her.

'Ah, glad you haven't gone home yet,' she says. 'Wanted to talk to you about the stereo.' I groan inwardly. The school's stereo system is Sister Hillary's pride and joy, one of the few tasks that Mother Superior feels confident assigning to her dim-witted charge. Because my love for music is legendary, because I was forever sitting in class banging away on imaginary bongo drums, I am the only girl that Sister Hillary trusts to handle the stereo system at socials and other functions. She does this with all the ceremony and dignity of a mayor handing the keys of the city to an honoured guest. But the downside of this is that every chance she gets, Sister Hillary engages me in arcane discussions about the proper maintenance and handling of her precious stereo system. Most of the time I don't mind but now, with smoke curling from behind my back and the heat of the cigarette beginning to make its presence known to my fingers, I feel trapped under the gaze of Sister Hillary's innocent, cow-like eyes. I brace myself for her to sniff the air in suspicion, to ask me what I am holding behind my back, to proclaim that where there is smoke there must be a cigarette, but she simply continues to talk to me. Behind me, I hear Jenny and Patty trying to smother their giggles. The cigarette continues to burn ever closer toward my fingers. Finally, I can't take it any more. 'Sorry, sister. Bad stomach cramps. Have to go ... bathroom,' I mumble and then sprint towards the bathroom before she can say another word. I pray to God that I don't run into anyone else along the way.

Not getting caught makes us bolder. A few months after meeting Jenny, I had refused to ride the school-bus anymore, preferring to catch a B.E.S.T bus. Tired of the daily dramas of trying to get me out of bed in time to catch the school-bus, Mehroo agreed. But not taking the school-bus means that I can stay behind with the other three at the end of the school day. Every few days, we collect our money together and head for the liquor store a few blocks away from school. For the first few weeks we take turns going into the shop and tell the man behind the counter elaborate stories of how we are running errands for our fathers, but it soon becomes obvious that as long as we have the money, he doesn't care how old we are or that we are buying beer while still in our school uniforms.

Hiding the brown bottles of beer in our school-bags, we head for Yasmin's house because her parents do not get home from work until much later. Just before reaching her house, we stop by our favourite paanwalla's stall and purchase three packs of Gold Flake cigarettes.

And then we consecrate Yasmin's religious, teetotaling, Muslim house by pouring our golden Kingfishers into glasses that have never held alcohol before. We play Abba's *Fernando*, Deep Purple's *Smoke on the Water* and Wings' *Band on the Run* over and over again. We sing along, with Pat playing a feverish air guitar while Jenny pretends to pound on drums, her straight dark hair flopping along like Ringo's. Greyish blue cigarette smoke fills the room while Jenny tries to teach me how to blow perfect smoke rings. I shape my mouth into the perfect O as she teaches me to, but somehow my rings look more like Cs or Ls. 'Girl, girl, girl,' Jenny says, shaking her head and displaying her dazzlingly white teeth. A lazy, languid feeling climbs up my legs and lodges in my stomach the more I drink. I feel ambition leave my body so that I no longer care about anything but how to prolong this mellow feeling.

This lack of ambition shows up in my grades. By ninth grade most of the teachers are on the verge of writing me off for lost and mummy is beside herself, reminding me that the board exams that determine whether I graduate from high school are only a year away. Dad repeats his threats of getting me a job as a packer in a factory if I don't make it through high school.

But I don't care. For the first time, I am discovering a world of pleasant oblivion, and it is a welcome respite from the prickly, nervous-making atmosphere at home. Also, there is the thrill of the four of us against the world, a kind of replay of *Butch Cassidy and the Sundance Kid*, going out with our guns blazing, going up in flames. After years of being the responsible, sensitive child who could always be counted on to do the right thing, I am revelling in being a bad girl and in becoming the kind of teenager that adults worry about. Being a bad girl is more freeing, liberating and infinitely more fun.

Soon, the boys are a greater distraction than even the booze. There are plenty of boys at Christ Church school, which is a stone's throw away from ours, but Jenny turns her nose up at them and says they are too young and immature for us. Of course we agree, because when it comes to sexual matters, Jenny is the undisputed leader. So Jenny hooks the rest of us up with friends of her current, college-age boyfriend and there are afternoons spent in dark movie theatres and much groping and touching and kissing. Then, Patty discovers that a cousin of hers is the deejay at a disco at Apollo Bunder and will allow us to spend Saturday afternoons in there for free, before the night crowd arrives. The cousin invites some of his friends and soon we pair up and dance a bit and then there is some groping and touching and kissing. It never goes much further than this, at least not for me, because years of propaganda about the virtues of chastity and how men don't respect women who give it up too easily and the importance of being a virgin when you marry, all this propaganda has worked on me. Besides, the thought of becoming pregnant is terrifying and everybody knows that good girls don't use condoms. So I make it a point not to come across as a tease, try to engage these boys in some conversation between the petting sessions, though sometimes that backfires because it is hard to go back to hot and heavy panting after you've asked someone what they think about the Emergency.

My grades are also falling because of The Pact. The Pact says that all four of us will try to get more or less the same grades. It says that each time one of us stops writing in an exam, the rest of us have to stop writing also. This is how we will prove our devotion to each other. I am dimly aware of the fact, as I suspect Yasmin is also, that she and I have more to lose by agreeing to this than Jenny and Patty. It is understood that Jenny will eventually make her way back to the United States and that the rest of Patty's family will soon be joining her brothers in Australia. But Yasmin and I will stay in India and be part of a mercilessly competitive educational system. We will have to make our way to college on the basis of our high-school grades and everyday we are bombarded with stories of kids who scored in the 99 percentile and could still not get admission into the city's top colleges. But I put these thoughts to the back of my mind and sign on to The Pact, although there are times when some lingering flake of ambition makes me hastily scribble a few more lines before I set my pen down when the others do.

✧

But when I get a lousy score on a literature exam, Greta Duke hits the roof. This time, I have gone too far.

Greta Duke has been teaching us history and English since seventh grade. I was home nursing a cold the first day that Miss Duke introduced herself to my class but when I showed up the next day, the entire class was buzzing with excitement. 'Wow, guess what?' Brenda burst out. 'Wait till you meet this new English teacher, men, you'll love her. She's not like any of the others. She is so funny and ...'

'Yah, and she looks young and active instead of like a shrivelled-up bora seed,' Anita added.

'And she said Shakespeare was really sexy,' someone else interrupted, a day-old amazement still fresh in her voice.

'Yah, she really said the word "sex",' Anita added. 'Said the word many times actually.'

'Hey, cool it, all of you,' I said, superiority dripping from my voice. 'Don't forget, she's a teacher. How cool can she be?'

But I was wrong. Three seconds after Greta Duke walked into the classroom, I knew that I was wrong. With her curly, shoulder-length hair, the thick, silver bracelet on her wrist and her bright-yellow dress that she wore shorter than most teachers dared to, Miss Duke was different from the other, worn-looking, irritable teachers we were used to. And when she opened her well-thumbed copy of *A Midsummer's Night Dream* and began reading from it, Shakespeare's words suddenly came alive with colour and passion. We had grown up hearing about Shakespeare, were intimidated by the thought of studying him, but the way Miss Duke explained his poetry, the bard seemed as accessible and contemporary as Nancy Drew had seemed a few short years ago.

'Well, what do think?' she asked a short while later, looking up from the book. 'So do you brats like Shakespeare?'

'Yes, miss, yes,' we answered in a chorus.

Miss Duke flashed us a mischievous, toothy smile. There was a small gap between her front teeth that made her look like a naughty teenager. 'Aw, you all just like him because of all the sex and romance.'

We looked scandalized. Imagine a teacher talking so casually about sex. And actually making a joke about us liking sex, as if it was the most natural thing in the world. 'No miss, no miss,' we protested. 'That's not it at all.'

'It's the language,' I said. 'It's just so beautiful.'

Greta Duke looked at me as if noticing me for the first time. 'You're Thrity, aren't you? I've heard a lot about you,' she said enigmatically. The other girls looked from one of us to the other, jealous at this special acknowledgment. I shifted in my seat, not knowing how to interpret her words.

'Well?' the other girls asked me at the end of class. 'Were we right or what?'

'Or what,' I answered automatically. But then it had to be acknowledged: 'All of you were right. She's fabulous.'

By ninth grade, about the time when my grades are tumbling like Newton's apple, Greta Duke and I have become best friends. She is the only shot of vigour and youth in a school where the nuns in their white habits and the invariably bespectacled teachers look more like fossils then live human beings. Unlike the other teachers – and even some of my more conventional classmates – Greta Duke is not scandalized or intimidated by my flights of fantasy and my talk about youth power. I keep threatening to come to school on a Saturday and paint yellow daisies all over the walls, talk about launching a coup against the nuns and taking over the school. Every chance I get, I organize signature petitions protesting all grievances big and small. The mad Parsi is alive and kicking and now she has added some political catchwords like 'revolution' and 'sit-in strike' to her vocabulary.

Greta Duke's response to all of my rantings is one of bemusement. One day, encouraged by my efforts to lead the entire class into signing yet another petition against a particularly cruel nun, I fling open the doors to the teachers lounge and burst in, my face flushed with excitement. Miss Duke is sitting at the long wooden desk while Mr Narayan is sitting at a corner desk. 'The youth revolution is here,' I yell and then wait for a response. Mr Narayan looks at me open-mouthed, his yellow eyes wide with anticipation.

Miss Duke looks up slowly from the papers that she was grading. 'Good. Let me know when it leaves,' she says evenly.

I exit the teachers' lounge duly chastized.

But now that my grades are tumbling like Jack and Jill, Miss Duke decides it is time to get serious. 'You listen to me, you little brat,' she says one evening. 'You have a fine brain and you're wasting it. I'm not like the other teachers – I've never had any problems with you being friends with Jenny and the rest of that lot. I know in many ways they've been good for you. But when all this business begins to interfere with your schoolwork, well, then it's time for me to speak up. From now on, you are going to stay behind after school and sit in while I tutor the other girls. I want you to start showing up at the library after school.'

I protest as the role calls for me to do but secretly I am thrilled. When I break the news to Patty and Jenny, they look surprised but then Jenny shrugs her shoulders and says she hopes I can still occasionally spend an evening with them.

When I tell mummy about my conversation with Greta Duke, she looks startled and then worried. She comes to school the next day and talks to Miss Duke in hushed whispers about how dad's business is not doing well and how we simply cannot afford another tutor.

'But madam, Thrity must've misunderstood,' Miss Duke protests. 'I didn't say anything about money. In fact, I'm not even going to spend much time on her. I know she will automatically pick up what she needs to just listening to me coach the paying students.'

And so I spend my evenings in the school library sitting at the table and pretending to not listen while Miss Duke teaches and grills the assortment of six or seven students whom she tutors after school hours. Once, I am sure she sees me stuffing back the pack of Gold Flake that was sticking out of my uniform's pocket but if she notices the cigarettes, she doesn't acknowledge my smoking habit or lecture me about it. Jenny and Patty walk by sometimes and I know they're headed to Yasmin's home for a beer and sometimes I'm jealous but what surprises me even more is how often I'm not. Because I am enjoying this atmosphere of learning and despite my studied disinterest I am thrilled when after all the paying students can't answer a question, Greta Duke turns to me with a silent, quizzical look and I casually blurt out the answer. On such days, if we are walking home together, she lights into me. 'Did you see how you answered that question today when none of those other duffers could?' she says in her deep voice. 'You think I'm not watching you, girl, but I see everything. Even with you gazing out of the window all the time, even with half of you living in God-knows-what fantasy land, you still absorb more than any of them. Just think what you could do if you applied that mind of yours.'

I say something self-effacing or smart-alecky but from the inside, I am singing. Greta Duke is the first adult I have ever known, who, even when she is criticizing me, makes me feel special and cared for. Unlike my mother's criticisms,

I never leave Miss Duke's presence feeling small and ugly. Rather, she makes me feel as if all of my shortcomings are born out of choices I have made so that I don't have that doomed, desperate feeling around her. After all, if I've made wrong choices, I can also unmake them. Even when she is exasperated with me, I can tell Miss Duke likes me, is amused by me and that takes the sting out of her words.

And then there is this: For all my declarations about not caring about grades and reputations, deep down I do. Years of lectures by my parents have done the trick and the thought of repeating a grade is so shameful, so unthinkable, that I know that flunking high school is not really an option. And I know that Greta Duke knows that I know this. That's why she's not ready to give up on me. One day, in an attempt to encourage myself to study, I copy lines from a Dylan song on a sheet of lined paper, fold the paper and hide it in my chemistry textbook. 'She knows there's no success like failure and that failure's no success at all,' Dylan sings and I think I know what he means. I know that Greta Duke is throwing me a lifeline, pulling me out of the dangers of the world that I am being seduced by. Even though I publicly pretend to disdain it, I hold on to this lifeline, sometimes fiercely, sometimes half-heartedly, but I hold on just the same.

After all, I may be the Mad Parsi. But I'm not crazy.

# Twelve

THE CHILDHOOD DREAM ABOUT THE city's poor has stopped visiting me. But the poor are still with me. Like ghosts, like shadows, they are everywhere and their presence exposes the contradictions and follies and hypocrisies of middle-class life, cracks it open like a rotten egg.

Going to Chowpatty Beach has become agony for me. Dad often takes us to the food booths that line the beach, where we eat bhel and mango kulfi and drink lassi or sugarcane juice. We are inevitably followed by a procession of half-naked children with distended bellies and snot-filled noses and young women with wild, uncombed hair, with a baby hoisted on one hip and another child at their side. Arms extended and palms turned upward for the coins of charity, the procession follows us from booth to booth, stares at us hungrily as we open our mouths to insert a puri, drowns out our conversation with a non-stop chorus of 'Arré, sahib. Child is hungry. No food for two days, sahib. Show some heart.' When the chorus gets too loud or aggressive, the irritated bhaiya who runs the booth steps out toward the mob, his hand raised in a menacing way. 'Chalo, move,' he yells. 'Let the poor people eat in peace. Shameless animals, making a nuisance of yourself.' As in a time-agreed ritual, the small crowd scatters but moves only a few feet away and within minutes they are back, one wary eye on the bhaiya, their mouths still curled downward in a piteous expression, their right hands (or the left hand, if there is no right hand) stretched outward. The older children sometimes kick the sand with feet made swift with impatience and desperation but are subdued by a quick look from the adults. Some of the bolder ones inch forward and touch us, pull on our sleeves with their dirty fingers and we cringe and take a step back, like in those horror movies when the monster approaches the virginal, golden-haired damsel in distress. If we linger at a particular booth for too long, with dad ordering a second round of kulfi say, some of the younger children sit down on the sand, bending their legs and turning their cracked, hardened bare feet toward their faces and pulling out splints or small pieces of glass or other debris from them. The middle-class people who flock to these food booths – the ones who vow to do a special pooja if Baby or Baba gets into Bombay Scottish or Cathedral school and who attend cocktail parties at Juhu and Breach Candy where they lament that the country is going down the toilet – watch these children and then look away.

I cannot eat at Chowpatty any more. The contradictions, the inequities that I live with everyday in Bombay, are too much in my face at Chowpatty. At home it is easy to ignore them but here, out in the open, there is no turning away from these dark and hungry eyes and from the questions about the accidents of birth and the randomness of privilege that they arouse in me. Guilt rises in me like bile, so that I lose my appetite and would like nothing better than to take my lassi and puris and kulfi and hand it to the children staring greedily at them. But I know that such a gesture will surely backfire, will arouse the lioness-like protectiveness that mummy feels for me when it comes to food, so that she will insist that I finish her dish of whatever it is she is eating, which in turn will compel dad to insist on buying something else for her and which gesture will make me feel even more guilty. So I make myself swallow whatever it is I am eating, trying to alternately ignore and smile at the children staring back at me. I somehow want to distinguish myself from the world that I belong to, want to silently plead my case to the ragged group that stands like a jury around me, want them to understand that I am not like my parents, that I understand their hunger and the resentment and fury that it must arouse in them. So I smile at the women carrying the dazed-looking children on their hips and sometimes they smile back at me, a quick, silver flash of startlingly white teeth and sometimes they stare back at me blankly, their faces a nylon mask that hide an entire world.

Part of the reason I so want to distinguish myself – and God, this is hard to admit – is because sometimes I feel the same cheated fury towards the beggars that my parents do. Sometimes I feel a wave of self-pity sweep over me: *Dammit, all we want to do is have an outdoor family outing at Chowpatty, have some fun and some food and how can we do that with these people circling us like vultures? It's so unfair, we can't ever go anywhere without having to think about the poor and dealing with the guilt their very presence elicits. I wish I was in London or somewhere, where I could walk down the street eating an ice-cream cone without someone wanting to snatch it away from me.* And then I hear myself and feel angry and embarrassed at how shallow my complaining self-pity seems when measured against the weight of their hunger and suffering. And so, as penance, I smile at the women and children.

And at around this time, as if this is part of the script, an old man and woman – he, leaning on a thick stick and wearing a long, white beard, she, with eyes grey and milky with age (or is it blindness?) and teeth red-brown with paan stains – walk slowly toward us. 'Arré baba, some change,' they say to my father in a pathetic sing-song voice. 'God will bless you, my son, some change for the poor.' The old man begins to cough but he needn't have bothered because my father has already dug his hand in his pant pocket and pulled out a handful of coins. 'God bless you, seth,' the couple sings, surprised and gratified at how easy the exchange is. They move away and one of the children – a boy of ten – chases after them, angry at their intrusion and their unexpected success at wheedling some coins out of my father. The old man picks up his stick threateningly at him and he backs away. But now the crowd of young mothers and children is tense and excited, knowing that their instincts are right, that this Parsi gentleman who has spent the last twenty minutes ignoring them, is a soft touch after all. They do not know what I know: that for whatever reason – perhaps because he lost his mother when he was four, perhaps because he loved and respected his father – dad can never turn away without giving alms to the elderly. The young mothers he will give money to unwillingly, the children he will adamantly refuse to give money to, instead keeping packets of Glucose biscuits in his car for distribution. 'Cannot spoil the next generation. They should be encouraged to work, not to beg,' he says, blithely ignoring the fact that there are Ph.D.s in this country who work as peons in small offices because there are no jobs. But the old men and women, he cannot say no to. To them, he feels a certain responsibility that borders on reverence. In his car, he keeps a stack of silver coins and if, while sitting in a traffic jam, he spots an old beggar a couple of cars down, he actually rolls down his window and calls her to his car.

Now our private processional is stirring, knowing that our food expedition is drawing to an end and having already seen proof of my father's generosity. Their cries for alms get louder and more dramatic. My stomach muscles clench and I feel my toes curl with guilt and embarrassment. 'Please, seth, memsahib,' one of the women cries. 'Children have not eaten in several days. Some money for food tonight.' She pushes forward one of the more pathetic looking children, a four-year-old boy with tousled hair and the liquidy, grey eyes that spell blindness. Having been thrust in the spotlight, the boy goes through his lines: 'Please, baba,' he says.

'Stomach is empty. God will grant all your wishes, seth. Please, something.' His small hand thrusts forward, and accidentally hits the bottom of my glass, spilling a bit of my lassi.

The bhaiya stirs, twirling his handlebar moustache angrily. 'Saala, badmaash. Sisterfuckers. Parasites. Get going all of you before I give you a good pasting. Harassing my best-of-best good customers.' This time the bhaiya looks serious and gauging this, the crowd makes to run. But just then, dad speaks up.

'Okay, you are hungry? No money from me. I don't believe in encouraging beggary. But Dilbar,' he says turning to the bhaiya. 'Give each of them a plate of bhel. I'll pay for the lot.'

A murmur goes through the crowd, as the women try quickly to calculate whether they should hold out for money or accept the offer. The offer for food is irresistible but accepting it would mean taking home less money to pay the local dada who owns them. But before they can act, Dilbar speaks, his mouth twisted in distaste. 'Please, saar,' he says. 'You are my good customer but these people are a nuisance. Bad for business, saar, if other customer sees them eating at my stall. Hope you understand, saar.'

Dilbar has made up their minds for them. The beggars turn on him, several of them speaking together.

'Bara seth said he would pay. Why you saying no?'

'You heard what the seth said. Give us our bhel.'

'God will bless seth for his generosity but He will curse you for your pride, you evil man. Treating us like we are animals.'

But Dilbar is adamant. He folds his hands across his hefty chest and shakes his head no.

The commotion has attracted the attention of the man who runs the bhelpuri booth two spaces down from Dilbar. He is a thin, ingratiating man with red, paan-streaked lips.

Now, he comes running up to us. 'What's the problem, what's the problem?' he says, in a thin, high-pitched voice. 'Dilbar, how can you send the Parsi seth away like this, unhappy in his heart? For shame, for shame. Tell you what, sir, I'll feed these poor, unhappy folks for you. Just move to my stall, sir, two steps away, sir, closeby only.'

Dilbar grunts. Dad is now anxious to be done with the whole scene. We move to the new booth, the urchins following us like a wedding procession. Dad pulls out his wallet and takes out some bills. 'There. This should be enough,' he says.

The thin man smiles a thin smile. 'Just a minute, saar, if you please. Er, need some extra baksheesh, saar.' He lowers his voice. 'Doing this as a favour to you, saar. You know how these people are, dirty and all. Will have to wash the dishes extra well, which is costing extra water, saar.' He points to the dirty metal bucket in which he washes the glass bowls.

Dad looks disgusted though I'm not sure if it's at the sight of the filthy water bucket or the man's avarice. He takes out another two rupees. 'There. And if that's not enough, we'll take our business somewhere else.' He turns on his heels and begins to leave, with mummy and I following. Mummy says something about wanting to stay long enough to see that the man actually feeds the crowd but dad has had enough. 'Coming to Chowpatty is no longer a pleasure,' he says to no one in particular. 'Fewer and fewer places in Bombay that one can go.'

I leave on that day, full of good will and affection for my dad. He is idiosyncratic in his beliefs, yes, but he tries to do the right thing.

But as I get older, I notice how my father's middle-class values rise to the surface at the oddest of times. By the time I am thirteen, we are both encased in our own ideologies and my simplistic dreams of feeding and housing the city's entire homeless population have hardened into a bitter contempt for well-meaning middle-class people who pretend to know what is in the best interest of a people they encounter daily but know nothing about. People like my father. Actually, people like myself, though I would've jumped into a vat of boiling oil before admitting this to myself.

✧

We are in the old, bulky Ambassador, just him and me in the huge front seat, making our way home from a business meeting that I had accompanied him to. The meeting has gone well and dad is in a cheerful, expansive mood. We are at Bori Bunder and the bumper-to-bumper traffic has crawled to a halt. Normally, this would bother him but today he sits patiently, not even getting angry when the cab driver behind us blows his horn for no apparent reason since there is nowhere else we can go. We roll down the windows, knowing we will be assaulted by the exhaust fumes of the old B.E.S.T buses but needing some air to combat the muggy, humid mid-afternoon heat. Just then, a healthy-looking, bright-eyed boy of about eight races to the car and swiftly approaches my dad. His hair is cropped close, his face is long and thin and this makes his toothy smile seem even more wide and infectious. 'Eh, seth,' he begins. 'Some money, please. Sister and mother are both sick at home. Please, kind seth. Bhagwan will bless you.'

Dad looks at the boy and then looks at me. 'See this?' he says to me, as if the boy cannot hear him. 'This is what is keeping our country backward. An able-bodied, active boy, begging for a living.'

Traffic moves a bit and the boy holds on to the window, trotting beside the car. He has heard my dad talk about him and maybe this makes him hopeful because as every beggar knows, the worst customers are the ones who ignore your presence, who stare through you as if you are made of air. At least this Parsi seth has acknowledged his existence.

Dad moves so swiftly that the boy jumps back a foot. Twisting in his seat, he reaches for the handle of the car's back door and opens it a few inches. The car to our right lets out a startled beep to make sure the ajar door doesn't hit it but dad has already calculated the distance and ignores the driver. 'C'mon,' he says to the bewildered boy. 'Get in. You can come to our house and work there. We are looking for a nice servant boy. You will get three square meals a day, decent clothes to wear. I will even send you to school. You can make something of yourself. C'mon, what do you say?'

The boy takes another step back, staring intently at my father. 'Daddy, please, for heaven's sake,' I say but he is still talking to the beggar boy.

'What is it? Don't want to work? Want to stay a beggar your whole life? Is there any future in this? At my house you can learn English, go to school. Perhaps be a peon or clerk in my office someday...'

The little boy looks at my father with wide eyes. Suddenly, he lets out a yelp and begins to run away from the car, twisting his way between the closely-packed vehicles. He looks over his shoulder once, to make sure that the strange man is not following him.

My dad sits back in his seat, disappointed yet satisfied. 'You see?' he says. 'They are just lazy. Prefer a free hand-out to working. That's why I never encourage these children by giving them money.'

I am not sure if this whole episode has been for my benefit but at the moment I'm too angry to wonder. 'Daddy, he was eight years old,' I say. 'What about his mother, father, sisters? You think a child can just leave his entire family and get into a car with a perfect stranger?'

He doesn't get it. 'You know we would've treated him well. You know he would've been safe with us,' his voice hurt, as if I have been accusing him of mistreating the boy.

'That's not the point. The point is, how does he know that? Dad, he's a child. And he has a family ...'

'Yah, a family which makes him beg for a living,' he cuts me off.

I am seething but I control myself. 'Dad, you know how when I was young you always told me never to get into a car with a stranger? What if his parents told him the same thing?'

Something clicks. I can see the struggle on his face as he tries to grapple with the seeming contradiction of parents who let their children beg for a living telling that child to beware of strangers. Dad sighs heavily. 'Maybe. Maybe so. But one thing I know – India's problems will not be solved by begging. Something has to be done.'

(And as if some twisted God had heard my father, something was done just a year later, in the dark years of Indira Gandhi's Emergency, when police routinely swept the streets clean of the homeless beggars. It was as if someone had taken my childhood dream of rounding up the poor and altered it, so that instead of providing them with shelter in my school basement, the beggars were discarded outside the city limits or warehoused in government barracks under terrible conditions.)

We drive home the rest of the way in an uneasy truce, both of us cocooned in the righteousness of what we believe. But in the coming months dad will talk about the incident at parties – how he had offered this able-bodied youngster a chance at a better life and how the lazy fellow had run away rather than take him up on his offer. And the other adults will nod their heads solemnly and shake their heads from side-to-side in expressions of dismay for where the country is headed. Sometimes I speak up and argue with them and risk the humiliation of their adult condescension as they tell me that this is the idealism of youth talking and that soon I will grow up and realize the errors of my ways.

But most of the time I keep quiet and instead help myself surreptitiously to the whisky and beer, downing the last of our guest's glasses as I carry them to the kitchen, taking a swallow directly from the bottle when no one is watching, so that I float through these parties in a blind haze. All that the adults see is a teenager who is extraordinarily helpful, who offers to mix their drinks for them and carry their empty glasses away for them. But the more I smile at them, the more hollow I feel on the inside, as if there is a bomb ticking inside of me. And in my drunken haze I imagine that there is such a bomb hidden inside all of the city's poor and that it is ticking all the time – while they arrange their faces into pitiful caricatures for our benefit, while they tell us that God will bless us even while they think that if there is a God surely he will destroy us for our blithe indifference, for our sinful self-absorption. I wonder how the adults can remain so blind to their precarious place on the top of the mountain. Occasionally someone brings up a news item about a particularly heinous attack on the Untouchables or Harijans by an upper-caste Hindu mob and then they all speak contemptuously about the damn caste system and how backward some of these rural Hindus are, to follow its ancient prejudices. The unspoken text is that we are lucky to be Parsis, lucky to be 'Bombay born and bred', and therefore free of the oppressive bigotries of people less civilized than us. 'What barbarians these people are,' a woman guest will say. 'Just imagine – burning someone alive in this day and age just because he is an Untouchable. After all, a human being is a human being.' And later that night, on her way home from the party, the woman will have her fleshy arm touched by a twelve-year-old beggar boy insistent on coaxing a few coins out of this kindly-looking woman and she, aghast at this violation by a filthy urchin, will shriek and take two full steps back, hereby losing her balance a bit and this sight will make the young boy lose his professional beggar's demeanour for a split second, so that he will let out a giggle before twisting his face into its usual pleading, piteous expression again. But it will be too late because the woman's husband will have noticed the touch and the grin and his manly pride will have been bruised and he will cry, 'Wicked pervert,' and raise his right hand as if to go after the boy, who, realizing that the inopportune giggle has cost him his coins, will flee into the dark night . . .

I want to tell our guests about an experiment that some of my friends have been conducting. One of my friends has made a brilliant observation about the rigid, stylized postures that beggars and donors both affect when money is changing hands. Middle-class Bombayites invariably plop their coins into the cupped hands of the beggars from a height, making sure that they never accidentally brush against what they imagine are hands contaminated with germs and disease. So, a bunch of us have taken to changing the rules of the transaction. Instead of holding the coin gingerly between two fingers and then quickly dropping it into the beggar's outstretched hand, I now hold the coin on the flat palm of my hand, silently urging the beggar to pick it up. This simple gesture reverses the social order, so that it is my hand that is now at the bottom. It also violates an unspoken, almost unrecognized taboo – in order to pick up the coin, the beggar's fingers must surely touch my palm, no matter how lightly. And an amazing thing happens: children as young as three are already so conditioned by omnipresent class distinctions that they freeze at this reversal of position. They stare at me with eyes wide open with confusion, apprehension, even fear. Something is wrong, unnatural, and you can almost see their young, uncomprehending brains churning, trying to figure out what is wrong and how to set it right. In the meantime, the offered coin rests on my palm, untouched. Moments pass. We lock glances, and I watch a caravan of emotions move across their bewildered faces. Occasionally, one of the bolder youngsters screws up her courage and grabs the coin quickly. But more often, they walk away, all the time staring at me as if trying to figure out this new perversion that they have encountered.

I know what will happen if I tell the adults about this experiment – they will look horrified and lecture me about how I, of all people, with all my health problems, should be extra-careful about not coming in contact with germs and did I wash my hands after these silly encounters?

At times like these, I look at the crystal beer mugs the guests are drinking from, the fine whisky glasses they are sipping from and I feel as though the whole world is made of glass, that it is fragile and tenuous and will shatter the moment someone from the outside casts the first stone. Somedays, the thought frightens me because, after all, I love these flawed, self-absorbed, well-meaning, sporadically kind human beings who are in this room with me. On other days I long for that moment of destruction, I can't wait for this facade to end, when the seemingly powerless display their strength and those who think of themselves as powerful realize how puny and small they really are...

Right then, Sheroo Nayak interrupts my murderous reverie. 'What about some music?' she says, gaily. 'What is that song I like, about a blue-eyed boy or something?'

I get up and put on *A Hard Rain's A-Gonna Fall*. The adults laugh and talk over the song, oblivious to its apocalyptic message.

# Thirteen

WATERGATE.
The word is exactly as complicated and bewildering as the word 'sex' was a few years earlier. 'Sex' was a word I saw in print all the time – *Stardust* would interview movie stars about what they liked about it, *The Illustrated Weekly of India* would have articles on the repressed attitudes of Indian men toward it – but no one would ever come right out and explain what the word meant. Somehow I knew enough to know that the word made people embarrassed and squirmy and that it was better not to ask adults about it but to figure it out for yourself, a little bit at a time. In sixth-grade the nuns had explained about the birds and the bees but the discussions were so clinical that I had failed to connect what they told us to the mysterious, magical three-letter word that was everywhere but still remained an enigma. In fact, my rudest awaking had come sitting on the marble steps of the school building during lunch recess one afternoon. 'Anita,' I said ponderously. 'One thing I don't understand about what Sister Ignatius told us. How does the sperm get to the egg from inside all the clothes?'

Anita stared at me for a long moment, delighted at this unexpected gift I had thrown her way. 'There are no clothes,' she said finally. 'People do it naked.'

I laughed. Anita was such a joker. 'Yah, right.'

'No joke. I swear, men, that's how it is,' Anita said, pinching her throat for emphasis. 'You don't believe me, ask Diana.'

I turned five shades of white. Being naked before a boy seemed too impossible, too preposterous, too outside the limits of my imagination.

The next day, Philomena D'Souza brought in a Viewfinder to school. All morning long, clumps of girls would peer surreptitiously through its square eye whenever the teacher was out of the room. Whatever they were looking at provoked much nervousness and giggling among Philomena and some of the older girls. Finally, just before lunch it was my turn. But instead of the usual slides of the Taj Mahal and the Eiffel Tower, there were slides of naked men and women entangled with one another. It was hard to see exactly what was going on but the pictures looked red and raw. 'Philo, what is it?' I said finally. Looking at me contemptuously, Philomena had replied, 'It's sex, stupid.'

But I was confused. Sex on the pages of *Stardust* had seemed sweet and harmless. Sex as described by the nuns seemed as boring as the snail races we used to organize in the playground behind the statue of the Virgin Mary. But sex as defined by Philomena seemed secretive and dangerous. How could one word have so many meanings?

Same thing with Watergate. Once, dad told me that it was the name of a building in Washington. But I also knew that it was a scandal and had something to do with Richard Nixon. Most of the people I knew had hated Nixon ever since he sided with Pakistan in the 1971 war over Bangladesh. So I figured anything that kicked Nixon out of office was a good thing. But then why did the grown-ups keep saying it was a terrible thing that had happened?

Pop culture comes to my rescue in 1976 in the form of *Mad* magazine's spoof on *All the President's Men*. I read the magazine carefully, trying to read in between the lines and connecting the satire to what little I already know about Watergate. And finally it all comes together – the burglary, the secret slush funds, the role of Deep Throat. (Of course, one of the pitfalls of learning history from *Mad* magazine is that for many years I will think of poor Gerald Ford as Deep Throat, because the very last panel of '*Gall of the President's Men*' shows Ford in a dark parking lot revealing shadowy secrets to Woodward.)

By this time, America has taken hold in my imagination as firmly as the world of midnight feasts and English bobbies once had. We have studied about America in geography class, learned the capitals to all fifty states and learned about its chief exports but all that is dry stuff compared to what I am rapidly learning. From the ads of music clubs on the back of comic books, I keep up with the latest rock-and-roll releases in America. That's how I choose what records to request when dad makes a business trip to Dubai or Kuwait. I stand on the balcony for hours wondering what 'Gee whiz,' sounds like in real life. After all, Archie says it all the time. I beg for a pair of blue jeans and when I finally get my first pair, I ignore the fact that they are three sizes too big for me. I promptly try to fade my jeans by pouring hydrogen peroxide acid over them but nothing happens. To my disgust, they don't even tear.

From Simon and Garfunkel I learn about Bleeker Street and New York City winters bleeding people, from Neil Young I learn about Four Dead in Ohio, from Neil Diamond about Brooklyn Roads. Woody Allen teaches me about therapists and Manhattan. John Steinbeck teaches me about Salinas Valley and Oakies and Cannery Row; Fitzgerald teaches me about the moth-holes in the American Dream; Hemingway teaches me about stoic, heroic Midwesterners who are strong in the broken places. Martin Luther King's Dream speech, which is included in one of our literature texts, has the amazing effect of making my hair stand on end every single time I read it. No teacher ever mentions that King had often mentioned India's freedom struggle as an inspiration for his civil disobedience movement.

Meanwhile, I struggle to learn Marathi, so that I can converse with the middle-aged woman who works as a servant in our home.

Every once in a great while, it occurs to me that I lead a schizophrenic life: I am a Parsi teenager attending a Catholic school in the middle of a city that's predominantly Hindu. I'm a middle-class girl living in the country that's among the poorest in the world. I am growing up in the country that kicked out the British fourteen years before I was born but I have still never read a novel by an Indian writer.

But this is what it means to be a secular Bombayite, I tell myself – to take all the contradictory parts of your life and to make a unified whole out of it; to know that you are a cultural mongrel, the bastard child of history and to learn to be amused, even proud of the fact.

Because the alternative is unacceptable. If, instead of bemusement you allow yourself to feel rage at being the product of a colonial education system that scarcely prepares you for the realities of living in your own country, if you question why you know the words to every Bob Dylan song instead of the words to songs by – but there you see, that's the problem, you don't even know who your country's Bob Dylan might be – then you are asking questions whose answers you will not be able to handle.

And the story is complicated and it is hard to know who is implicated in it. The British, with their famous declaration of building an Indian elite who looked Indian but were English 'in taste, in opinions, in morals and intellect,' yes, of course the British are implicated but that's too easy. And then you examine the complicity of those Irish nuns whom you adored as a child and who left their green, fertile island to come to this dry, sunbaked subcontinent in order to educate the pagans and you are swept in a tidal wave of mixed feelings, resentment and good will battling each other for supremacy. But wait, the moving finger moves on and now it points at your community, the chauvinistic old women who kept framed photographs of 'apri' queen on their peeling walls, and the old Parsi men who carried parasols in order to protect their light skins so as to distinguish themselves from the Hindu hordes, and your parents, who insisted you take piano lessons instead of learning to play the sitar, as many of your Hindu friends did. And finally, you yourself are implicated because surely you could have sought out the novels of Tagore as you did those of Hemingway, surely you could prevent the others from teasing the Hindi teacher in ways you would not dream of teasing those who brought you the works of Shakespeare?

The only hint of my childhood love affair with Britain now comes from adoring The Beatles and the Fabs are not really British any more, seeing how they now belong to the world and seeing how George Harrison himself was infatuated with India.

I subscribe to a youth magazine called *J.S.*, which features full-size blow-ups of pop stars like Peter Frampton and Gary Glitter, that I paste on the walls and ceiling of my small study. A moment of reckoning arrives along with a huge, glossy poster that I have traded for a Queen album. The poster has the Jackson five on one side and the Osmonds on the other. I know that my decision to honour one or the other group on my wall will say something about my musical taste and sophistication and I know that in order to be considered cool and sophisticated, I must choose the Jacksons. But my heart belongs to Donny. Call it puppy love.

The punk movement that is sweeping across the West does not reach us. As always, we are about five to ten years behind. We are still singing *Puff the Magic Dragon* at school picnics, although thanks to Jenny's worldliness I am also playing air guitar to Queen's *Bohemian Rhapsody*.

But the biggest influence on my life is Bob Dylan. The nuns had taught us *Blowin' in the Wind* in school and we all know Peter, Paul and Mary's airy-fairy version of it. But I don't really discover the raw power of Dylan until Arvind, my pen pal in Calcutta, plagiarizes the words to Dylan's *Shelter from the Storm* and tries to pass them off as his own. When, embarrassed by my effusive praise, he finally confesses the poem's true author, I check out *Blood on the Tracks*. And fall in love with the ingenious word play, the effortless rhymes, the worldly humour and yes – even the voice. Soon, I am greedily seeking out every Dylan album that I can find. And my own poems begin to change. Gone are the earnest, Robert Frost-influenced poems about hard-working old men and rainy nights. Suddenly, I am writing about one-eyed gnomes and moth-ball mirrors and the Ticks of Tanzania.

Discovering Dylan also unwittingly provides me with the perfect weapon in my ongoing battle with my mother. Mummy is convinced that Dylan, with his nasal whine, is a joke on her, somebody whom I've invented with the express purpose of irritating the hell out of her. The voice of a generation, the conscience of a nation, the bard of the 1960s is reduced in my mother's mind to a toad with laryngitis. 'Listen to the lyrics,' I say, in an unconscious echo of the words spoken by Diana's older sister a lifetime ago. But mummy has a ready answer: 'If God had wanted us to understand what he's saying, he would've given him a better voice.'

✧

Mummy is trying to end my friendship with Jesse. After a year of singing her praises she has suddenly turned on her and is bad-mouthing her to anyone who will listen.

Jesse has become good friends with my mother's nephew, who lives around the corner from us. They often meet at the bus-stop near his apartment building and ride together to college. This has my mother apoplectic. She is convinced Jesse will scheme to have her poor, innocent nephew fall in love with her and then break his heart. All of my mother's shame at having grown up poor is now brushing up against Jesse's privileged, affluent upbringing. She casts this budding friendship between Jesse and her nephew in sinister, suspicious terms. 'Everybody knows she was in love with that Muslim fellow in her hometown,' she says, contempt dripping from her voice like fat trimmings. 'Now to get over him, she's trying to trap my poor Dinshaw.'

My father, Mehroo and Babu stare at her blankly. They have no reason to dislike Jesse – other than the fact that my nightly chats with her make me skip dinner – and they don't think Dinshaw is the unworldly saint that mummy is making him out to be. She turns away from them with dissatisfaction, her hissing hatred needing a better audience.

She finds it in her sister Villoo. 'Do you know what that wicked son of yours is doing, nachoing, dancing with that Godless girl?' she says. 'You know she's an atheist? Says so herself, and wah, that too with pride. You mark my words – she is going to use our Dinshaw and then abandon him like a banana peel in a garbage dump. She's not in our league – everybody knows her father is worth millions.'

Villoo aunty says a reasonable thing. 'If she's such a bad girl, why do you let your Thritu be friends with her?'

I want to applaud Villoo for her logic. But mummy speaks first. 'My Thritu is not having an affair with her. She is not a boy, who will go all lattoo-fattoo over some arrogant Godless girl. But he's *your* son. Follow my advice, don't follow, what do I care?'

Dinshaw's sister, Persis, gets into the act. So does her best friend, Shinaz, a nice-looking woman with a hooked nose that she generally keeps hidden behind an embarrassed handkerchief. They are good girls, respectable, sexually inexperienced, conventional, who accept without question the authority of their priests, parents and teachers. Jesse's very existence, the way she carries herself – her jaunty, assertive walk, the joyous angle of her head, her eccentric crackle of laughter, her merciless mimicry of the affected, pseudo-British way in which upper-class Parsis speak – is an affront to them. In my kinder moments, I understand how threatening and alien someone like Jesse must appear to them, how she must make their own lives seem so miserably constricted and small and without possibility, how she must make them wrestle with sleeping dreams they don't even know existed.

But my charitable moments are few. I love Jesse too much to be kind to her detractors. Most of the time, I fight battles on her behalf, battles that she is blissfully unaware of because I cannot bring myself to tell her how much resentment she inspires in people who barely know her.

'What the hell does she think wearing those pink pants?' Persis says.

'I tell you, this girl has no sense of taste,' Shinaz adds.

'It's not taste. It's shame. She has no shame,' Persis says, as if she is a world-wide authority on the matter.

'What does shame have to do with how you dress?' I say. 'Someone might say the way the two of you dress, in your short dresses and all, is shameful.'

Persis addresses the air, the way she does when she's very angry. 'Just listen to her,' she says, not looking at me. 'Always leaping to Jesse's defence, right or wrong. Totally and utterly brainwashed. Now she, too, is running around wearing keds and all. And talking like this to her own cousin, for the sake of someone she barely knows. Well, we'll see when she comes running back to us in two-three months.'

Shinaz fixes me a baleful look which I ignore.

My cousin Dinshaw is a strange fellow and apparently does not share my need to defend Jesse against his family the way I do. In fact, he goes out of his way to create misunderstandings and ill-will. It appeals to his sense of humour that his new friend arouses so much negativity within his family.

So he goes for the jugular – or rather, for the nose. Shinaz's nose.

'Jesse was commenting the other day on Shinaz's long nose,' he tells his sister in a conversational tone. 'She said it was more hooked than the hook on Captain Cook's arm.'

World War III has just been launched.

My mother stomps around in a cloud of fury, refusing to even acknowledge Jesse's presence when she runs into her on the street. Persis is dripping venom and outrage. 'Who does she think she is?' she mutters repeatedly. 'The bleddy bitch. Just because they have money...'

Shinaz plays the part of a beatific martyr as if she was born to play the role. Villoo aunty mutters every foul word and curse she knows, going back to Jesse's great-grandfather.

I fight back with what I think is scientific detachment. 'Look, I know Jesse's patterns of speech, okay? She'd never say something stupid and crude like that. If she wanted to insult Shinaz, she'd think of something better than a silly, personal insult.' My words land without even creating a ripple in their rage.

Things get so out of hand that I finally confront Dinshaw. 'Why don't you tell Persis the truth that you made this shit up?' I say. 'Here they are hating Jesse's guts because of you and your damn lies.'

But Dinshaw only winks. He is enjoying himself.

Mummy finally takes it upon herself to tell Jesse what Dinshaw's whole family thinks of her. She accuses her of playing with her nephew, of insulting family friends. She returns to our apartment smug and full of herself. 'Told her off, got it off my chest,' she brags. 'My family – we are honest, direct people, unlike some I could mention,' and here she throws a glance at Mehroo. 'If we want to say something, bas, we just say it, regardless of consequences. I just spoke my mind. She just listened chup-chap. After all, what could she say? But it will teach her not to try any stunts with my family.'

I am mortified, repulsed by my mother's language and at how completely she has turned on Jesse. This is not the first time mummy has turned on an erstwhile friend but her unpredictability has never impacted on me before.

I know that my friendship with Jesse is over. I mourn its passing, going over each sweet memory, holding it in my mind like a piece of hard candy in the mouth. Anyway, I should've known. If there's any goodness in my life, it will be taken away. That's just the pattern to my life, as irreversible as the patterns on a zebra. It has always been this way. I was foolish to think that the friendship with Jesse was truly a break from the past, that the sheer fun and joy of it would propel me into a different future.

Two days later, Jesse bangs on the balcony door. I do not answer. I know she wants to tell me off, to make formal what I already know in my heart. Mummy is off visiting her mother, as she does each evening. Mehroo looks at me inquiringly when I don't answer Jesse's shouts, but she doesn't say anything. Finally, the calling and knocking stop. The next day, she knocks again. This time, I go to the balcony, dragging myself there. I feel numb, without hope. There is a metallic taste in my mouth, as if I've gnawed on tin.

Jesse looks angry. Well, after what my mother did, who can blame her? 'I called and called yesterday but you didn't answer,' she says. She waits for me to say something but I just shrug lightly.

She starts again. 'You have been avoiding me. Why?'

She won't make this easy for me. 'Well, after what my mother did to you ...' I say.

She interrupts me. 'But that was between your mother and me. Why have *you* been avoiding me?'

Do I really have to spell out the obvious? 'I didn't think you'd want to be friends with me after what mummy did. I thought you'd never want to see me again.'

The silence drags on so long, I think this is how it's going to end, with both of us drifting away...

When Jesse speaks her voice is raw with ... pain? anger? 'I can't believe you hold me in such contempt,' she says. 'You must think so little of me if you think I'd let your damn mother or anybody get in the way of my friendship with you.'

Is it possible to feel two contradictory emotions at the same precise moment? It is. I did. A sharp sting of hope pierces my heart like a needle. A boulder of remorse at having lost Jesse because of my own stupidity rolls down my body.

'Jesse, please,' I say. 'I'm so sorry. I thought ...' I am so close to tears I can't go on. 'You have no idea,' I start again.

She reaches out over the partition between the two apartments and grabs my hand. 'Don't be stupid, Thrity,' she says. 'You know we're surrounded by silly, petty people. They have their own reasons for being that way. But we don't have to get caught up in all that.'

That night, I wish I still believed in God because I want to shout my thanks to the heavens. Instead, I stand on the balcony and talk to the stars. One of them winks back at me.

## Fourteen

BABU IS PERTURBED, I CAN tell. He paces the balcony and stares at the end of the street to where it meets the main road, as if looking for something on the horizon. Then, he comes in and fidgets with the buttons of his shirt. In contrast, dad is calm but obviously angry. 'Pesi,' he says sternly. 'Don't worry so much. After all that we've been through, this is nothing. Just a minor embarrassment, that's all.'

But Babu is taking this personally. He is, after all, in charge of the workshop. Dad's duties mostly take him out of the office, canvassing for orders, submitting tenders, meeting with customers, doing on-site inspections. The factory is Babu's province, his responsibility, and his casual, hail-fellow-well-met relationship with the labourers is a source of pride to him. He swears at them, jokes with them, yells at them, steals an occasional chappati from them, gives them extra money when they go to their villages once a year. And they, in turn, worship him, grin when he calls them sisterfuckers, perk up when they hear the dry cough that precedes him into the factory each morning, beg him to share the modest meals they prepare on their kerosene stoves each evening.

And now, these same workers are on strike. Worse, any minute now they will show up at the house, armed with placards and red banners and bullhorns. They will stand on the street below our balcony and shout slogans condemning dad and Babu. It's a strike tactic commonly used in Bombay these days, everybody knows that, but we have never been picketed before and all of us are embarrassed and afraid. But of all the family members, Babu and I are taking it the most personally – Babu because of his almost-fraternal relationship with the striking workers, and I, because of my childhood bond with Jamal.

When I was little, I loved Jamal. He was a young, tall, handsome man in his mid-twenties, with enormous white teeth and an ever-ready, quick smile. Dad said that if only Jamal had been educated, there was no telling how far in life he could've gone because he was smart and learned things in a flash. Among all the workers, he was Babu's favourite because although he didn't talk as much as Babu did, they were alike in some ways – gregarious, generous, quick with a laugh. Whenever there was extra work at home – if the apartment had to be washed and cleaned from top to bottom or if some heavy trunks were to be brought down from the loft in the kitchen or if ice-cream had to be hand-whipped in the wooden churn – Babu would always ask Jamal if he wanted to earn some extra money. Always, the answer was yes, so that Jamal was a regular presence in our home.

'Jamal,' I would scream and rush toward him whenever he showed up at the door and he would laugh and pick me up and perch me on his shoulders while mummy followed him around the house saying, 'Careful, careful.' His body was muscular and carried the same clean, sweet scent of sawdust that was on my dad and uncle when they came home from the factory each evening. Sometimes, when he was cleaning the house, he would toss me a rag and allow me to wash the walls with him, with me scrubbing the section closest to the floor while he stood on a ladder beside me, occasionally looking down to throw me a quick smile, his dark black eyes twinkling. I would scrub until my hands ached and then he would climb down the ladder and pull the rag from my hands. 'Enough, baby,' he'd say. 'You go play now.' How impossible it was to explain to him that working by his side was more fun for me than anything I could do on my own, that I was tired of making up an only child's lonely games of invention and this act of working side by side with another person felt happy and exciting to me.

As I grew into my awkward teenage body, my relationship with Jamal changed as we both became more guarded and self-conscious around each other and as the invisible taboos against physicality and horseplay took hold under my family's protective gaze. Our relationship became more complex and we were more reserved around each other but beneath that exterior reserve was the knowledge of the past, of the years that I had hero-worshipped him and he had treated me like his younger sister. Jamal's affection for me now took different form. When I would show up at the workshop during summer vacations, he would confidently order someone to go get a Coke for me, in contrast to the old foreman who would go through his litany of, 'What will you drink, baby? Mangola? Limca? Gold Spot? Coca-Cola? Hah, one Coca-Cola then, icy-cold.' Jamal had now started calling me memsahib instead of baby but there was an irony in the way he did it, as if the two of us shared an old joke.

I, too, was less exuberant in my pleasure at seeing him but I still acknowledged our past bond by lingering to talk with him in front of the other workers, asking about his family and how his father's asthma was. Often, Jamal would point to the book I invariably clenched in my hand, asking to see it, flipping through the pages although we both knew that he could not read. When he returned the book, his face shone with pride. 'You keep reading, memsahib,' he'd say. 'You learn everything in the world there is to learn. Then you come and educate poor Jamal.' We'd both laugh at that but sometimes I had to look away, to beat back the tears that would inexplicably sting my eyes at his words.

And now here's Jamal, standing below our balcony, leading a group of about twenty-five other workers, as they chant their slogans and raise their fists in the air. Even from this distance, I notice that those twinkling dark eyes are now flashing with fury, and his open mouth is twisted with rage. Along with their flags and placards, they have brought drums and bells and are using these to tide over the silence in between the slogans. Our entire family is lined up on the balcony, too stunned and embarrassed to move until dad takes charge. 'Okay, come on,' he says. 'Everybody get in the house. The longer we stand here, the worse their antics will get.' There is real anger in his voice. But it is Babu's face that catches my attention – he looks as stunned by Jamal's transformation as I feel. And there is something else in his face – a pained look of betrayal as well as a hopeless confusion, as if he is realizing for the first time that all the jokes and back-slapping in the world cannot alter the basic fact that people like us and people like Jamal occupy different worlds, that the walls that separate us are too thick to be torn down by only goodwill. Right at that moment, the union leader – a stranger who has shown up to organize the workers only two months earlier – leads the workers in a particularly lewd slogan about the women in the family and hearing this, a light goes out of Babu's eyes and his shoulders slump. But the next second, he lets out a roar. 'Bloody motherfuckers,' he says. 'I'm going downstairs right now and grabbing that bastard union leader by his throat. They can do all their maja-masti about me but if they say a thing about our women ...' He looks around for a shirt to throw over his sadra but dad steps toward him. 'Pesi, calm down. This is exactly the reaction they want from us, don't you see? Then they'll accuse us of breaking the strike by using physical violence. No, let's get on with our day. Sooner or later they will get tired of acting like monkeys and go home.'

But I feel a compelling urge to go back out on the balcony because I have an insane thought that if I can just make eye contact with Jamal, I will be able to re-establish our old friendship and then ... then ... but here my imagination fails me. I venture out anyway, but it is of no use. Upon spotting me, the bells and drums get louder and the chanting more frequent. I try to catch Jamal's eye but the distance is too great and he is no longer in the forefront. I stand there, wanting to do something, make some grand gesture that expresses equal parts solidarity and disappointment, but nothing comes to mind. Just then, Roshan spots me. 'Come in, you idiot,' she yells from the living room. 'Why do you always want to make a fool of yourself?'

The strike is settled four days later. The outside union leader had approached dad and Babu the day after the demonstration and asked them how much they were willing to pay him to simply declare the strike over and skip town. 'Of course, bhaisahibs, you'll have to give the workers a small wage increase, just so I can save face,' he added with a sly smile. 'Otherwise, they'll come after my throat.'

Dad did not try to hide the contempt on his face. 'So all this hero-giri was just for show? Disrupting my business, coming to my house and embarrassing me ...'

The union leader looked sheepish. 'That was just theatre, sir. Something to make the workers feel good.'

'And if we do not pay your ... bribe?'

The man remained unperturbed. 'Not a bribe, sir. Baksheesh. A little reward for calling off the strike.'

And so the strike has ended. But the easy, chatty relation between Babu and Jamal is gone, with Babu being wary and Jamal being uneasy and awkward. Sometimes, Babu cannot hide his bitterness at what he considers to have been Jamal's disloyalty. Jamal, in turn, is increasingly sullen and quiet. When he greets me at the factory now, his face is blank and although he still automatically orders a Coke for me whenever

I visit, it is a conditioned response, with none of the old knowingness or authority. The exuberant man with the ready grin seems to have fled along with the vanishing union leader. Occasionally, I try to engage him in conversation but the answers are brief and perfunctory.

✧

I am at the factory on a day when, four months after the strike has been settled, Babu's lingering bitterness spills over. Jamal has screwed up on an order, has cut the logs of timber half a centimetre too short and Babu is furious at the waste. In his usual manner he cusses at Jamal but this time, the old teasing, the wink that used to take the sting out of Babu's words, is missing. Jamal says nothing, which only seems to infuriate Babu more. 'So where is the Lion of the Punjab these days?' Babu cries, berating the man in the presence of the other workers. 'What has happened to his roar? Did he sell it for a fifteen-paise an hour pay raise?' All heads turn to Jamal, expecting a fiery comeback. Instead, he smiles a self-effacing smile, lowers his head and walks away.

But three days later, he shows up at our home in the evening. It is the first time he has been to the house since the demonstration and so when a startled Freny opens the door, she hesitates for a second before letting him in. 'How are you, memsahib,' he says to her and then spotting me behind Freny, he flashes me a quick but subdued smile. 'Are both seths at home?'

Freny leads him to the living room and then leaves to go get dad and Babu, so that Jamal and I are alone for a brief moment. 'Ae, Jamal,' I say brightly, desperately trying to reprise the easiness of our earlier encounters. 'You want something to drink? Chai? Soft drink?'

He smiles again but shakes his head no. We are quiet for a moment and then suddenly he says, 'Pesi seth is very angry with me, baby.' I open my mouth to say something, to contradict him, to reassure him but the sadness in his face takes my breath away. Before I can say anything, he continues, 'I made a bad, bad mistake.'

And now I am seized with contradictory feelings, so that one part of me agrees with him but another part also wants to lecture him on his right to strike and how he has nothing to apologize for. Again, he speaks before I can: 'This family has been very good to me, baby.' I look away from him, and when I can trust myself to look at his face again, I notice that his eyes are red and teary.

Babu and dad enter the room, their faces guarded. 'Salaam wa'alaykum,' Jamal says and they automatically reply, 'Wa'alaykum salaam.'

'Everything at the factory okay?' Babu asks and visibly relaxes when Jamal assures him that everything is fine. I realize that they have no idea about the reason for this visit.

We soon find out. Jamal has come to take his leave. He thanks us for giving him a job when he'd come to Bombay from his village in the north as a gauche, unworldly boy of twenty. He tells Babu that he has been like a father to him, thanks him for the numerous times he has bailed him out of financial situations. He flushes and apologizes for the whole strike business and says he realizes that things will never be the same because of that situation. He says he knows that now he has lost dad's and Babu's and Mehroo's trust and because of that he has come to take his leave because he cannot continue working at the factory, not with the fallout from the strike still floating like dust particles in the air. I hear myself gasp when Jamal says he is leaving but I don't know if he hears me because he goes on. He has another job lined up at a factory in Chembur but wherever he goes, he will always remember us and our many kindnesses towards him.

No one has interrupted Jamal while he has been talking. Now, I wait for someone to say something – for Mehroo, who has come into the room, to say it's time to let bygones be bygones, for dad to say he is in no position to lose his favourite worker, for Babu to call Jamal a sisterfucker and put his arm around him. But no one moves. Finally, dad clears his throat and thanks Jamal for his years of service and asks when his last day will be. He touches Jamal lightly on the arm and wishes him good luck and Jamal nods his head to acknowledge the gesture. I am stunned at how easily Jamal is being let go, like a discarded piece of machinery. But I do not say a word because I sense the unspoken disappointment and hurt that all four adults in this room are experiencing and I suddenly feel very small and inexperienced.

After Jamal leaves, Dad and Babu decide to give Jamal an extra month's salary for his long years of service. I know that I should be glad about this but I'm still reeling from how casually the relationship has been severed. I am also struck by how broken, how defeated Jamal had looked while the rest of us have recovered unscathed from the strike. I think of him starting out afresh in a new place, and wonder if this new, serious, sad-faced Jamal is permanent or whether the old, impish Jamal will resurface again. And I realize that I will never know because I will never see him again. I am angry at myself for having ever believed that Jamal and I were friends, for believing that friendship was possible between us. I realize that on those occasions when I pretended to work by his side – when he indulged me by letting me wash the walls with him, for instance – he was working until he was bone-tired, working in addition to his full-time job at the factory, in order to earn some extra money for – for what? To send home to his family? To save in a bank? To buy himself a new set of clothes? I realize that in all the years that Jamal had ordered Cokes for me when I visited the factory, I had never seen him sip a soft drink. Here I thought he was treating me as his friend when actually he was treating me like a spoilt princess, a visiting dignitary who had to be entertained with soft drinks. And that day of the demonstration on the balcony – what did I think he would do if he caught my eye? Walk away from the strike? Decide that his friendship with me was more important than a fair wage? What kind of arrogance on my part did it take for me to stand on that balcony? And what I'd thought of as solidarity, wasn't solidarity at all. It was just liberal guilt.

No, Jamal and I were never friends. He probably always knew that, aware as he had to be of the class barriers between us. I had been blithely unaware of those barriers, or, had felt good about myself for ignoring them. Now, I realize that ignoring those barriers had not been an act of humility and democracy but of hubris and privilege.

I go to bed that night, angry and disappointed at myself. When I sleep, I dream of Jamal. His face is in the sky, cloud-like, and his eyes are opaque and dripping with tears. I am on the ground, looking up at Jamal's face in the sky, watching his tears turn into rain as they fall around me. I want to say something to him, console him, but he is very far away.

We are both very far away from each other.

✧

For only the second time in my life, my father has lost his temper with me but this time, we have gone almost four months without speaking to each other despite living under the same roof. He is open about the fact that the months of my punishing silence have been hell for him but my teenage pride will not let me concede the same point.

For the last four months, a flag of sorts, the emblem of my defiance, has held a pride of place in my closet. It is a striped, blue-and-white cotton shirt given to me by a friend and it is what inaugurated my period of silence. The shirt is about three sizes too large for my ninety-nine-pound frame but baggy shirts and blue jeans are in fashion among the arty kids in college and I love the fact that the shirt hides my small but growing breasts. My well-dressed, dandified father, with his starched collars and pressed pants, hates that shirt. He is embarrassed at the thought of his only daughter walking around the neighbourhood wearing an ill-fitting shirt and jeans torn at the knees. My head is filled with images of scruffy, long-haired rock-stars like Bob Dylan. He still remembers the impeccable dress style of a Sinatra or Cary Grant. We are from two different worlds and soon, those worlds will collide.

For months, he keeps his silence. But it all comes to a head one evening, hours before he is to catch the overnight train to leave on a business trip. That afternoon, he is giving his banker friend a ride home when he spots me at the bus-stop near my college. Instinctively, his foot hits the brake to stop but when he notices how 'shabbily' I am dressed, he speeds by. He is not sure if I have seen him. But for the rest of the afternoon the fact that he did not stop for his only child shames him, makes him disgusted with himself and by evening, the shame has hardened into anger. That evening, he is glowering as I answer the doorbell and let him in. Oblivious to what has transpired earlier in the day, I make small talk while he hastily throws his clothes into his suitcase. Mehroo tells him that dinner is ready but he mumbles something about picking something up along the way. 'Wait then,' she says. 'I'll just wrap the cutlets up for you to eat on the train.' She hurries into the kitchen.

We are alone in the hallway as he waits for Mehroo. The blue fluorescent light blinks and hums overhead. Suddenly, my father's eyes narrow as they focus on a tiny hole on my right shirtsleeve. When he speaks, his voice is choked. 'Wearing torn clothes outside. My own child. Even when the business was really bad, when we had no orders, when all we ate every night was daal and rice, even then, nobody in this family ever went outside with torn clothes...'

'It's not really torn,' I reply. 'The hole's so small, no one can see. Besides, that's the fashion...'

'*I* can see it. That's what matters. I can see it.' And he takes a step toward me, puts his index finger in the hole and moves it down the length of my arm, the shirtsleeve tearing to expose my arm and hanging near my wrist.

There is a sudden silence. We stare at each other, both of us unsure of what to do next. I am breathing hard, willing myself not to cry. My dad looks as horrified as I feel. Mehroo walks into the silence and gasps as she sees me, standing in my torn shirt, looking like a street urchin. 'Wh ... what happened? Burjor?'

In reply, my dad picks up his suitcase. 'I'm ... I'll miss my train.' He opens the front door and then stops to look at me. 'I'm sorry,' he says. 'I ... we'll talk when I get home. Stay well.'

I do not reply. For the rest of the evening, I ignore the pleas of the grown-ups and walk around in my torn shirt. Each time I glance at the torn sleeve, I feel a warm sense of satisfaction, like blood rushing into a cold limb. My father's action has given voice to something I have felt but could never vocalize, has exposed some essential truth: I am a misfit, an alien in your midst, my torn shirt proclaims. I am different from the rest of you. My values are different. I do not love or fear the same things that you do. And that makes me different.

Two days later, I receive a blue aerogramme from my father, the first letter he has ever addressed to me. 'Darling Thritu. I'm about to board the train,' he wrote. 'I'm sorry for what happened ... But I am right.'

I hate him and admire him for the last sentence. But I don't acknowledge the letter when my father returns from his trip. Mostly, I don't acknowledge him at all, despite

Mehroo's cajoling. When he asks me a question, I make my eyes focus elsewhere while I answer in monosyllables. As the months drag on, my hostility begins to feel silly even to me but now, I don't know how to walk away from it and toward him. It seems terribly important, a matter of life-and-death, to not be the one to give in, lest I be perceived as weak. At times, seeing the hurt look on his face, I weep hot tears into my pillow. Then, I force myself to look at the tattered shirt hanging in my closet, to buttress my position. Finally, at the end of four months, he breaks down at the dining table one day, his eyes filling with tears. That is all it takes. I go over and hug him while the other adults sigh in relief.

But it takes me another three weeks to remove the torn shirt from where it's hanging in my closet. Even then, I neatly fold it and place it on a shelf, where it will remain for years.

✧

The channawalla wanders up to the car and my dad buys a rupee's worth of roasted peanuts. This is the first time since our estrangement that we have come to the seaside. He tells me how ashamed he is for having lost his temper with me, how the memory of the aborted trip to Hanging Gardens still hurts him. This is the amazing thing about my father – unlike most adults I know, he has no problems admitting he is wrong. In fact, his relentless drive for self-improvement, his paroxysms of self-doubt, his candidness in talking about his life, both embarrass and fascinate me. In contrast to him, I am already closed, emotionally guarded. In some ways, my dad is younger, more trusting, more innocent than I am. It occurs to me that just as he can still outrun or outwalk me, my dad can also emotionally outdistance me.

We started doing this several years ago, dad and I, coming to the seaside after dusk, sitting in the car and talking. Mostly, he talks and I listen. Or rather, he talks and I let my mind wander down its familiar paths – daydreaming about being older and out of the house and wearing cotton saris to my journalist job at *The Times of India* and perhaps even having my own little apartment somewhere far from my childhood home. But my dad does not know my futuristic fantasies and he still talks to the teenager that I am. Sometimes he notices how my head tilts away from him as he lectures me about the importance of honesty ('Don't even pick up a ten-paise coin from the ground, if it doesn't belong to you'), the value of education ('If you don't finish college, the best I can promise you is maybe I can get you a job as a packer at a box factory') and the dangers of premarital sex ('Boys want different things in a girlfriend than in a wife'). Then his voice gets even more intense than usual. 'Listen to me, Thrituma,' he says urgently. 'Learn from my life experience, don't make all the mistakes I have made. I want to spare you all the pain I've gone through. I had no one to advice me. Everything I've learned, I've learned the hard way, through trial and error. Even if you forget eighty-five per cent of everything I am telling you, just the fifteen per cent will come back to you when you're older. That is why I say the same things over and over again, like a broken record.'

I hear him, even understand what he's saying, but I can't help myself. I am bored. I have heard this lecture too many times and I am bored. Besides, I have now begun to realize the gulf between our worlds. My father had quit school in the sixth grade. He is a self-made man and everything that he knows he has had to teach himself. He has never read a Shakespeare play in his life. Already, I have read books whose very existence my father is unaware of. I know things about art and music that my father does not. Nor does he realize how those things have changed me. For instance, my father is unaware that ever since I read *Lust for Life*, the biography of Vincent van Gogh, two years ago, I have stopped asking him for car rides, preferring instead to ride the public buses. I identify so strongly with Van Gogh that I even develop a stutter to sound like him. I walk around with what I imagine is a haunted, crazed look and cultivate Van Gogh's contempt for the bourgeois life. Hermann Hesse's *Damien* and *Steppenwolf* give further voice to the alienated stranger I have become. I am no longer the earnestly good child who gave all her lunch money to the nuns. I am no longer a child.

In contrast to the intellectual, passionate, art-filled world that I am reading about – a world, it is clear to me that I have to die trying to be part of – the world described by my father sounds tediously conscripted, pale and bloodless. His is the world of virtue and practicality. But my soul hankers for a greyer world, filled with ambiguity and complexity. My father promises me a world of answers – 'Honesty is the best policy', 'Cleanliness is next to godliness', 'A stitch in time saves nine'. but I am increasingly enthralled by a world in which people ask impossible questions, questions without answers.

It is impossible to communicate all this to my father. The few times that I have tried he has turned to me with worried eyes, as if I have become one more problem in his life that he will be forced to solve. I know only too well the other pressures on him and do not want to be part of the problem. So I say nothing. Or I say it obliquely: at the dinner table I will suddenly ask the adults if they know of a place where I could get my Michelangelo print of David framed to hang in the living room. I brace myself for the inevitable answer: 'There's too much dust from the textile mills. Any picture on the wall will have to be dusted every single day and you know how lazy the servants are. '

So I sit in the pictureless living room, with its solitary calendar from Batliwalla and Sons being the only thing hanging from the walls. I notice that even the calendar does not have a picture on it. Someday, I promise myself, every room in my house will have pictures on the wall. And I will buy fresh flowers once a week. Someday.

I sit crouched like a tiger, biding my time.

MRS BEATRICE D'MELLO HAS THROWN me out of her physics class yet again, so that I have now spent five days in a row in the hallway. Most days it is a badge of honour to be kicked out of Mrs D'Mello's class but today, Mother Ignatius had passed me in the hallway, raised her eyebrows when she saw me leaning against the cream-coloured walls and said, 'Out in the hallway again, eh, child?' and I had felt my face flush at the injustice of it all. I wanted to explain how Mrs D'Mello had a vendetta against me, how she kicked me out of class at the slightest provocation, how she would ask me question after question until she threw me one I couldn't answer and then ask me to leave the room. But Mother Ignatius was already walking away.

There was a time when Mrs D'Mello was genuinely fond of me though it seems so long ago it's hard to remember. There was a time when she laughed at all my jokes and would even allow me to interrupt the class by turning on my pocket transistor radio and listen to the cricket score when India was playing Pakistan.

In seventh-grade, I was the first girl to come to school with a pocket radio. It was a yellow Philips radio that Babu had bought for me. The radio made me feel connected to the legions of cricket fans who brought the city to a virtual standstill when there was a test match going on. Bombay, when gripped by cricket fever, was a transformed city. White-collar workers called off sick in record numbers. A middle-aged businessman in a white Impala would think nothing of rolling down his car window and asking a street urchin if Sunil Gavaskar was still at the bat. Strangers walked up to each other and asked, 'What's the latest score, yaar?' Firecrackers went off all across the city whenever Bedi bowled another batsman out. During the India-Pakistan matches, the Muslim shop owners at Bhendi Bazaar would hand out sweetmeats each time an Indian wicket fell, while nearby Hindus glowered at them. A panoramic view of the office crowds at Churchgate or Flora Fountain would have shown men and women leaning slightly to one side, pocket transistors glued to one ear. The air filled with the crackle of these radios, the rapid-fire voices of commentators Vijay Merchant and Lala Amarnath rising and falling like ocean waves. No war, it seemed could bring Bombayites together the way a test match did and if I had to be at school and away from the excitement, the least I could do was carry a pocket radio.

I would turn the radio on low, flip open my desk top and lay it on top of my books inside the desk. Every few minutes, I would cradle my head in my hands and rest my ear against the desk. Then I would whisper the score to the girl sitting next to me, who in turn would pass it to the next person until the whole class knew. For a few days, Mrs D'Mello watched me go through this elaborate charade. Then she said, 'Okay, child, let's do this. I'll let you listen to the radio every once in awhile and you can tell the whole class. Then we go back to our studies, eh?'

I thought she was the coolest teacher in the world.

But the friendship between Mrs D'Mello and myself was short-lived. It ended the day my classmates and I were standing in the hallway during a class change and I made what I thought was a brilliant anthropological observation. 'Hey, do you notice how much Mrs D'Mello looks like a horse when she laughs?' I said to Anita. 'Such big teeth she has.'

Anita gulped hard. Her eyes grew big as she stared at a spot over my shoulder.

I turned around. Mrs D'Mello was glaring at me, her eyes narrow and mean. She had a tremendous scowl on her face. My stomach dropped.

'I ... I ... It was a compliment ... I love horses ... I didn't mean anything bad ...' I stuttered but it was too late. Mrs D'Mello had turned on her heel and was marching into the classroom.

Thus began my long and lonely exile in the hallway. Most days, I was fine with it, would walk out of the classroom with a swagger, making sure that everyone noticed the novel I was carrying to keep me company in the hallway. But today, embarrassed by Mother Ignatius' words, I am fuming about the unfairness of it all.

It is lunch recess and about seven of us have decided to go across the street and get a plate of pyali, a spicy mixture of potatoes and beans. On the way back, Tasneem decides to buy some boras, the red, tangy berries, and slices of raw green mangoes dipped in salt. The old street vendor deftly slices the mango and I stare at his small, sharp knife. 'I swear, yaar, if I had a knife I'd go and kill Mrs D'Mello right now,' I say almost to myself.

But Anita Khalsa hears me. 'I dare you,' she says immediately.

'Dare me to do what?'

'I dare you take a knife and go up to Mrs D'Mello and say the words, "Mrs D'Mello, I'm here to kill you." '

The other girls crowd around us. My mind is working fast. This is my chance to once and for all be the undisputed holder of the title of Mad Parsi.

'What's the bet worth?' I ask.

And they think for a minute. 'One LP,' Rukshan says, knowing my love for music.

'Not enough, men,' I say. 'This could get me thrown out of school, for God's sake. No, this is worth at least four albums.'

That stops them for a minute and I'm almost hoping they will back out. But then Anita says, 'Yah, we can all chip in the cash, so what. Okay, four albums.'

I gulp hard, wondering how I manage to get myself in these situations. Nothing to do now but see this through.

Tasneem's first-floor apartment is adjacent to the school and we decide to go there to borrow a knife. She decides not to run up to the apartment, convinced her mother will be suspicious if she looks her daughter in the eye. 'Ma, ma,' Tasneem yells from below and when her mother appears at the balcony she asks her to toss us a knife.

'What you need a knife for, beta?'

Tasneem thinks fast. 'For biology class, ma. We have to cut up a frog.'

Even from this distance we can see Tasneem's mother grimace. But she goes inside and returns with a knife wrapped in newspaper, which she throws down at us after asking us to get out of the way.

So there is no way out now. My last hope, that Tasneem's mom would smell a rat and refuse us the knife, has faded. The presence of the knife makes the dare seem more real. As we walk back to the school and climb the two sets of stairs that lead to the teachers' lounge, word spreads, so that a procession of about fourteen girls is now following me. I hold the knife, still wrapped in the newspaper, and try to think of how to extract myself from this situation in a way that will fulfil the spirit of the dare and still let me save face. And then it comes to me: while the others wait outside the glass doors of the teachers' lounge, I will walk up to Mrs D'Mello and say loudly, 'Mrs D'Mello, I'm here to kill you.' But here's the tricky part, here's where I will prove myself more wily than Houdini – I will also add, in a voice soft enough for only Mrs D'Mello to hear, 'Don't worry, this is just a joke.'

It does not occur to me that Mrs D'Mello, who has hated my guts for more than two years, may not think much of this joke. I feel confident of my secret plan as we march toward the teachers' lounge.

More confident than the others, it turns out. As the group sees that I am determined to see the deed through, the enormity of what could happen begins to dawn on them. We are at the end of the hallway that leads to the teachers' lounge when Tasneem chickens out. 'Ae, come on, yaar. This is going too far. If my mother finds out what I wanted the knife for she will make mincemeat out of me.'

Mary pipes up. 'Yeah, we'll all get into solid trouble. And after what happened only two weeks ago, none of us can afford to get into any more trouble, no?'

We all know immediately what she's talking about.

✧

The troubles that Mary is referring to began with a song. It was a song I had written in tribute to our school's patron saint, Claudine Thevenet, and was sung to the tune of The Osmonds' *I'll Be Your Long-haired Lover from Liverpool*.

We were to have performed this song at a special assembly being held at a nearby Catholic school but everything was running behind schedule on that day and Sister Ignatius instead gave up our block of time to the graduating tenth-graders and we returned to school without having sung our song.

What happened next took me by surprise: A strange brew of hurt pride, teenage angst, mass hysteria and bubbling hormones erupted in spontaneous combustion, so that the entire class was shedding tears of indignation by the time we returned to school. As the song's creator, I was initially flattered by the outrage its non-performance had provoked and then I was shocked by the hysterical outpourings of forty very emotional girls. I had never seen my friends like this. Most of the time, we tried to outdo each other by being cool, unemotional and devil-may-care. At first I tried to reason with them but when I noticed that I was the only one who did not believe that we had suffered a great injury, a terrible insult, and that we were continually being oppressed, patronized and humiliated by the graduating seniors, I, too, got swept up in the tidal wave of emotion.

Two hours later, an unsuspecting Mother Ignatius asked us to gather in our assembly hall to practice the song for next day's performance. Since we had not had an opportunity to sing today, she declared, we would perform the song during tomorrow's school assembly.

Boycott. The word spread quickly throughout our ranks. We would not participate in today's practice and we would not perform tomorrow. It did not occur to any of us to communicate our hurt or our new decision to Mother Ignatius. We took our places in the stands as usual and when Mother Ignatius asked Mary to come take her place at the piano, she complied.

Mary was older than most of us because she had repeated several grades. She was a tall, athletic, Anglo-Indian girl with straight brown hair and beautiful grey eyes. It was well known that Mary was one of the school's handful of charity cases and it was rumoured that the family has fallen onto hard times because her father was a drunk. But what Mary lacked in scholarly abilities she made up in her cheery willingness to help and she was a favourite with many of the nuns.

Mother Ignatius raised her baton. 'Ready?' she said. 'All right, Mary, give us the opening chord.'

We remained motionless. Mary sat perched on the piano stool, her head bowed.

Mother Ignatius looked surprised. 'C'mon girls, let's get to it. Let's try again. Ready?'

The big room was silent. Mother Ignatius turned toward Mary. We could tell she was struggling to hold on to her patience. 'Okay, Mary. Let's hear that chord.'

But Mary bowed her head even further, so that her chin was resting on her chest. Mother Ignatius looked from her to us. It was obvious that she had no idea what was going on and it occurred to me that one of us should fill her in but the atmosphere in the room was suddenly so charged, we were all so caught up in that web of defiant silence, that I was afraid to move.

Mother Ignatius was not afraid to move. With a few deft steps, she was standing before the piano. 'Play, Mary,' she said softly, and when Mary did not move, she repeated, 'Play, my child. Play the piano.'

Mary sat with her head down. Mother Ignatius stared at her for a few moments. 'Get up,' she said suddenly.

Mary stood but her eyes were averted. The rest of us looked on helplessly, holding our breaths. 'Look at me,' Mother Ignatius said ... 'Talk to me. Tell me what is going on.'

Her words fell on deaf ears. 'Look at me,' Mother Ignatius repeated, her words precise as bullets this time. And the next minute, a bullet landed, as her right hand flew over Mary's face in a slap.

We gasped. Mary and Mother Ignatius both flinched and looked stricken. And then, all hell broke loose. 'It's not fair, it's not fair, it's not fair,' Anu began to wail, sounding like a police siren. Anu was a short, homely girl from a conservative Hindu family and most of us avoided her because it was well known that Anu was a snitch and a tattletale. Anu's uncharacteristic outburst had a mesmerizing effect on the rest of us. Soon, everybody was talking and crying and yelling all at once.

Mother Ignatius took in the situation. 'Okay, everybody back to your classroom,' she said crisply. 'I still have no idea what's going on but will settle that later.'

But Mother Ignatius had made a wrong calculation. Being left alone and unsupervised in our classroom only gave room for the hysteria to grow. For a moment I thought I was the only dry-eyed girl left but then I caught Patty's eye and she gave me a quick, bemused look as if to say, What the hell is going on here? I shrugged in reply.

'We have to do something. We cannot let ourselves be treated like this by those senior girls,' Barbara was saying and now I was convinced that the sun has risen in the South today. Barbara was Mrs Pinto's daughter, an obedient, goody-two-shoes type, who spoke so softly it sounded as if she always had laryngitis.

But Barbara's little speech had an effect on me and gave flight to all my fantasies about youth power and student revolution. Seize the moment, seize the hour, I said to myself. 'Okay,' I yelled decisively. 'Here's what we will do. Let me quickly draw up a signature petition and we'll personally deliver it to Mother Ignatius.'

All forty of us signed the petition. All forty of us moved like a dark cloud of angry bees from our classroom, made a left turn and walked the short distance to Mother Ignatius' office.

I knocked on the door. She looked up and smiled, as if she was happy to see me. I felt a sudden rush of affection for her, which I tried to suppress. I remembered the many conversations Mother Superior had had with us, conversations where she had shared parts of her life both before and after she became a nun, talks which had removed some of the mystique that surrounded the nunnery and made us look at the white-clad figures less as space aliens and more as flesh-and-blood human beings.

'You girls can ask me anything,' she had once said to us in one of her informal talks.

A dozen hands went up at once.

'Why did you become a nun, Mother?'

'Is it true that all nuns were jilted by their boyfriends and so they joined the convent?'

'Do you miss not seeing your mummy-daddy?'

'How old are you?'

'Is it true you are bald?'

'Have you ever been in love?'

Mother Superior had raised her hand, laughing. 'Girls, girls. One at a time.'

And she told us about how long and thick her hair had once been, how it had been her pride and joy, an object of vanity, really. How her boyfriend – yes, she had had a boyfriend – used to compliment her on her hair. And no, she wasn't quite bald now but yes, she'd cut off her hair after she'd joined the convent because it was easier to manage under the habit and all and also, because it had been a source of pride and vanity and God did not like pride. 'So off it came, chop-chop,' she smiled.

I had felt an inexpressible sadness when she told us about her hair. I couldn't decide if what she had done was foolish or admirable.

But now, standing outside her office, I casted these sentimental memories out of my head. 'May we come in?' I asked.

'Of course, of course,' she replied but then jumped up from her chair with a start as all of us walked into her small office, crowding her.

'What is this?' she said, and I was surprised to hear a tremor in her voice. Her body stiffened and her eyes darted around the room. 'How dare all you girls march into my office like this.'

The day was getting away from me like a tumbling roll of yarn. 'But, Mother, I just asked you if we could come in,' I replied in confusion. Mother Ignatius looked more angry than I have ever seen her. What's worse, she looked – *scared*. And then it dawned on me: Mother thought this was a sit-in. She thought we were here to surround her in her office and not let her leave.

I was about to explain when Anu came to my rescue. 'It's not fair, it's not fair, it's not fair,' she wailed and despite the charged atmosphere, I wanted to giggle. But then I heard it from behind me, a wall of sound that was pushing forward. It started low and deep like a growl and then got high-pitched. Everybody was talking all at once and what was really astounding was that girls like Anita Khalsa, who had made a reputation for themselves for being as tough as nails, were sobbing as if they were at a funeral.

'You slapped Mary,' Barbara cried and Mother Ignatius flinched and took a step back as if to escape the accusation in Barbara's tone.

'Will somebody please tell me what on earth is going on?' she said . . . But most of us were too hysterical to talk. Mother looked around the room helplessly. Her eyes finally fell on me, one of the few remaining dry-eyed girls in the room. 'Thrity? Can you tell me what this is about?'

In response, I handed her the petition. She read it, once, twice, but when she looked up she seemed as confused as ever. 'That's what all this is about? Because your class was not allowed to sing?'

I heard the incredulity in her voice and felt embarrassed by the theatrics of my classmates. Our cause suddenly seemed puny and silly to me. But I banished these treacherous thoughts and when I spoke, my voice was calm and steady. 'It's not just that, Mother. There are so many other problems. The seniors always seemed to end up with the best of everything and we are made to feel like...'

Then I lost my train of thought because just then I had glanced sideways to look at Patty for support and to my amazement I noticed that her shoulders were shaking. She was standing with her head bowed and her hands crossed in front of her and for a moment I thought that she was laughing and then I realized that Patty – unsentimental, tough-assed Patty – was also crying. I lost it then. I tried to go on and list our grievances but now I was caught in the sea of adolescent grief and resentments that were swirling around me and I felt myself going down. To my mortification, I realized that there were tears streaming down my cheeks.

Mother Ignatius did me the favour of looking away. 'All right, I think I've heard enough to know what the problem is,' she said. 'Now all of you have to trust me to fix it. I will place a phone call to the principal at St Agnes and invite her students to a return visit and you can sing your song then. Now, go back to your class and compose yourselves.'

But there was still one unfinished business. Minutes after we returned to our classroom, Mother Ignatius followed us in. 'Come here, Mary,' she said and Mary got up from her seat in the last row and walked to the front of the class. 'I'm sorry for hitting you, my child,' Mother Ignatius said. 'I just lost my temper and I was wrong.' Then, she did a classy thing. First, she kissed Mary on the forehead. Then, she made a small sign of the cross on her forehead.

A thrill ran through all of us. Mary beamed.

But Mother Ignatius was not yet done. Her eyes fixed on me and narrowed slightly. 'The next time you decide to bring forty girls into my tiny office, please ask permission first,' she said icily.

'But Mother,' I protested. 'I did ask...'

But she was walking away and did not hear me. Shit, I thought to myself. How do I end up in these situations?

'That's absolutely not fair, yaar,' said Zarina, the girl who sat in front of me. 'I'm solid sure you asked her permission. These adults are half-deaf, I tell you.'

I smiled weakly at Zarina. But I couldn't help but feel that I was suddenly on Mother Ignatius' blacklist through no fault of mine.

✧

Less than two weeks have gone by since the song incident and now I am actively courting more trouble. We are close enough to the teachers' lounge now that I suspect they can hear us. The crowd following me has shrunk to four intrepid girls. But now that we are moments away from the glass doors, they are wavering also.

'Thrity, men, this is stupid,' Kajal says. 'Let's just forget about this.'

I am in two minds. Part of me is scared at seeing this through but I am equally scared at the prospect of word getting around that the Mad Parsi had chickened out from under a dare. Reputations are like pets – you have to groom them, feed them, and not abandon them. Besides, I notice that Anita Khalsa, my main rival and the girl who started this whole thing, has not spoken a word yet.

But the next moment, Anita speaks up. We are at the door of the teachers' lounge and several of them are peering at us curiously from the glass doors. 'Okay, I withdraw,' Anita says hastily. 'Kajal is right. I don't want to get you thrown out of school or something. These teachers are so unsporting, you know?'

This is my chance to stage a graceful exit with no loss of face. In fact, I have stared Anita Khalsa down and she has blinked first. I even have two witnesses to this moment of supreme victory. And yet, I hesitate, my right hand beginning to reach for the doorknob.

'But what about my four albums?'

Anita looks exasperated. She knows she has given me an out that I am too obstinate to take. 'Screw the albums,' she says. Then, seeing the determined look on my face, she blinks some more. 'Okay, tell you what. We will give you a free album just for not doing anything.'

I think fast, trying to size up the situation. 'No, yaar, that's not good enough. Tell you what, let's compromise on two albums and I'll give up right now.'

They hesitate, reluctant to shell out all those bucks for nothing. For a moment I think I have aimed too high and that Anita will call my bluff. I tighten my grip on the golden door handle. Seeing this, Anita folds completely. 'Okay, you bloody Shylock, you damn bloodsucker,' she says. 'We will give you two albums if you stop right now.'

And so, the following Saturday, a bunch of them take me to Rhythm House and watch silently as I pick out Elton John's *Greatest Hits* and Neil Diamond's *Hot August Night*. I pay the difference in price because the second is a double album.

For the next few weeks, I listen everyday to *Candle in the Wind* and *Song Sung Blue*. When Elton John sings, 'Daniel my brother, you are older than me/Do you still feel the pain of the scars that won't heal,' I invariably think of my cousin Roshan and my complicated relationship with her and my eyes fill with tears. At the next school social, I carry the album to school and Mother Ignatius teaches some of us how to tango to *Crocodile Rock*.

And Mrs D'Mello sleeps well at night, undisturbed by nightmares of vengeful students breaking into the teachers' lounge with knives hidden in newspaper, who expect her to smile even while she is being told that they are about to kill her.

# Sixteen

B Y BUYING ALCOHOL AND CIGARETTES while underage, I break the law many times during my high school years. I also commit at least two sins during my junior year.

The first sin is winning first prize at a government-sponsored essay-writing contest extolling the virtues of family planning during Indira Gandhi's draconian Emergency. Of course, this was in the still-innocent period of early 1976, when news that the government's birth control campaign had run amok, had not yet reached us in Bombay. We didn't know about the roving vans that cruised the streets of New Delhi, looking for men – and boys as young as fourteen – to forcibly sterilize them. I had grown up watching adults screw up their noses when they talked about how the lower-classes repeated their endless cycles of poverty by reproducing like rabbits, had read textbooks blaming overpopulation for all of India's ills. So when a group of bureaucrats show up at school one day and the nuns fawn over them and then hastily organize the essay-writing contest, I write a composition that would've gladdened the hearts of the snip-snipping thugs who were prowling the streets of Delhi even as I wrote.

But that was a sin born of ignorance and therefore pardonable. What I do to Jaya is deliberately cruel.

Jaya is the only classmate I ever have who scores higher than me in composition class. That alone is enough to make me notice her and to fear her as a competitor. She is a tall, pencil-thin Catholic girl with bad skin and long, skinny legs.

She is also bitingly witty, though she is so shy and mousy-looking, that it takes me months to appreciate her caustic humour although she sits at the desk next to mine. I have an uneasy, complicated friendship with Jaya – on the one hand, I am attracted to her obvious intelligence and political awareness. On the other, I know that she thinks I am wasting my time hanging out with Jenny and the others and this unspoken judgment makes me prickly and awkward around her. It also doesn't help matters that she dotes on me and talks to me in a manner that assumes we share similar values and sensibilities. There is an air of intellectual superiority to her that makes me bristle, even while I understand that the circle of superiority is large enough to include me. I know that my other friends feel patronized by her and that is enough to make me align myself with them. But I also take in the thin lips that tremble with emotion when she recites a Shakespearean sonnet, I know that Jaya's thick, Catwoman glasses hide eyes that are kind and that the sarcastic wit makes up for a deeply sensitive nature. The truth is that Jaya and I are alike in that we are both thin-skinned and hypersensitive and we both have a secret desire to be writers. She knows this and assumes a friendship based on that unspoken knowledge. But I do not want to align myself with someone who is so vulnerable and shy because I am exposing myself. After all, I have a reputation to uphold and my personality is larger and more extroverted than hers. Then too, Jaya gives off enough of a whiff of possessiveness that it makes me feel constricted being in her company, so that when I am around her my jokes get cruder and I am louder, more expansive and boisterous. Sometimes, she laughs with the others at one of my jokes. Most of the time she just peers at me from behind those thick glasses, her thin lips stretched in a line that I take to mean disapproval. Like many of the adults around me, Jaya seems to think that I am better than who I am spending my time being, and there is always a faint air of disapproval around her that sets my teeth on edge.

It is 1976. We are in ninth-grade, a year away from graduation. The Emergency is almost a year old when Jaya comes up to me one day and says she needs to talk to me in private.

'What is it, men?' I say immediately. 'Can't you just tell me here?'

'No, I told you, it's private. Let's walk out in the hallway, okay?'

Jaya has a boyfriend, I say to myself. Goddamn it, who would've thought? Old Jaya has a boyfriend. And still so serious and all, not even cracking a smile.

I fly off my chair and follow her into the hallway. But she is still not smiling.

'What is it?' Then, seeing that she's about to cry, 'Jaya, what's wrong, men?'

'Nothing's wrong. It's just that ... nobody in school knows but ... my mother's in jail.'

I freeze. In my middle-class brain, jail is forever associated with criminal behaviour. I don't know Jaya's mother well but the dark-haired, petite, smiling woman in a white kurta-and pants whom I'd seen at school on a few occasions, did not look like a criminal to me. Still, one never knew...

'Wha – what did she do? What crime did she commit, girl?'

Jaya looks shocked. 'Crime? She committed no crime. She was the head of the teachers' union. She was simply organizing the other teachers at her school. But under the Emergency, you know, the right to strike has been criminalized...'

Jaya continues to talk but I stop listening. I am still in shock. I have never known anybody who has had a relative in jail. The concept of going to jail for one's beliefs is alien to me. I come from a resolutely apolitical family, where the only ancestor who participated in the freedom struggle against the British, was an object of derision in family lore. I come from an ethnic community that has held itself aloft from the turmoil of its adopted country, a minority that has thrived by not choosing sides, by existing peacefully with its neighbours. All my history and civics textbooks tell me that India is a democracy where the rule of law prevails. When I was a kid, dad used to chuckle as I saluted every traffic cop we passed. The hair on my arms stands up involuntarily when I hear the national anthem and I love watching the Republic Day parade on TV. And now Jaya is trying to convince me that her mother is in jail just for trying to start a union. It makes no sense. Jamal tried to start a union, too, and nobody threw him in jail. No, Jaya is lying. Everybody knows how it goes: jail is for criminals.

'I don't know, baba, I don't know,' I interrupt her. 'All I know is, people don't go to jail if they haven't done anything wrong. That's just how the law works.'

Jaya's face crumbles as if I have landed a punch on her jaw. She stares at me open-mouthed. 'But ... I swear ...' she stammers.

I can't look Jaya in the eye. I am ashamed of myself but then self-righteousness smothers my embarrassment and makes me land the knockout blow. 'If your mummy's in jail, she probably deserves to be,' I say and then walk away.

I resolutely avoid looking at Jaya the rest of the day.

Two weeks later, the edifice of my conformist, middle-class existence lies in ruins at my feet. It begins innocently enough with a bus ride to Homi Bhabha Auditorium to listen to a recital by a visiting German orchestra. As always, Jesse and me catch the double-decker bus from its terminal and scramble for the front seats on the top deck. This is our favourite seat and often, we stick our faces out of the window to feel the wind against our faces. As always, we talk about art, music, literature – or rather, Jesse talks and I listen, storing up all the information she so casually imparts, memorizing some of her funnier one-liners so that I can pass them off as my own in school the next day. My heart swells with joy and I feel the wild, mad, happy-drunk feeling that I always do when I am in Jesse's company. Every conversation with Jesse affects me the same way – I feel as if my brain has received a good scrubbing, so that it is bright as brass. Nobody in my circle reads, knows or thinks as much as Jesse does and even now, after several years of being close friends, I am awed that she has overlooked the five years that separate us – I am fifteen, she is twenty – and sought out my friendship. I feel totally inadequate in this relationship, as if I am doing all the taking but when I tell Jesse this she always looks offended and tells me I am wrong.

Now she is talking about some obscure Pacific island and suddenly, I can't wait another minute. 'But Jesse,' I interrupt. 'How do you *know* so much?' There is a lifetime of deprivation, awe and admiration in the question but Jesse shakes her head impatiently, brushing off my overly-eager, fawning question as if it were a fly. She looks embarrassed and then mumbles something about my talking nonsense.

We talk about other things, poke fun at the strange business names – Rassiwalla Rope Company; Chimneywalla and Sons – and signs – Stick No Labels Here; Horn OK Please; No Spitting or Sitting on Grass – that we pass. We also go past several of the giant billboards that have sprung up overnight during the Emergency: Work More, Talk Less; Indira is India, and the omnipresent family planning slogan, Hum Do, Hamare Do: We two, Our two.

And then Jesse mentions a name I've heard before: Karl Marx. I vaguely know that Marx was a Communist and that Communists are enemies of the state and silly people to boot, because everybody knows that without a profit motive people will never work.

'Yeah, he was a Communist, right?' I say. 'Like those people in China? Ae, did you know that those Chinamen don't get to vote or anything? That's why Nehru went to war with them – they hated us for our freedom.'

I am blithely repeating what I've always heard and so I'm unprepared for Jesse's reaction. 'Don't talk shit,' she says abruptly, in a tone harsher than any she has ever used. 'Who do you think is free in our country? The people living in the slums? The servants in our houses? And we all see what freedom of speech even we actually have, with all the media cowards running scared of the Emergency.'

I stare at Jesse in amazed silence. This is a side of her I have never seen before. What was she getting so angry about? And was she angry at *me*?

'Well, anyway, the Communists want to distribute money equally,' I attempted, repeating what I'd heard at school. 'But if everybody makes the same, what is the incentive for people to work? It sounds nice but it would never work, na, if people could just šit at home and all?'

She looks at me directly for the first time since we've started on this subject. 'Do you know what the basic principle of Communism – rather, I should say, Socialism is?' she says rhetorically. 'It's, "To each according to his ability; to each according to his need." Do you understand what that means?'

I don't. She explains. I ask more questions. She answers them. She tells me about Mao in China and Lenin in the Soviet Union and the various grassroots movements that she claims are going on in India.

While Jesse is talking, I think back on those childhood dreams about the city's poor. After years of being told by the adults that the poor would always be with us, that the poor were poor because they were lazy and didn't want to work, that nothing could be done about poverty so it was better not to think about it – at last someone is telling me something different. And to hear Jesse say it, entire countries had reorganized themselves according to these revolutionary principles. To each according to his need. It is the most life-affirming thing I've ever heard. Everything that I've always believed about people – that people usually only did mean things when they were deprived, that given a choice they'd do the right thing – all of those beliefs are boiled into that line. The adults around me are wrong, wrong, wrong.

I had boarded the B.E.S.T bus that day an ordinary schoolgirl, self-indulgent and self-absorbed, occupied with my own changing body and its pleasures. When I threw around words like youth revolution and revolution, I was thinking Woodstock, not Russia.

I disembark from the bus that day, baptized in a new faith. I feel as if I had been given a pair of X-ray glasses because I can suddenly see the inside structure of things. 'Distribution, not production, is the problem,' Jesse had said and isn't she right? Can't I see evidence of that all around me – the skyscrapers growing up from the armpits of the slums, the hungry children sleeping on the pavement in front of the dazzling jewellery stores, the belching Share Bazaar traders ignoring the one-eyed beggar at their side? Bombay does not seem depressing any more. I will no longer be able to see it as a dirty, crowded, bankrupt city on the brink, on the edge of falling into the void. Instead, every beggar, every impoverished worker, every domestic servant, every new immigrant suddenly seems made of stardust, bursting with unrealized power, untapped potential and infinite possibility. Brother, I want to say to the next person I see, if only we could see what we are truly made of…

I go back to school on Monday, a new person. One of the first things I do is go up to Jaya. 'Hey, I've been thinking about our conversation the other day. Sorry, men, I was a total bitch. But actually, I want to learn what happened to your mother. You know, with the Emergency and all, stuff like this is happening a lot.'

Jaya eyes me suspiciously. 'But I thought you wrote an essay praising the Emergency just a few months ago.'

So she remembers that. 'I know. I was a total idiot. But I understand more now. And, well, I was wrong, you know. And I'm very sorry I was so mean to you.'

Jaya comes to school the next day with a crudely printed pamphlet detailing the abuses under the Emergency. I take it from her silently, not asking her any questions and tuck it inside a book. Later, I read it in the hallway after I am kicked out of physics class. I am shocked by what I read: political prisoners being mercilessly tortured, beggars being rounded up and chased out of the city, slum colonies being razed, the press being gagged, union officials being imprisoned, the constitution being revised, the police being given absolute powers. This is happening in the country where I live and until last week the only thing I knew about the Emergency was that the buses were running on time.

Indira Gandhi has been Prime Minister most of my life. My generation had grown up automatically applying the female pronoun when talking about that office. Like many middle-class Indians, my family worshipped her, believing what Indira herself insinuated on several occasions – that without her, India would disintegrate into chaos, that the country needed a Nehru to rule it. The Nehrus were India's Kennedys – urbane, charming, sophisticated, good-looking, charismatic. My aunt Freny often spoke with pride about a foreign news conference where Indira had answered questions in fluent French. My dad had been excited as a schoolboy when she had inaugurated one of the government housing projects that he had been a contractor for. Unlike many of the bald, paunchy, dhoti-clad, heavily-accented Indian politicians, the light-skinned, sharp-featured Indira spoke fluent English, dressed smartly when she went abroad, and seemed at ease among Western leaders. For a country still recovering from the national inferiority complex that was a leftover from British colonial rule, watching Indira flirting with Lyndon Johnson and going toe-to-toe with Richard Nixon and Pakistani President General Yahya Khan, was better than winning a test match against the Aussies. Unlike the other paan-chewing, pot-bellied doddering leaders, Indira was the kind of politician you could dress up and take out. At cocktail parties, businessmen spoke of how much easier life was under the Emergency, now that the union troublemakers had had their balls cut off; office workers returning wearily to their homes in the suburbs each evening were thankful that the trains were running more efficiently; ordinary citizens were just plain grateful that the constant bickering between politicians had ceased. And if that meant that a few fundamental rights had to be temporarily given up, well, one couldn't have everything. Perhaps India was too large, too diverse a country to support democracy anyway. Look how efficiently those generals ran Pakistan. And if Indira's familiar face – with the famous white mane running through her dark hair – graced every magazine cover and chastized us from every billboard, so much the better. After all, we needed Mother Indira to look over us and keep us from chaos and self-destruction. If there were rumours of her son, Sanjay, siphoning off money and rewarding his corrupt cronies, well, the guy was a technocrat and wasn't a pragmatic, dynamic technical guy just what India needed at a time like this? And after all, Sanjay was a Nehru, the grandson of the great Jawaharlal Nehru. How bad could he be?

I take Jaya's pamphlet with me when we go over to Yasmin's house that evening for a beer. I listen as the others chat about a Cat Stevens album that Jenny has just bought, listen to them make plans about going to a disco on Saturday but I feel strangely aloof from the conversation. When there is a lull, I pull out the pamphlet. 'Hey, you guys, listen to this,' I say and begin to read.

They listen in uncomfortable silence. 'Yuck,' Jenny says when I read the lines describing the torture of prisoners. I can sense from their body language that they want me to stop reading but I can't and they are too polite to interrupt.

Nobody knows what to say when I finish. 'Geez. Yeah. Well, that's too bad,' Jenny says lamely, trying to break the silence.

Patty picks up the thread of the conversation. 'Wow, gosh. That's terrible. What a country. But listen, we should decide because I need to let my cousin know. Are all of us going to the disco on Saturday?'

For the first time since I've been friends with them, I feel ashamed of being in Yasmin's house, for whiling away my evening drinking beer. For a split second I see it all clearly and with revulsion: The four of us, indulgent, narcissistic, seeking thrills and wasting more money in one evening than someone else might earn in a week.

I get up. 'I have to get home,' I say. 'I'll see you all tomorrow.'

Jenny gives me a quizzical look. 'You all right, girl?' she asks.

'Yeah, I'm fine,' I lie. I head into Yasmin's bathroom and finger toothpaste onto my teeth, trying to gargle away the smell of cigarettes and beer before I go home. I also try to gargle away the faint but bitter taste of shame and self-disgust. On the way to the bus-stop I pluck two leaves from a nearby tree and grind their fragrance between my fingers to cover the smell of tobacco on my hands.

Then, I go home.

✧

It is January 1977 and Indira Gandhi has called for new elections within two months. The opposition leaders have been released from prison and have formed a coalition called the Janata Party. India is in convulsions, a new order trying to emerge from the dark womb of the Emergency. The suddenly-unmuzzled newspapers are filled with stories of the atrocities committed in New Delhi. Living up to its reputation as the charmed city, Bombay has been spared much of the trauma but now even ordinary Bombayites are feeling the shame of knowing that we have lived in a cocoon of ignorance for the last two years. I have recently turned fifteen but even I can tell that, like the fresh pau baked at the bakery across the street, history is being made daily these days.

The four of us have plans to go see a movie at Sterling. I almost don't go because business is bad again and when I ask Babu for money he takes out his wallet and opens it for me to see its bare contents. I turn away in embarrassment for I know what it costs him to refuse me anything. 'That's okay,' I say, trying to laugh. 'It's a stupid movie anyway and I didn't really want to go. I'll just call them and cancel.'

I am dialling Patty's number from the living room when Babu comes up to me and presses a ten-rupee note in my hand. 'Found this under my pyjamas in the cupboard,' he says. 'Must've forgotten I had some money there.'

I protest but he insists. 'Go enjoy,' he says. 'This little money is not going to help me anyway. And who knows when you'll next be able to go?'

But riding on the bus with the three of them, I am feeling uncomfortable. Guilt at taking Babu's last bill from him, unease over this new distance I'm feeling between myself and the other three, makes me jumpy. Also, earlier that morning Jesse had mentioned to me that there was to be a large student march at Flora Fountain that afternoon, protesting the Emergency. She was planning to attend along with her college friends. I wanted to invite myself but felt shy about doing so, as if I'd be gate-crashing a private party. But news about the morcha had made my afternoon plans with Jenny, Patty and Yasmin seem small and insignificant.

The single-decker bus we're riding is crowded and for most of the distance, Yasmin and I have been standing not too far from the open door. Jenny and Patty have found seats a short distance away from us. As the bus approaches Flora Fountain, it slows down, blocked by what seems like a wall of people walking on the streets in front of it. It's the student demonstration. I push my way to the door of the bus, hanging on from the steel rod at the entrance. My pulse quickens as I notice the determined expressions on the faces of the students marching past, holding aloft their homemade signs and banners. They are talking, shouting slogans. 'Indira Gandhi, shame, shame,' they chant. Then, the singing starts. My hair stand up on end before I can even place the song. They are singing *We shall Overcome* in Hindi. The song shimmers in the bright sunlight of the day, a haunting combination of defiance and wistfulness, a battlecry and a prayer. As the bus crawls past the marchers, I notice a police officer in his khaki uniform tapping his fingers lightly against his baton, to the beat of the song. And then I notice that the place is crawling with policemen, notice the grey Jeeps behind the long procession.

I turn away from the door and make my way back to the others. 'It's a demonstration against the Emergency. I know some of the folks who organized it. Let's skip the movie and join the march instead.'

They stare at me as if I've gone crazy. 'Aw, come on, Thrit,' Jenny says. 'You know we've been waiting weeks to see this movie. Don't be a wet blanket, please.'

A moment passes between us. A stage in my life ends and a new one begins during that moment, although it will be a long time before I figure that out. An old allegiance falls apart, a new one waits to be born. Perhaps Jenny knows this too, because as I turn away and head back toward the entrance of the bus, she makes a move, as if to grab me but then sits back in her seat.

I lean out of the bus, knowing I'm at a crossroad. If I jump off the bus now, it will end the closeness of my friendship with the other three. If I stay on, I won't be able to look at myself in the mirror. I scan the crowd for Jesse, knowing that the decision will be easier if I can spot her. But I get no easy help. The decision is mine alone.

'Stop watching, join us instead,' the students are chanting in Marathi to the crowds of office workers who are standing on the sidewalk with their mouths open, watching the antics of the college students. But I think their words are directed specifically at me. I can continue riding this bus to the movie theatre, where I can be a passive spectator in someone else's story. Or I can jump off this bus and help these kids write their own. A brand new story, Made in India.

It happens so suddenly, I don't even realize I've made a decision. My hand loosens its grip on the steel rod and I jump backwards off the slow-moving bus. The students next to me let out a cheer. 'Hey,' Yasmin shouts and I wave to her. 'Enjoy the movie,' I yell. 'I'll see you all Monday.'

The next second I am swallowed by the large crowd that shifts like sand around me. If I stood still now, the energy and momentum of the crowd would propel me forward. But I have no intention of standing still. A jittery excitement and a shouting happiness move my feet. A college girl in a white kurta and blue jeans puts a casual arm around my shoulders. 'I heard what you said to your friends. Glad to have you here,' she smiles. I smile back and then laugh, for no apparent reason other than the joy of marching on a Saturday afternoon through the streets of downtown Bombay with thousands of idealistic, intense-looking young people. I can't wait to go back to school on

Monday and tell Greta Duke about this adventure. She can only teach history.

I'm making it.

✧

The joy is short-lived. We gather behind the statue of Flora Fountain and sit cross-legged on the street when I spot him – Fali Mehta, the Parsi chief of police who is an old childhood friend of dad's and Babu's. Fali uncle is sternly surveying the crowd, his hands on his hips and looking quite different from the jovial, back-slapping man I am used to seeing at parties and wedding receptions. My mind freezes with terror so that I forget to listen to what the student speaker addressing the crowd is saying. If Fali uncle spots me in this crowd, I am dead. The news will definitely get back to my dad and with his fear of radical politics, I know what my father's reaction will be. My moderate, peaceful father has an instinctive dislike for zealotry or conflict of any kind and to him, challenging an omnipresent figure like Indira Gandhi is akin to challenging God. I cover my head with my hands and stare at the ground, trying to convince myself that Fali uncle will never spot me in a crowd of thousands.

The next minute I hear his familiar voice, with its flat, broad Parsi accent, blasting through a bullhorn. 'Now listen here,' he booms. 'You are prohibited by law from going any further. The area around Mantralaya is closed to demonstrators. Now, settle down and have a peaceful demonstration and there will be no trouble.'

A murmur flits through the crowd, like a silver fish parting the waters of a lake. There is some movement in the front of the procession and I surmise that the student leaders are trying to decide whether to defy the ban. Several minutes pass. Somebody begins a new chant and it floats over the crowd in successive waves. Then there is a lull, as if we are all getting drowsy under the mid-day sun. A policeman sits on his haunches at the edge of the crowd and trades good-natured remarks with the nearby crowd. 'Give up your uniform and join us,' a student says and the cop grins at him and then yawns. My earlier excitement abates as other emotions kick in – fear at being spotted by Fali Mehta; remorse at having abandoned my three friends so blithely; a slight boredom at the endless speeches denouncing the Emergency.

Then, there is a shift in the weather. A cry goes up. 'Onto Mantralaya,' someone yells from the front and the rest of the crowd picks it up and leaps to its feet.

'Stop,' Fali Mehta yells into his bullhorn. 'You are violating the law. There is a ban against gathering at...'

'To hell with the ban,' a younger voice competes on another bullhorn. 'This city belongs to the people, not the government.' The crowd roars its assent.

I am pushed forward by the moving crowd, like a blade of grass bopping on a heaving ocean. There is no time to think now, and no way to leave or head in the opposite direction. All is movement, a surging sea of clenched fists, raised hands and pounding feet. The singing, the shouting, the sloganeering have a new urgency now, louder, more frequent, more taunting, as if the tension and fear that we all feel can be kept at bay by a wall of sound.

The front of the procession is going past the police barricades. And now there is a new sound in the air – wholly unfamiliar to me but so ominous, like the slithering of a snake, that I feel sick to my stomach. They are lathi-charging us. Policemen who minutes ago were trading quips with us are now attacking us, their thick, wooden batons raised high above their heads. They hold the batons in the air and whisk them around, making that horrible, slippery sound. *Sik-sik-sik*, the lathis go in the air, singing their deadly music seconds before they find their mark on somebody's head or arm.

I stand immobile, paralysed by a fear so numbing, it feels like a physical disease, as if I've had a stroke. Out of the corner of my eye I see a policeman heading toward me but all I can think of doing is closing my eyes and covering my head with my hands, as if not seeing the approaching danger will make it disappear. I have long since given up on my legs to carry me out of here, seeing how they have turned to rubber.

Somebody grabs my left arm and drags me. 'Come on,' I hear a male voice say. 'Run.' He pulls me by the hand and together, we run, this way and that, avoiding crashing into other people, dodging the reach of the batons that whisk over our heads. I hold on to the warm but sweaty hand of my unknown rescuer, thinking I will never let it go. My legs are still rubbery but now they move as if they have wings beneath them. We are both gasping and heaving but still we run, hand in hand, crossing several streets, looking over our shoulders every few minutes, running to put as much distance as we can from the madness behind us.

We finally come to a bus-stop that looks safe because it is populated with office workers and other non-student types. 'Okay,' says my rescuer. 'You should be safe here. How old are you, anyway?'

'Fifteen,' I say.

'Fifteen,' he repeats, shaking his head and wiping the sweat from his brow. I look at him. He has a thin, narrow face, a scraggly beard and John Lennon glasses. He is wearing a blue checked shirt and loose, ill-fitting pants with sandals. His feet are dusty from our run.

'This your first morcha?' he asks, chewing his lower lip and when I say yes, he nods. 'I thought so. That's why I helped. I saw you jumping out of that bus. But if you do this again, you'll get used to the lathi-charges. The bastards attack us every time.'

'Thanks for your help. I don't know what I would've done otherwise.'

He is already turning away. 'No problem. Well, I should head back.'

'Head back where?'

He grins. 'Back to the demonstration. Can't let those police goondas win, no? Well, see you around.'

The next day I read in the *Indian Express* that at least half of the students had re-gathered after the initial lathi-charge. My throat clenches with pride.

I decide not to tell Jesse about my presence at the march, knowing that she is forever torn between her own growing political militancy and her older-sister desire to protect me from all harm.

But the image of the students, bruised, beaten, scared, returning to the place of their victimization, stays with me long after the story fades from the newspaper headlines.

# Seventeen

KAMALA HAS BEEN WORKING AS A domestic servant in our home since I was eleven. She herself is a woman of indeterminate age. Her tight, fleshless face, her scanty hair, her tobacco-destroyed teeth, make it hard to guess how old she is. Her face reminds me of a boulder – it is yellow-brown, smooth and polished as if time and circumstance have removed every unnecessary ounce of flesh. And like an archaeologist, I have excavated Kamala bit by bit, starting with her name. When she came to work for us, she was known by the generic name of Ganga, the name that we confer on every servant who works for us. For years we called her Ganga until one day I asked her the revolutionary question: 'What's your real name?'

Kamala, she replied and a whole universe opened up before my eyes – a human being with a name and suddenly there were other trails to follow – family, marital status, children, where she lived, where she disappeared to when she left us in the evening ... and then, likes, dislikes, preferences, allergies, past illnesses, what made her laugh...

It is the nature of revolutions that one change follows another and soon, another cataclysmic event: I hugged Kamala. First, an arm around the shoulder, then, a quick, sideways hug, pulling her closer toward me and then, finally, a full, frontal hug, the same way I would hug Mehroo or one of my friends at school. Physical space, not to be violated because of the invisible walls of class, religion, tribe, language, education, all the things that divided us, that physical space suddenly, effortlessly, trampled over – and nothing happened. The heavens didn't open up, the Gods didn't send their lightning bolts of wrath. Just ... the adults raising their eyebrows and looking silently at each other for guidance. Just ... Kamala giving a short, embarrassed laugh if I hugged her in front of one of the adults and then quickly moving out of my embrace. Just ... the sharp, pungent smell of Kamala's hard-working sweat, unfamiliar, new. But other than that, nothing.

And so I excavate Kamala, bit by bit, coax her out of the mask of silence she usually assumes in front of the adults (unless she is angry and then she rattles off indignant words like the rat-a-tat of a machine gun, her flat chest heaving), make her laugh, have her tell me stories, have her describe her nieces and nephews to me. Filling in the blanks, drawing a picture of this mystery woman who shows up at our house at seven a.m. each morning and then disappears into the evening shadows until the following day.

Most days, it is like moving mountains because the very presence of the adults makes her freeze, withdraw into silence. When they are around, her movements are stiff, her speech stilted and self-conscious. Even while she is talking to me, I notice her looking at them out of the corner of her eye. But when we are at home alone, her face gets animated when she talks, her light brown eyes grow round and wide, her hands gesturing wildly. But along the way to getting her to trust me, there are many missteps on my part. In the beginning, I take my lunch plate and set it beside hers on the floor, my silent, ineffectual protest against a social system that allows Kamala to cook our food but not sit at the dining table with us while we eat it. Roshan giggles, dad is torn between thinking it's a silly gesture and wanting me to stop, mum is annoyed and Kamala is embarrassed – and pissed. She scolds me, making sure the adults understand she wants no part of this.

Finally, after several days of sitting on my haunches like she does and eating my food, I give up.

My next mission is to get Kamala to sit at the dining table with me though even I know better than to try this in the presence of the adults. But when we are alone, I refuse to eat my lunch until she comes and joins me at the table and there is much eye-rolling and head-shaking but finally she does. But she looks so damn uncomfortable sitting on the brown chair, that there is no pleasure in this for either her or me. If I don't insist on it, she automatically squats on the floor in front of me when we are talking. Until...

Until that glorious day the summer that I am fifteen. I am in the living room playing *Let It Be* on the stereo and Kamala comes sailing into the room and asks me to change the music, to stop playing this record in a language she doesn't understand, to instead play the record I had brought home two days earlier. It is an old fishermen's folk song, sung in Marathi, which is Kamala's language and she knows the song and now she is demanding that I play it. And I am leaping off the couch before she can even finish her request, my heart singing at the maternal, authoritative manner in which Kamala is ordering me about. Success, I think, at last. And it gets even better: she comes and sits on the couch next to me and we listen to the record in silence. She looks straight ahead and her face is expressionless. If she knows the words of this song she doesn't let on. I have no idea what she's thinking but I don't care. I am enjoying sitting on the couch with this woman I have come to love and respect so much, this quiet, hard-working, decent, dignified woman who, I think, deserves to inherit the earth. I wonder about a system that considers this woman ignorant and illiterate when she is clearly wise; that allows her to work for people who do not even call her by her own name. Usually, these thoughts would depress and anger me but today is a day of celebration. Even as I realize that this brief moment of spontaneity will not change anything, I still feel a rush of hope, a tantalizing glimpse of possibility. I allow myself to romanticize and sentimentalize the moment even while I realize that this sentimentality is something I can afford but Kamala can't. And so I savour this unguarded sweetness between us, even after the doorbell rings and Kamala jumps guiltily off the couch and hurries to the door to let the others in.

Two days after this incident she comes to me and asks in an off-hand way whether I'd like to go with her to her nephew's engagement party. Before I can express my pleasure at the invitation she begins to recite all the reasons why I probably shouldn't go: We would have to leave very early in the morning and change two buses, her nephew lives in an old, rickety building with a common bathroom and I probably have to study for my exams anyway. 'Kamala,' I say. 'I really, really want to go. I've always wanted to meet your family, especially your nephew. I know he's your favourite.'

So Kamala broaches the subject to Mehroo, who, she knows, is in charge of these decisions. And to my surprise, Mehroo says yes.

Kamala breaks into a wide, surprised grin when she comes to pick me up on that Saturday. I look clumsy in my a green and gold cotton sari and the sight of me in clothes other than my usual shirt and jeans makes her laugh. She smiles even more broadly as we walk toward the bus-stop and I awkwardly navigate the folds of the sari and try to make sure I don't trip. 'Baby, why did you bother with all this?' she asks. But I can tell that she is happy I made the effort.

It is a wonderful day. Kamala's family is warm, welcoming and friendly toward me. For the first hour or two they fawn over me, give me a chair to sit on while the rest of them sit on mattresses on the floor but after a while I tell them that this attention is making me uncomfortable and to my great surprise, they get it and stop their fussing. Still, I can tell that Kamala is keeping a protective eye on me, pulling me away when one of the neighbourhood boys gives me an insolent, knowing smile and escorting me to the community bathroom that's down the hall from her nephew's apartment, muttering all the way about the dirty habits of some of the people who live in this chawl. But she is also glad to be among family she doesn't see too often and I see a side of her I've never seen before. The controlled, silent woman who moves like a ghost through our house, has disappeared. In her place is a colourful, boisterous woman with a sharp tongue and a hearty laugh. I thrill each time Kamala laughs, knowing it may be years before I ever see her this free again. Kamala's nieces and nephews call her 'Kaku,' and they all laugh when I start calling her by that name.

'Better not call me Kaku at home,' she says on the way back. 'What will your mummy-daddy think, if you call me aunt?'

'I don't care,' I say. 'You *are* my aunt.'

And so the woman who was once Ganga and later became Kamala, now becomes Kaku. And I suppose it is a good thing, this progression from the anonymous to the familial but I can't help but know that even this power to name, is a sign of privilege. What does it mean that a fifteen -year-old teenager has the power to give a woman at least three times her age her name back? And if a name can be given, can it also be taken away?

And then there's this: After that time on the couch, after the adults came back home and Kaku jumped off the couch to answer the door, she went back to resume her kitchen duties. And I, I stayed in the living room, listening to the

Marathi folk song one more time. Then, when the song ended, I lifted the stylus and changed the record.

And *Let It Be* played through the house once again.

# Eighteen

BABU IS DEAD.

The man who has been a second father to me all my life, who saw me seconds after I was born, who has loved me as proudly and steadfastly as he did his own daughter, is dead – suddenly, shockingly, at the age of fifty-four.

The doorbell rings at seven p.m. The whole family is at the dinner table except for my aunt Freny, who is spending the night by her husband's side at the hospital. We have come home from the hospital a few hours earlier, relieved to find Babu in such good spirits a day after his kidney stone surgery. Now, we are almost done with dinner when the doorbell rings. Mehroo looks startled as she pushes back her chair to answer the door. We are not expecting any more visitors tonight.

From the dining room, I hear Sam uncle's voice. He is out of breath and talking fast, which makes his voice sound even more high-pitched than always. 'Mehroo, come quick,' he says. 'Pesi is not doing well. I just went to the hospital to see him for a few minutes and Freny sent me to fetch all of you. Dr Sethna is on his way in also.'

Dad is already on his feet and toward the door. My mom, too, rushes out of the room, leaving me and my cousin Roshan all alone in the suddenly empty room. I stare at Roshan, not knowing what to say and she stares back, her nose and eyes getting red. Then, she gets up and I hear the flip-flop of her rubber slippers on the floor of the hallway. I gaze at all the abandoned dinner plates on the table and look down at mine. It is almost empty – just a few more morsels to go. And then it happens: A quiet, cold voice says to me, 'Finish your dinner. You will need all your strength to run around if Babu is sick.' So I continue eating, the only one in my family to do so. I eat fast and guiltily, afraid that someone will enter the room and catch me in the act. It is the first time I have encountered the hidden ruthlessness in myself, that cold-eyed practicality that will surface whenever I face a situation of crisis. This is a side of myself I have not yet experienced and I feel like a mercenary, a soldier of fortune, as I gulp the food down.

The potential seriousness of the situation hits me as I notice how furiously my dad drives us to the hospital. Dr Sethna has reached the hospital before we get there and is in the room examining Babu. We wait outside the room. Freny is in the room with Babu so we have no idea what is going on. Finally, Mehroo grabs one of the nurses coming out of the room but the woman only says, 'Doctor should be out soon. Then you can ask him everything.'

Finally, Dr Sethna steps out. He is a handsome man in his fifties with greying temples and a calm manner honed from years of serving in the army. He had removed my appendix six months earlier and now he smiles at me and murmurs, 'Hi, girlie.'

Without waiting for me to respond, he turns to the adults. His brow creases as he sees the worried look on their faces and he exhales loudly. 'His stomach is filling up with gas,' he says without preamble. 'We don't know why. I've written a new prescription and we'll watch how he does all night. Beyond this, there's nothing I can tell you right now.'

Dad steps forward. 'But doctor, is it ... serious?'

Sethna sighs again. He has known my dad and uncle for years, ever since they were all young men. 'I don't know, Burjor. It could be. I'll do everything that I can. Pesi is my patient but first of all, he's my friend.'

His words fail to reassure Mehroo. 'Just this afternoon when we were all here, he was fine,' she says. 'Talking, making jokes. We were all marvelling at how well he was doing, touchwood.'

'Yes, well. Well, I know you're anxious to see him. But please, I must warn you – don't be shocked by his appearance. As soon as the medication works, things should be better.'

But we are shocked. Shocked speechless. The gas has filled up Babu's belly to the point where we cannot see his face from the foot of his bed. The white sheet covering him is like a giant tent over him. And what's really upsetting is that it seems to us that his belly is growing larger even as we watch.

Freny's eyes are red and I go up behind her and give her a quick hug. 'Don't worry,' I say. 'We're all here now. He will be fine in a few hours.'

My dad and Mehroo are on either side of their brother's bed. 'Pesi? How are you, brother?' my dad asks. 'You don't worry at all, okay? Whatever has to be done, you know we will do. I will be by your side, night and day. I will take you home myself in a few days. '

Babu's eyes flutter awake. He looks as if he's trying to respond but all we can see is a wave of emotion cross his face, like the sun's shadow across a field.

I am sitting by the foot of Babu's bed and decide to rub his feet because he's forever asking me to massage his feet. I reach under the blankets and my heart stops. His feet are freezing cold, colder than ice, colder than the coldest object on earth. I am fifteen years old and not acquainted with death but even I can sense that there is something alien and dangerous about this kind of coldness. It feels to me as if I'm touching death itself, as if death is creeping up Babu's body. I tip over the edge of the blanket to look at his feet and they are a hideous shade of white. For the first time,

I am really afraid. Leaning over, I touch his hands and they are cold, also. I take Babu's feet in my hands and start rubbing furiously. In a few seconds, I'm in a trance. If I can just keep this pace up, I think, I can make him well. My hands move as fast as those of the shoeshine boys who polish my father's shoes each morning.

A nurse comes into the room and says Freny's younger sister, Mani, has just called the nurse's station to ask one of us to stop by the house and pick up an ointment for Babu. Freny mentions that Mani had been at the hospital earlier, just as Babu was beginning to get bloated and had remembered an ayurvedic ointment that apparently worked wonders with stomach pain. I volunteer to make the short trip to Mani aunty's house, anxious to get away from the claustrophobic atmosphere of the small hospital room. To my surprise, none of the adults protest. By now it is 9:30 p.m. and although the Bombay streets are crowded and well-lit, somebody would've normally stopped me from going out alone at night. But tonight, nobody is paying me any attention. All eyes are focused on Babu's stomach; all of our breathing follows his rasping breath.

I half-run the few blocks from the hospital to Mani aunty's house. She is waiting for me and answers the door on the first ring. Mani aunty goes to the bathroom to get the small tube of ointment and gives me instructions on how often to apply it. 'How is he?' she asks and I start to reply but suddenly I can't speak because I am heaving with sobs. I want to tell her about how cold Babu's feet are and how, touching them, I felt as if he were already dead. But no words emerge. Mani watches me cry for a minute and then she speaks: 'Stop it. Stop your crying. This is not the time for tears. This is the time to fight with God, to wrestle with Him for Pesi's sake. Now come on, be brave. This is the time to be strong, not weak. If you fall apart like this, who is going to take care of my Freny?'

Mani's words greet me like a slap in the face. I stare at her open-mouthed, knowing instinctively that she has said exactly the words I need to hear, realizing dimly that she has selected for me, like a black woollen coat, the role that I must wear. All I have to do now, is slip into this role of guardian and protector. Mani is absolutely right. This is the time to wrestle with God, to use my youth and vitality to thaw the iciness that is creeping up Babu's limbs, to combat the cold fear that is growing in my own heart.

I feel myself straighten up. 'I'm sorry, Mani aunty,' I say, and my voice is firm. 'I'll take care of everybody, don't worry. Thanks for the balm.' She pulls me toward her in a quick, tight hug and then I'm running down the stairs and into the night. There is a moon in the sky and it follows me like a dribbling basketball as I walk fast toward the hospital. I look at the moon and begin my quarrel with God, fighting so desperately for Babu's life, talking to the moon with such intensity, that I feel the sweat running down my face. People look at me strangely and I realize I'm talking out loud but I don't stop. 'I'm not giving in to You,' I say to the moon. 'We need Babu in our family – you know the role he plays. We need him more than you do, God. Please, please, please God. I'll give up drinking beer for six months – for a year – if you let him live.'

Later that night, Roshan and I are standing in the hallway of the hospital, looking out over the gardens. I tell her what Mani aunty had said to me and urge her to do the same. She looks at me and nods but doesn't say anything. Instead, we both look up at the moon, so serene, so aloof, it seems to mock our desperation. We stand there, utterly alone and yet silently leaning into each other, first cousins who are more like sisters, thanks to the generosity and love of the man who, across the hallway from us, is battling for his very life.

I am back at the hospital by ten a.m. the next day. Mummy has made omelette sandwiches for dad, Mehroo and Freny, all of whom have spent the night at the hospital. I hand each of them a sandwich but they just glance at it and put it away. I quickly figure out why.

Babu's stomach has grown even more than last night. It is hard to believe and for a second I'm tempted to think that this is just another of Babu's many practical jokes, like the way he wriggles his ears and turns his eyelids upside down. But this is no joke. Babu's face is pale and puffy and his fingers and toes are a greyish white. Dr Sethna has already been by earlier this morning and pronounced that my uncle has kidney failure though he has no idea why.

Dad leaves the room and when he comes back he announces that he has just consulted with Dr Sethna on the phone and it is decided – we are shifting Babu to Jaslok Hospital. None of us have ever been to Jaslok but have often driven by the tall skyscraper in the posh side of town. Jaslok is where the movie-stars and politicians go when they're ill but it also has the best facilities for kidney failure in town. If dad is worried about the cost, he does not let on.

Now that a decision has been made we are all anxious to get going. Masina Hospital, with its lemon-coloured whitewashed walls suddenly seems incredibly two-bitty and small-time. Of course they can't figure out what's wrong with Babu here. But the specialists at Jaslok, why, one look at him and they'll be able to tell us what's going wrong. And then they'll fix it. Optimism courses through my veins like a drug, so that when Babu is lifted and placed in the ambulance, I feel relief rather than apprehension.

None of us is prepared for the curt, remote, inaccessibility of Jaslok Hospital. Babu has already been whisked away into the Intensive Care Unit by the time we get to the hospital. We are not even given time to say goodbye or to reassure him that we are all nearby. Unlike Masina Hospital, where we could crowd in his room and be participants in his illness – some one rubbing his hands, someone applying massage oil on his hands, someone else soothing his brow – we are mere spectators, as the high-powered doctors hook Babu up to metallic machines and rubber tubes, rendering him unrecognizable. We have to beg to even be let into the lobby of the ICU and then we are reduced to going up in twos to gaze at him through a glass partition. It is as if Babu no longer belongs to us, as if the hospital has now taken over his care, as if Jaslok has usurped all the vital relationships in his life, as if it has now become his surrogate brother and wife and child. All of a sudden, Babu seems far away and remote to us, in a way that he wasn't at Masina. I have a sudden, terrifying thought that this is a dress rehearsal and Jaslok is readying us for the final, awful separation; the hospital is telling us, *This is how it will be when he dies – he will feel close enough to touch and yet, you will not be able to.*

Hours go by and we fall into a routine. The entire family has gathered in the waiting room on the seventeenth floor but every half hour two of us take the elevator to the ICU on the fifteenth floor, stare at Babu from behind the glass partitions for a few minutes and then take the sad ride up back to the waiting room. Already, it seems as if we've been doing this for years, as if all life on the outside has ceased to exist, that the hospital is the only life we've ever known. Already, it seems to us as if the world outside has been drained of life and colour, like the colour has drained from Babu's face.

As the miserable afternoon wears on, we try to be judicious of our time in the ICU lobby, considerate about giving each family member a turn to go to the fifteenth floor. As his wife, Freny has first rights to as many visits as she wants but there are so many people in this room who love Babu – my aunt Mehroo, who has practically raised him; my dad, who is walking around as if he's the one attached to a ventilator; my cousin Roshan, who, at nineteen, is too young to watch her father like this. So we take turns.

At about eight p.m., it is my and dad's turn. Shankar, the young man who operates the elevator, has started his shift a while back and already he is familiar with my family and seems to understand our growing fear and grief. Mani, with characteristic generosity, has already pressed a ten-rupee note in his hand and now we tip him every time we ride the elevator. As the doors of the lift close, my father suddenly doubles over, as if someone has struck him hard in the stomach. His shoulders heave and tears stream down his cheeks as he cries wordlessly. Shankar looks aghast. Clucking his tongue in sympathy, he murmurs, 'No, no, sahib. Bas, bas.' I put my arms around my father. Suddenly, I remember the other time that I have watched my dad break down hard.

It was three years earlier, a day in 1974, at a time when the global oil crisis of 1973 had snaked a long, tortured and unlikely path toward my father's business and driven him to the point of bankruptcy. The optimism of the late 1960s had affected my father – he had broadened his line of work to become a developer and had successfully bid for a large government contract to build low-income housing. But the oil crisis struck; the cost of raw materials doubled, then trebled; and the small print on the contract held the contractors responsible for the rise in prices. Along with several other developers, my father lost his shirt on the deal.

All that day, the mood at home had been tense and subdued. Mehroo had told me that morning that today was a vitally important day, that daddy had a big meeting with his bankers, who would decide whether to loan him more money so that he could try saving the business. At nine p.m. that night we heard the fumbling of the key and dad let himself into the house and to the dining room, where we were gathered. He looked haggard and tired and, I don't know, *defeated* – in a way I'd never seen before. I think we all knew the answer to our silent inquiry before he even spoke. When he did, he looked directly at his brother. 'Bhai, we're finished,' he said quietly. 'They refused any more loans. We have nothing left. I don't know where the money will come from for food tomorrow. I don't know what to do next – if I'm very lucky, maybe I'll be able to drive a taxi for someone.'

If dad had said he was going to become a coolie at Victoria Terminus station, he couldn't have shocked me more. Nobody we knew in our social circle drove a cab. Driving a taxi was something *they* did – they being the illiterate, uneducated, working-class, paan-chewing, kurta-pyjama-wearing, non-Parsi men, with whom we had nothing in common. I don't know what shocked me most – the uncharacteristic pessimism with which my father spoke or his bewildering choice of profession or the fact that he suddenly burst into tears in front of the entire family. His sobbing was the sound of a man at the end of his rope, a man on the verge of – bankruptcy? suicide?

Nobody spoke for a moment. Then, there was a rustle and then a roar. It was Babu. 'Nonsense, Burjor,' he shouted. 'This is no time to lose your courage, bhai. Cab-fab, nothing. We have our factory and we will rise again. We are not dead yet. Tomorrow morning, first thing, I will make the rounds of the market and get us some credit. Even if we have to pay twenty-five per cent interest, so be it. You concentrate on getting the outside orders, bossie. I'll get the work done. We will pay the workers from our house money, if we have to. Freny will turn over her entire pay cheque to us if we need it. Now, saala, stop your chicken-shit crying.'

It was a reversal of roles. Babu was usually the nervous, cautious sort. Dad was the dreamer, the visionary, the one who dared to cast a wider net. But that was the secret to their success – one of them was always there to pick up the other. So that I know what dad is saying as he sobs in the elevator. 'He was – is – more than my brother. He's my partner, my best friend.'

We reach the ICU in time to see one of Babu's doctors coming out of his room. As he walks past us, dad reaches over to stop him and introduce himself. Then, his eyes fill with tears again. 'Doctor, this man is very important to us,' he begins. 'Please, spare no expense in looking after him. You have no idea what he means ...'

The doctor's lips tighten. 'Please, sir,' he says curtly. 'Pull yourself together. We have no time for such sentimental theatrics in here. I am too busy and have many other patients to worry about. You people bring your relatives here after it's too late and expect us to pull a miracle.' Then, he turns on his heel and walks away, leaving us standing open-mouthed. A ward boy who has heard the whole exchange tsk-tsks in sympathy and disapproval. 'Badmaash doctor,' he says to us in low, confidential tones. 'No heart in this man. Treating everybody badly. You don't worry, saar. He got bad manner but he's a top-class doctor. Your patient will be A-OK.'

But dad is not appeased. I see the blood rising from his neck to his face and his eyes have a murderous look in them I have never seen before. 'I should kill him,' he mutters. 'If I was half a man I would just go get a knife and kill the bastard.' But even as he talks, the anger leaves his eyes and is replaced by a kind of bewildered hurt.

We walk back into the waiting room defeated. The doctor's rudeness has shattered the last bit of hope that I was still feeling. Babu is not going to make it, I know that now. All the king's horses and all the king's men will not be able to put Babu together again.

Slowly, the hours pass. Most of the families of the other patients have left, so that as the hours crawl toward dawn, it is only my family that waits in that large waiting room.

But we may as well be stranded on the moon, given how isolated from the rest of the world we already feel. We walk around in a daze, we talk in fragmented whispers. From the picture windows we can see the distant streets but even Bombay is quiet and subdued and unrecognizable at this late hour. From this height, we are closer to the sky than to the forlorn city streets. I keep waiting for the sun to rise, trying to trick myself in to believing that if Babu survives another day, lives to see another dawn, he will make it. That he will turn a corner. So this is what it means to keep a death watch, I think. I think of Babu lying all alone in a strange room, covered in a confetti of tubes and hoses, and for the first time I don't feel pity for him. After all, all of us gathered here are surely as alone as he is, lonely planets orbiting around each other in our own fog of confusion and pain and regrets.

Regrets. I am choking on my own. So many moments to trip over, to feel guilty about. A few weeks before he went into the hospital he had asked me to join the family for a Hindi movie. And I had said no. Such contempt in my voice. Because by now, I hated the song-and-dance, formulaic, masala Hindi movies. The pretensions of being an intellectual so strong now and what easier way to shorthand that change to the family than by expressing contempt for the commercial movies that they so loved? The cracks in the facade, the faultlines already appearing now – I only want to see small, low-budget movies by Shyam Benegal and Satyajit Ray, I'd said to him and Babu had looked at me with confusion and hurt. Roshan had piped in, the contempt in her voice matching mine: 'Yah, you want to see films where the camera focuses for fifteen minutes on a fly sitting on a chappati. So booooring, those movies. I go to movies to be entertained, not to be put to sleep.' I shut up then, the gap between the two of us too enormous to bridge, the gap between where I come from and where

I want to go, too immense to fathom. But the hurt look in Babu's eyes as the rest of them left for the movie had taken away all the pleasure at having said no.

The truth is, he was beginning to embarrass me. All the things about him that had thrilled me as a child – the loud laugh that always ended in a coughing fit, the casual dropping of four-letter words in his conversations, the abandon with which he farted – now made my toes curl with embarrassment. When Pervez, the slim, delicate-looking man who used to come to the house to tutor me in math and science, would express amazement at the liberal sprinkling of four-letter words in Babu's conversations, I would not hear the obvious delight and affection in Pervez's voice. Instead, I would fume inwardly at Babu's lack of sophistication and manners. What I had once seen as lack of pretension, now appeared to be crudity.

And he knew it too. Could see the distance in my eyes. Was too hurt to mention it directly because after all, what could he say? That he didn't feel my love as strongly as he once did? That he had always loved me as faithfully as he had loved his own daughter, Roshan? Remind me of those childhood years when I would sit by myself and try and decide once and for all, who I loved more, Babu or daddy? Remind me that he had held me in his arms the day that I was born before my father even made it to the hospital? Remind me of that wonderful day when I was seven and cuddling with him one evening when he said to me, unexpectedly, 'You are my first darling of the morning.' I turned that phrase over in my mouth like toffee, toyed with it with my tongue. 'What does that mean?' I finally asked, not wanting to ask, afraid that the explanation may be more prosaic than the tingling feeling the words conjured up for me. He shrugged, laughing. 'Nothing. Just what it says. I just made it up. You decide what it means.' I wore the words like a silver medal the rest of the day.

Two memories from the week before he went into the hospital: Joan Baez' *Come from the Shadows* was playing on the stereo in the living room. I was lying on my stomach on Freny's bed and hanging from my waist, my hands dangling toward the floor. 'And we'll raze, raze the prisons to the ground,' Baez sang and I pondered the seeming contradiction: how do you raise something to the ground, I wondered? Must be poetic licence, I finally decided. To my left, Babu and Freny were leaning on the railing of the balcony, talking to each other in soft, low voices. They were relaxed and leaning into each other, a stark contrast to the stiff, cautious way in which my parents carried themselves around each other. I was suddenly filled with an insane happiness. So that when Babu asked me a little later if I want to go with them to see *Witness for the Prosecution*, I immediately said yes. On the way to the theatre, Babu talked about what a classic the movie was, how brilliant Charles Laughton was in the main role. And Tyrone Power, he breathed, the admiration for the actor he must've felt as a young man still coming through. At his side, Freny smiled. Soon, they were talking about the other Hollywood movie-stars they grew up with. Cary Grant. James Stewart. Ethel Merman. Humphrey Bogart. Spencer Tracy and Katherine Hepburn. The names tumbled off their silver tongues, like beads of mercury. I sat in the backseat with Roshan, warm and drowsy from this replay of their youth.

And now, a week later, this man whose eyes had lit up with pleasure when I told him how much I had loved *Witness for the Prosecution*, who had bought us chicken rolls and potato chips during intermission, who had taken us out to dinner after the movie, was lying in an isolated hospital bed, dying? dead?

I must've dozed off because the noise of the elevator doors opening makes my eyes fly open and I'm just in time to see Shankar the elevator operator step out of his steel cage and go toward where Mani aunty is sitting. She looks up at him silently, questioningly and he simply shakes his head from side-to-side, once. But his meaning is awfully clear. Shankar is the angel of death, the messenger of doom. He has come to bring us bad news from the ICU two floors above us. Babu is dead.

Mehroo, noticing the silent exchange between Mani and the elevator boy, jumps up from her chair. 'What?... Is he ...?' she asks Shankar and he nods, averting his eyes, gazing at his feet. Sobbing hard, Mehroo heads over to Freny. The sound of sobbing fills the room. My dad is standing by himself at one of the windows, his shoulders shaking. His older brother is dead. He is now the only surviving male in the family.

And just then, there is a flash of dazzling light flooding the room. It is the sun, red and angry as a chilli pepper. And it is immense, a red cannonball in the sky. Despite the immense grief that I feel, I am distracted and mesmerized by the close beauty of the sun, as seen from this height. People who live in skyscrapers must know the sun so much more intimately than the rest of us, I think.

But today, the rising of the sun, the dawning of a new day, feels like an insult, rather than a thing of hope. Or rather, it feels like a burden, this new day, because it is the first day that Babu will not be alive to share with us. This is the first day of a new life that we will all have to get used to but right now, living, the simple act of putting one foot in front of another, seems impossible. I feel like those astronauts walking in space, clumsy, heavy, everything in slow motion.

I look at the sun until my eyes smart from its red sparks. The long night of waiting is over and so is praying to the moon. A new morning of horror has replaced the waiting and I now change allegiances and pray to the sun. But instead of wrestling for Babu's life, I now pray for death.

A long sleep. Oblivion. Because to be awake is to be stabbed a million times a second with the pinprick realization of Babu's death and how it will change our lives forever. 'Please God,' I pray. 'Just give us all an injection, something that will just let us sleep for forty-eight hours, past the point of having to deal with this. Because none of us is ready.' For an absurd moment, I flirt with the fantasy of rushing up to the nurse's station and stealing some drugs that will spare us this long, horrific day that is dawning.

Because I know sure as anything, that my role as the baby of the family is about to end. Has ended. A freight train has roared into our lives and has flattened everything in its path, including my childhood.

It's growing up time. I will not cry. I will not lend my voice to the sobbing in this room. I am no longer a child. I have responsibilities, several broken people that I have to put back together. All the king's horses ... All the lonely people where do they all come from? ... No one was saved ... But I must. Save them all, these people that I love. Repent for all the ugly thoughts I ever had about any of them. Fighting with the moon. And losing. Empty-handed.

I am no longer a child. I will not cry.

## Nineteen

W HITE. THE FUNERAL IS ALL white. The women in their white, cotton saris. The men in white daaglis. The white of the sheet that is covering Babu's body as it rests on a simple wooden platform on the ground. The white robes of the priests and the white masks that cover their mouths as they sit mumbling their prayers for the departed soul. The white of the sandwiches that some thoughtful relative has brought for us to the Tower of Silence and that lie untouched. The whites of Babu's eyes, eyes that have been donated to another human being somewhere across this miserable city where blindness is so common. The white of Babu's feet, so cold and hard when I touched and kissed them one last time at the hospital. The whiteness of fury, the pure rage that I feel at this aborting of life, the obscene haste with which Babu's body is removed from the hospital, the surreal absurdity of finding ourselves in a funeral home, praying over Babu, *Babu,* who was so alive, so vibrant, so attuned to the world. The whiteness of the world, this blurry white world that grief creates, where everything loses colour and taste and shape.

And then, colour. The flare of the fire that burns in the small silver urn before which the priests sit cross-legged on the floor. The grey of the smoke that rises from the urn, obscuring Babu's face at times. The brown fur of the dog that is led into the funeral home and made to witness Babu's still body. I tense up at that, my body turning into stone and Jesse, sitting at my side notices immediately. 'It's nothing to be afraid of,' she says, taking my hand in hers. Her hand is a warm nest, a welcome relief from the cold that has nestled in my heart since the moment I touched Babu's feet at the hospital. Jesse is still talking. 'Just see the dog in anthropological terms. It's just a ritual that's meant to act as a diversion, something to take the mourners' minds off their grief.' And it actually works, so that I can feel my body relaxing as I think of the genius who invented this diversionary ritual. I am so grateful for Jesse's analytical, rational presence at this moment, that I could kiss her.

But then my body tenses again. It is time to say goodbye to Babu forever. The skinny, hollow-eyed corpse-bearers stand in their tattered, dirty clothes, ready to hoist the body and take it to its final path to the big well with the circling vultures. For a moment, the pallbearers themselves look like vultures to me and I hate them for their greedy eagerness to get started and finished with their task. But then I remember the stories of how these men drink in order to be able to perform their unpleasant task, I think of how their sunken, sad eyes must witness the unwitnessable – the sight of the dark-winged birds descending like death into the huge well into which the bodies are laid. I think of how their nostrils must be filled with the smell of death, a smell that must cling to them at all times, a smell so irrefutable that why bother showering or shaving or wearing clothes other than the rags that they dress in? I think of their dirty, wax-filled ears trying to block out the sounds of tearing flesh and cracking bones and suddenly I am heaving, heaving and then my heaves turn into choked sobs, my mouth opening and closing soundlessly. Everybody is crying now, Mehroo with her piteous cries of 'Bhai, bhai', Freny with tears streaming down her cheeks, stunned at becoming a widow at fifty-one, Mani aunty bawling like a baby for the brother-in-law whom she loved like a brother, my dad looking as dazed and lost as a boat out at sea, the old men from the nearby apartment buildings shaking their heads at the irony of their being alive while the man they called the prince of the neighbourhood is dead, the old women remembering how he used to flirt with them and make them laugh with his bawdy irreverence, the destitute widows telling stories of how he would press a five-or ten-rupee note in their hands whenever they saw him on the street and how he treated everybody, from a king to a beggar, the same. And everybody saying how he was too young to die, that this was not the proper age to die and me being confused by that because at fifteen, Babu's age of fifty-four seems old to me and besides, I wonder what the proper age to die is? No age is the proper age to die, I say to Jesse and she looks at me for a minute because she hears the rawness in my voice and then she nods understandingly.

Dad follows the pallbearers as they carry Babu's body out and down a trail. I want to go with him but someone puts out a restraining arm and whispers that only men are allowed to accompany the body from this point. Several of the other men walk desultorily behind the pallbearers, so that the large room now holds clusters of white-clad women, many of them bent with osteoporosis, whispering and murmuring in small, hunched groups. I walk aimlessly from one group to another, introducing myself to those who don't know me as Freny's younger daughter. They look startled until someone else explains to them the closeness of my bond with Babu and Freny and the peculiar geometry of my family alliances. But I am already walking away. The rawness in my throat, the rage that I feel at the events of the last few days is so strong that I feel that I will vaporize if I stand still.

'Bechari Freny,' I hear one of the bent old women say to another, as I approach another cluster of *tsk-tsk*ing mourners. 'Poor Freny. Widowed at such a young age. What will happen to her now, the poor thing? Who will care for her and her daughter?'

And finally, my rage has found a path. 'Bechari Freny, nothing,' I say. 'No need to feel sorry for her. And what do you mean, who will take care of her? She has her whole family with her. We will take care of her, who else? Just because Babu has died, doesn't mean she's not part and parcel of our family. Please don't worry about her – and please don't call her bechari any more.'

I have never spoken to an older person this rudely and I'm unsure who is more shocked. In either case, the effect is electric. The poor woman looks aghast. 'Hah, yes, no ...,' she stammers. 'I was only saying ... so glad to hear. May God bless you, deekra.'

But I am already moving away, looking to find Freny in this crowd. I finally spot her, sitting on a chair in the front row, staring at the spot where Babu's body was a half hour ago. There are several people standing around her but Freny seems completely alone. I stare at her for a moment, struck by how young and beautiful and wistful she looks. Then, I make my way through the crowd and go sit on the chair next to hers. I take her hand in mind and make her look at my face. 'Kaki,' I say, using the honorific I use when I'm talking to her. 'Listen to me. You have always had two daughters – Roshan and me. But from today, you will also have a son. From today, I will be a son and a daughter to you. I will take care of you, I promise. You don't worry about anything.'

I am so intent on looking Freny in the eye, wanting her to see how sincere I am, that I am startled when I feel the splash of tears on my hand. Freny is crying hard and she puts one hand around my neck and grabs my head to her shoulder. We stay this way for a minute, holding each other hard. 'Thank you,' she whispers when she can talk. 'I will never forget these words. Pesi and I have loved you as our own from the day you were born.'

I want to cry then, want to cry as hard as Freny is crying but this is not the time. I have to be strong for Freny's sake, for Roshan's sake, for all of their sake. I have to keep my composure, I have to fight with God, battle with the moon. I must be strong, I must be strong. I have responsibilities now, I have a family to support, whose burdens I must carry. I am a coolie, my job is to lift their burdens. I am no longer the baby of the family.

There will be time for tears later.

✦

We do not observe the customary period of mourning. Two weeks after coming home from the funeral home, dad insists that we turn on the stereo and television. There is enough sorrow at home, he says, and he wants to do everything he can to alleviate it. Nobody contradicts him though mummy makes noises about how Babu deserves more of a mourning period and how heartless we all are. Still, she watches TV with the rest of us.

Ever since we moved Babu to Jaslok, mummy has been talking about what a mistake it was to take him to that cheap Masina Hospital in the first place, what a tragedy it was to let that hajaam, that barber, Dr Sethna operate on him. I know the words are calculated to wound dad, to make him feel that he put money over Babu's well-being. The words have their intended effect. Dad goes around explaining that he wasn't thinking of cost, not really, that they picked Masina Hospital because it was convenient and close to home and also, he had no idea that a kidney stone operation was such a big operation. He points out how casually Babu had come home one day and announced that he'd put up with the bastard kidney stones for long enough and had decided to get rid of them once and for all. Dad mentions that it was Babu's choice to go with Dr Sethna, after he'd done such a wonderful job with my appendix surgery, a few months earlier.

None of the adults know that I feel guilty about the choice of Dr Sethna. At the time of the appendix surgery we were all so happy that everything went off without a hitch. Now, I wish there had been some complication, anything that would've made us think twice before using Masina Hospital and Dr Sethna's services again. I secretly believe that I killed Babu so that the next time mummy brings up the issue when the two of us are alone at home, I turn to her, eyes flashing with anger, and tell her to please shut up about this. She is startled into silence but then her lips get thin and she accuses me of asking her to not speak the truth just to protect my dad. 'Everybody knows that this could've been prevented,' she hisses. 'Everybody knows that if they'd all listened to me Babu would've still been here.' Her words are so wounding that I turn away from her and lock myself in the bathroom until I trust my emotions enough to step back out.

But the fact is, none of us know what killed Babu. His death is an unresolved mystery in our lives and it makes amateur detectives out of us. Dad even makes appointments with other doctors just to question them about what could've possibly gone wrong but their instinct is to protect their colleague. There are rumours and speculations and conjectures that come back to us. About how the anaesthesiologist screwed up. About how the operating room was not properly sterilized. About how Dr Sethna accidentally left a pair of scissors in Babu's stomach before he sewed him back up. Mehroo makes frequent trips to Masina Hospital, trying to chase down all the rumours, arranging to meet with off-duty nurses to get them to spill the beans but she invariably comes back empty-handed. The code of bewildering silence holds.

I am with Mehroo the day we accidentally run into Dr Sethna at the local drugstore. It is the first time we have seen him since the funeral. Dr Sethna's appearance at the

Tower of Silence had created quite a stir. Half the mourners were awed and touched by his presence; the other half said he had something to hide and guilt had brought him to the funeral. Sethna himself had a simpler explanation – Babu was his friend, he said. And although he was an atheist and didn't believe in all the religious mumbo-jumbo he was here simply to pay his last respects. (While I was recovering from the removal of my appendix, he had visited me one evening and engaged me in a discussion about religion to get my mind off the pain. 'Christ is not even a historically accurate figure,' I remember him saying. 'There's no public record that he even existed.')

And now we were face-to-face with Sethna at the pharmacy. Here he was, the man Mehroo was no longer sure was still a family friend or her brother's killer, leaning on the glass counter and laughing and chatting with Behram, the store-owner. Sethna was short and stockily built like Babu and I remembered Babu in almost the same pose – leaning casually on the counter and talking to Behram. All of these men were around the same age and had grown up around each other and despite the different paths their lives took – Behram joining his father's business, Sethna serving as a surgeon in the army for years, Babu joining my father at the factory after flunking the exam to join the Merchant Navy – they talked to each other easily, with cuss words and slang liberally sprinkled into their language, their friendship forged during endless hours spent in their youth working out at the Parsi Gymkhana.

As his eyes fall on us, Sethna stops in mid-laugh and immediately makes his way toward us. He glances quickly at me and then moves to hug Mehroo. When he lets go of her, both's eyes are wet with tears. 'Kem che, Mehroo?' he asks. 'How are you keeping?'

Mehroo shakes her head. 'So-so. Still missing Pesi a lot.'

Sethna nods. 'I understand. He was a great person.'

This is the encouragement Mehroo needs. 'The worst part is, not knowing what happened. I lie awake at night wondering ... when I'd last left the hospital, he'd looked so good. Told me he'd see me tomorrow.' And now Mehroo's tone is openly beseeching: 'Doctor,' she says, 'just tell me the truth about what happened. You know our family, we are not interested in revenge or lawsuits or anything. We won't do anything, I promise. This is for our satisfaction, only. I just need to know the truth about what happened to my brother.'

Sethna's face is kind and his eyes red. 'Mehroo, try to forget it,' he says gently. 'I myself don't know what went wrong. As far as I'm concerned, the surgery was a success. Now don't ask me this question again. Just get on with your life. I'm very, very sorry about your loss. It's my loss, too. Pesi was my friend. This is one of the biggest blows of my career.'

We leave the drugstore that day with different interpretations of what Dr Sethna has said. I think that he has admitted to not knowing what went wrong. But Mehroo insists that he made it clear he didn't want us to know what had really happened, that we wouldn't be able to handle the truth. Sethna as good as admitted that there was a cover-up, she says, and said that we should let sleeping dogs lie. I also leave the store convinced that we will never know what happened that day. Mehroo leaves convinced that the truth is out there and it is only a matter of digging for it. Dad looks from one of us to the other, torn between wanting to arrive at the truth but not sharing Mehroo's obsessive need to know. 'Well,' he says finally, 'whether we ever find out or not, it won't bring Pesi back.'

In some ways I am glad we have the mystery of Babu's death to distract us from the dark grief that is stalking us. At home, we listen automatically for Babu's dry cough that would announce his return home at the end of the day and when it hits us that we will never hear it again, the realization feels like a fresh wound. Freny has resumed going to work and she still returns from work on payday loaded with the usual treats – bars of Cadbury's chocolates, Kelvator's raspberry syrup, packs of Tiny Size Chiclets, Kraft cheddar cheese in a blue tin, copies of *Stardust* and *Filmfare* – but it is not the same without Babu there to make some joke or comment about what she brings home.

'Do you remember how he used to tease me?' Freny asks me one evening and I know immediately what she is talking about. At the start of every school year, Freny, my mom, Roshan and me would go shopping to Colaba Causeway. Roshan and I would feel like queens on that day. Freny would buy us everything new, top to bottom, from the ribbons in our hair to the patent leather shoes on our feet. Salesmen lit up when they saw us approach, stocks of goods came tumbling down from the shelves because Freny was legendary for her generosity. Later in the day, loaded down with our new shoes and socks and dress materials and school uniforms and school-bags, even new soap dishes, we would take a cab to Paradise for a lavish dinner. Then, another cab to take us home, where all the adults would gather to admire our spoils. Amid the oohs and aahs, Babu would stay silent. Winking at me, he would turn to Freny and in a deceptively soft voice ask, 'This is all fine and good, all the things you've bought for Roshan. But have you bought the same things for my Thritu?' No matter how often Babu repeated this line, the effect on Freny was electric. 'How can you even ask me that? You know I love both girls equally. Each one owns half my heart. I have never treated Thritu as anything but my own daughter. I may not have given her birth but ...' And then Freny would stop, knowing that she'd been had, while Babu and I would erupt in peels of laughter.

Now there is nobody who calls me his first darling of the morning. And anyway, that time of youth and innocence has long past. We are all drifting now, dark patches of grief walking around each other. Now it is up to me to step into Babu's shoes, to make sure Freny still has someone to take her to the movies, to make my dad lose that hurt look that has muscled its way onto his face, to distract Mehroo from trying to solve the riddle of Babu's death. Even months later, the grief is so strong at times that I revisit the idea of drugging all of us until this time has passed. I want to cry in dark, private corners like the rest of them, want to sit huddled in the living room talking about Babu like the rest of them do. But there is no time. Grief is not a luxury I can afford because I have a drowning family to rescue. There will be time for tears later, I assure myself.

My chance finally comes six months after Babu's death. Roshan is out with her friends; the adults are attending a late afternoon funeral service for an elderly acquaintance. I am blissfully, unexpectedly, alone at home. As soon as I realize that I will have about two hours to myself, I resolve that this is the day to shed those tears that I've held back so many times, to mourn Babu in a way I've never allowed myself. No more fighting with the moon – this will be a day of surrender.

At the appointed hour, I sit in the living room, clutching a picture of Babu and await the tears. Nothing happens. I force myself to remember details of Babu's face and hands. I can feel the muscles in his forearms as clearly as on that day a month before his death when he and I had walked home from the factory, with me holding his arm all the way home. Still no tears. Not crying has become a habit, a reflex. This calls for drastic action, I realize. I look through my record collection and pull out every sad song that I can find. Terry Jacks' *Seasons in the Sun*. Neil Diamond singing *If You Go Away*. I am very aware of time slipping away, knowing that my time alone at home is limited. Any minute now there could be a knock on the door that could end this private time. It may be months before such an opportunity arises again. But my tear ducts remain unconvinced. I cannot shed tears for the man who had literally given me the last ten-rupee note in his wallet, a man whose face was one of the first ones I'd seen after being born. I am a freak, a cruel, heartless bitch, a frigid, emotionally constipated piece of shit. I had finished my dinner when the rest of the family had left their plates untouched upon learning that Babu was ill. I had been mean to him, had looked down on him once I'd gotten myself some intellectual friends.

I sit in the living room thinking evil thoughts about myself, knowing that I am berating myself at least in part out of clear-eyed calculation. Because I want to feel something and if I can't cry for Babu perhaps I can shed tears of self-pity. But the ruse doesn't work.

The tears didn't come that day and they didn't come until years later on a cold winter's day in Columbus, Ohio, about eight thousand miles away from the hot, foetid city in which Babu had spent most of his life. The tears finally came that day because I was homesick and I suddenly thought of Babu, all alone in the England of the early 1950s, studying for his Merchant Navy exams and failing. And suddenly I was weeping for that disappointed young man who came back to Bombay having labelled himself a failure and for how lonely and scared and alone he must've been in England. I was crying because I realized that Babu never talked about his year in England because the stench of failure was too strong. And I wondered what he would've thought of me, the second member of the family to venture out in the big wide world. Would he have been proud? Nervous? Even a little jealous? And then it hits me that I'll never know because Babu stopped knowing me at the age of fifteen and I remember how his death changed my family forever, made us all grow up and grow old before our time and then I'm crying, crying, crying for the years that Babu never had with his beloved Freny and crying for my father whose youth ended that day in April 1977 and above all, I'm crying for me, finally, I'm crying for me, for that frightened, lost kid who tried her best to hold her unravelling family together, for that poor, miserable fifteen-year-old who was charged with fighting with the moon, and for that ugly, awkward, skinny girl who would never be anyone's first darling of the morning any more.

# Twenty

IT'S BEGINNING TO UNRAVEL. I can tell by the way they won't look me in the eye.

It begins as a trickle and at first they have the decency to look away, their faces pinched with embarrassment, but after awhile the trickle grows into a regular stream and now they are simply looking through me, ignoring me as if I am a pebble in their way.

I look around frantically for Vinny but he has gone to fetch us some battatawadas and bread for lunch. I have been on my feet in the hallway outside the college admission office for four hours and I am tired.

This is my second year of college. After years of mouthing empty platitudes about youth revolution while in high school, I finally have a chance to make it happen.

We had launched the fee boycott campaign six weeks ago to protest Bombay University's plan to hike tuition by twenty per cent, thereby making a university education inaccessible to thousands of low-income students.

For weeks now, I have been standing at the same spot each day begging, pleading, and arguing with my fellow students to return home without paying their fees for the upcoming semester. And Vinny and I have been successful beyond all wildest dreams. Many of the students have travelled to college from their faraway homes in the suburbs during the summer-break to enrol for the following term. But I have looked them in the eye, slapped their backs, read them statistics about how many students would have to drop out if the fee hike goes through, beseeched them, appealed to their sense of justice, laughingly told them that I would pay their return bus fare home, and amazingly, miraculously, I have succeeded in getting most of them to turn back.

The clerk at the office window scowls at me each time I am victorious, each time I convince another student to continue the fee boycott. I smile at him on occasion, an appeasing smile as if to say, We're really on the same side, brother, but he looks away. Principal Singha frequently walks by the ground floor office where Vinny and I have stood guard for the last six weeks. Most of the time he ignores us, simply sweeps past us, but sometimes he shakes his head and stops to talk to us, as if his curiosity is greater than his contempt for us. 'What do think you're achieving with this, Red?' he says to me in his gravel-like voice, using his favourite moniker for me. 'Wasting both your time and the college's time. You think the chancellor of Bombay University is going to be scared of your little tactics?'

In his usual earnest way Vinny steps forward to argue with Mr Singha. He pulls out his little fact sheet about the number of students affected by the hike but the principal shakes his head impatiently, grunts, and resumes walking.

I go home each day shaking with fatigue and excitement. Although we are on summer-break, I am working eight-hour days. I get to college a few minutes before the tuition window opens, stay on through lunch and leave only after I make sure that the fee clerk has left for the day. But after the ambitionless years spent with Jenny and Patty, after years of self-absorption and navel-gazing, after all the high-school talk of youth power and youth revolution, I feel as if I have discovered my life's work. Each evening I knock on the door that connects our apartment to Jesse's and give her the day's report. 'You know what's really great about this?' I say to her one day. 'I feel as if I am using my very body in the service of people I do not even know. I mean, it's one thing to sit in endless political meetings at Elphinstone College or somewhere, smoking cigarettes and sipping glass after glass of chai, but this is something else. This is like actually using your body, standing when you are dying to sit down, talking when you don't feel like saying another word, looking and touching and talking to people. I don't know – this feels more real to me, I guess.'

Jesse nods. I can see a look of almost maternal pride in her eyes.

But now it is just a few days before the term starts again and the kids are panicking. The first few ones mumble their apologies to me, explain that their parents will skin them alive if they miss any classes, brush aside my explanations of how we could win this thing if we only stuck together, and go ahead and pay their fees. 'C'mon, yaar,' Anand says. 'God only knows how many classes I've bunked last term. You know that Mr Singha is just waiting for a chance to kick me out of here. I just can't risk that, yaar.'

Once a few of them pay, the others follow, until Vinny and I are floundering like fish on the shore. They are not listening to us now, the mesmerizing, magical hold that we had on them until a few days ago, has been broken.

I glance at the face of the clerk. He is grinning at me, a victorious, gleeful smile. I look away. Weeks of fatigue are catching up with me, making me teary. We had been so close. A few more days of unity and we could have defeated the system. For a split-second I ask myself if I was wrong to have refused Pranab's offer from a week ago and then I hate myself for my moment of weakness.

Pranab is an overweight, burly guy whom we jokingly refer to as a professional student. At twenty-six, he is considerably older than the rest of us but seems to have no intention of graduating from college, content to spend his time cruising down the streets of South Bombay on his

Yamaha motorcycle. Pranab belonged to the youth division of the Congress Party and I knew that he and his ilk looked upon student activists like Vinny and me as idealistic idiots. So I was reluctant to go when I heard that Pranab wanted to meet with us in the college cafeteria for a chat. But Vinny convinced me otherwise.

'Arré, Vishnu, bring two more glasses of tea, fatta-faat,' he yelled to the young server when we showed up. I was irritated by his presumption at ordering tea for me without even a cursory inquiry, but I didn't show it. After all, Pranab had many other qualities, which irritated me even more greatly.

He smiled at us, and I noticed that his teeth were beginning to yellow from the constant cigarette smoking. 'Hey, yaar, thanks for coming,' he said, shaking hands with Vinny and nodding at me. 'I've been watching both of you for days, keeping the students from paying their fees and all. Not a bad job, yaar, considering and all. Most days you get what? Ten-twenty students to turn back? And maybe two-three cowards go ahead and pay anyway? If I had my way, I'd kill those bleddy bastards.'

We listened to him cautiously, silently, unsure of where this was heading. Pranab kept talking. 'Yah, men, two of you are giving all of us student activists a good name.' I bristled at that, at his presumption at equating his thuggery with the kind of work we were doing but Vinny kicked me gently under the table and I held my silence.

'So here's what I have to offer,' Pranab was saying. 'Me and my boys can get this whole college shut down in two hours flat. Nobody will dare set foot in it to pay any tuition-fuition. You two can go home, relax, or take in a flick or two. In exchange, all I ask is that you don't challenge me in the next student election.'

Vinny and I exchanged a quick look, unsure of whether to laugh or be offended. This bloody idiot with his bristly moustache and shifty eyes actually thought that we would waste our time running for a meaningless college election.

'What, you mean you can shut down the college in two hours?' Vinny asked, although we both knew what Pranab meant.

'Oh, come off it, yaar,' Pranab said. 'You know I have good contacts. A few stones thrown, a few windows broken, maybe one or two beatings and this college won't open until we want it to.'

We were wasting our time. I got up. 'That's not how we operate,' I said, trying to sound as nonchalant as he did. 'Any goonda can close something down with violence. We are trying to appeal to student's sense of justice and solidarity.'

Pranab raised his right eyebrow. 'Sense of justice?' he repeated, snickering a bit. 'Sister, just wait till it's time for college to start. Then you'll see them all lining up at the front office, baaing like sheep. Even your best friends won't know your name when they're in that queue, paying their fees.'

Well, he was right. As I watch them lining up behind the open window and averting their faces from where we stand, Pranab suddenly seems to be a genius in human psychology.

'Sheep,' I mutter to myself. 'Disgusting, fucking sheep.'

So much has happened since I impulsively participated in my first demonstration. The Emergency ended on March 20, 1977 with Indira Gandhi's ignoble defeat. I received the final grades for my high school board exams the next day. (When Greta Duke saw that despite all predictions, I had actually done well in my exams, she shook her head and said, 'You have the devil's luck, Umrigar. The devil's luck. Never forget that.') Indira's nemesis, the doddering Morarji Desai, became Prime Minister at the age of eighty-one. Babu died in April of that year. Three years later, a repentant, desperate India brought back Indira Gandhi in a landslide. By then, I had finished three years of college.

✧

College: Steam and smoke rise from endless cups of tea and cigarettes while we sit in cafeterias discussing how to build a student movement; afternoons spent sitting cross-legged on the grass at the Bombay University campus, debating politics and 'the Indian condition', with members of opposing civil liberties organizations; counting the money from selling mimeographed booklets to the rush of sweaty factory workers that pours out of the textile mills after twelve-hour shifts; looking over my shoulder constantly to make sure I don't run into any of my father's business friends who might let slip that they spotted me half-way across the city from where I'm supposed to be.

College: Requesting the office clerk to fix up the attendance rolls to masquerade the fact that I have not attended classes in months; mornings spent gossiping and eating tomato-chutney sandwiches on the marble steps outside of college; writing and directing plays for the All-Bombay Intercollegiate competition; going to Jehangir Art Gallery to take in the latest art shows and then stopping at nearby Rhythm House; skipping class to sit in the rain at Nariman Point, gazing out at the sea while Vinny lights cigarette after cigarette and lets me take deep drags off them.

College: Coming close, *this* close, to doing my bit to shut my college down to protest the tuition hikes and then watching the tide turn, watching it fall out of my grasp like sand out of a fist, watching them pull away from me, as relentlessly, as remorselessly, as the ocean pulling away from the sand. It's one thing, at age eighteen, to talk about how we will work for the revolution even though 'we won't see it during our own lifetime'. It's another thing to experience the truth of that.

The tuition hike went through. Our predictions about the number of students who wouldn't be able to afford college came true. Nobody seemed to notice. Thus hope yellows into cynicism.

✧

But that's not the full story either. There are other dis-illusionments.

There is the day in my final year of college when the whole gang is sitting on the marble steps and Abbas says he needs to go home to study.

We protest but Abbas is already on his way. 'Okay, see you, then, John Travolta,' Hanif yells after him.

We call Abbas John Travolta, because several years ago he had walked into the theatre to see *Saturday Night Fever* as plain old Abbas Hakim and strutted out as John Travolta, swinging his hips and walking on his toes, the way the Tony Manero character does in the movie. He also began to talk in a faux New York accent, pronouncing coffee as *kofee* instead of *cawfee*, as we did.

Now, Abbas swings around. 'You all should be studying too, yaar. Final exams are less than two weeks away.'

'Yah, okay,' I say dismissively. 'Two weeks, my foot.'

Hanif turns to me. 'No, he's right about that. Imagine, two more weeks and we'll never meet again like this. All of us will be out in the world.'

My brain freezes. I realize that college life is drawing to a close. I suddenly feel woefully inadequate to tackle the working world. My lifelong dream to work at *The Times of India*, slips off my shoulders like an ill-fitting cape. I am nowhere close to being ready to be anything but a college student. The world suddenly feels too big a place for me to navigate.

Also, there is this...

Reluctantly, hesitantly, at first in a whisper and then a little louder, is this voice that points out to me that our Utopian vision of what the world should look like does not match up with the personalities of the people trying to build that world. I want to ignore that disconnect, that gap that looms between the purity of our dreams and the narrowness of our daily lives. I have already lost so much – my faith in religion, the escapism that my druggie friends once offered, my faith in my ability to make things right between my parents – that giving up my belief in politics seems too unbearable a loss.

But I am growing up. Dreams that used to once thrill me – like Natasha's vision of a world that was a good place not just for humans but for animals too, which meant nobody would eat meat in a socialist paradise, or Shekhar's imagined world where every person could afford to drive a Cadillac – have lost their hold on me. I notice instead the self-aggrandizing poses struck by the student leaders and the way activists from upper-caste, affluent Hindu families scorn the label 'intellectual' and instead refer to themselves as the working class; I notice that all the lefty kids dress and speak the same way, until we all have the same intonations when we speak about 'the people', and 'the masses'. I notice how we write off former comrades whose politics differ even slightly from ours, I remember how, once when we were planning a women's rights event, Suresh yelled at his girlfriend for forgetting to add sugar in his tea and how nobody commented on the irony.

And then there is the fatigue. I am tired of sitting in endless meetings and study groups, discussing whether Lenin or Trotsky was correct. I am tired of constantly fighting everybody, from the police to the thirty-year-old thugs who masquerade as student leaders, to my own father, who is petrified that my political views are going to land me in jail.

It is draining to sneak around behind his back, to constantly look over my shoulders, to always feel as if I am going to get caught. Also, I have the kind of personality that needs at least occasional successes to keep going. And in this line of work, there is no instant gratification, no tangible success. With every new student whom I talk into attending one of our meetings, joining our organization, it seems as if someone else has dropped out.

The sour taste of disillusionment rises in my throat. I try to force it back down. But it keeps popping back up, like a tag-along younger sister who shows up at the wrong times and places.

I also try to block my ears to an unmistakable sound. It is the sound of another door closing.

# Twenty-one

I HAVE TO GET OUT of here no matter what it takes to do so.

The thought is so clear in my head that it takes my breath away, so that I feel as if I have to sit down on the wooden steps that I am climbing. I am at the bottom of the stairs leading up to our second-floor apartment but even from here I can hear mummy's voice, loud, hysterical, and thick with rage. It is this thickness that makes my stomach collapse, because it is the sound of madness and this is how she sounds when she is totally out of control. I have grown up hearing the same harshness in her younger sister's voice, the sister who has fought her own lifelong demons. And now mummy has inherited this bellow and the ugliness of it makes my hair stand up on end.

I know that mummy is having one of her daily fights with Mehroo. I stand at the bottom of the stairs, my head light with nervousness, my legs suddenly feeling as if they are made of hay and unable to carry me another step to the apartment. Occasionally, I can hear Mehroo's voice, quivering and thin with frustration and emotion. Then, mummy's voice rises again, covering up Mehroo's in a torrent of words. Even from this distance I can make out the curses that she is hurling at Mehroo, cruel, poisonous words that land like darts in my heart. I automatically do what I've done all my life when mummy curses Mehroo. *Please God*, I say, *whatever bad thing she wishes for Mehroo, let it happen to me instead twice as strong.*

Now I am at the first floor landing and I stand there debating what to do next. I know that I am here on borrowed time because any minute now the first-floor apartment door will be flung open and one of the neighbours will join me on the landing, watching me with eyes made narrow with inquisitiveness, trying to gauge my reaction, storing up the information so that a nugget of gossip can be dropped at the appropriate time into the jaws of salivating, news-hungry neighbours. Worse, the woman may say something to me, either something flippant and snarky about the daily fights, or worse, something meant to be kind and understanding that might bring a tear to my eye, which in turn will also be duly reported to the other neighbours.

I suddenly feel claustrophobic, as if I am trapped on this tiny strip of space where I am standing, unable to continue standing here and reluctant to climb the flight of stairs that will take me into my apartment and face-to-face with the hysterical, raging woman who has given birth to me. I feel a hatred that rises from my stomach into my mouth and tastes like sour milk. For a moment, I flirt with the idea of turning around and racing down the stairs and into the freedom of the streets, of walking around Bombay until dusk gives way to night and my feet grow heavy and tired from walking. I want to run away from the misery of prying neighbours and the red-hot embarrassment that flows through my limbs like lava, at the thought of everybody around us knowing every intimate detail of what goes on within our apartment because of my mother's bullhorn voice. But while I am fantasizing about flight, I also fantasize about rushing into the house and cupping my mother's open mouth with my hand and pushing her torrent of hateful words back down her throat, my hands rougher on her mouth than they need to be. I feel a blinding fury then, at the thought of this reception that I am receiving at the end of a long day in college.

I continue standing on the landing, unable to move, paralysed with indecision. Part of me wants to rush out without a look back and never return again, to lose myself in the crowds of Bombay. Part of me wants to rush upstairs and throttle my mother, silence her, cause the buffalo sounds coming from her throat to stop. And all this time, while I debate what to do next, I am aware that any minute now the first floor apartment door will fly open and then I will have a third dilemma to deal with. I want to lay myself down on the cold stone floor of the landing, curl up within myself, cover myself with a warm blanket knitted from silence, and fall asleep. This, of course, is not an option. There is a decision to be made.

When I was nine years old I stood in the bathroom one day with the sharp, pointed edge of a steel compass in my inner ear. I had learned that a punctured eardrum could cause deafness and it was deafness that I craved, the white, snowy silence that would block off my mother's voice. I wanted to lose myself in silence, wanted to occupy a world where adults did not scream their hate at each other, where mothers did not dissolve in gut-wrenching, soul-searing sobs, where beloved aunts did not cry to the heavens for help.

The compass was part of a geometry set that my aunt Freny had bought for me that year. The pale yellow metal box also contained a six-inch plastic ruler and a protractor.

I stood in the bathroom for the longest time that day, trying to picture what a world of silence would feel like, trying to imagine the pain that would invariably follow a pierced eardrum. Would there be blood? If so, how much? Would it trickle out of my ear in a thin stream or would it gush out? What explanation would I give the adults when they asked what I was doing with a compass in the bathroom? Would I be able to fool them into believing that it was an accident? And most important, once I felt the pain and saw the blood, would I have the guts to follow through by piercing the second eardrum, also? What if I chickened out? What good would one deaf ear do?

In the end, I didn't have the guts to go through with it. Because just as my fingers tightened around the cold metal .of the compass I realized that deafness would mean more than escaping from the sound of my mother's shrieks and curses. It would also mean never hearing music again or the sound of the birds or the roar of the ocean or my father's humming as we drove along Marine Drive. Indeed, I would be losing an entire world in order to gain the escape from angry words that I was seeking and bad as I was at math, even I could figure out that the gain was not greater than the loss.

But this craving for oblivion did not end on that day. For years, I fantasized about killing myself and leaving behind a note that simply said, 'Let there be peace at home.' I was sure that this was the only way to make the adults end their daily bickering. A few years after the compass incident, when I was fourteen, I snuck into the medicine cabinet and stole the bottle of iodine that stood next to the bottle of mercurochrome. Each time Mehroo applied iodine on my bruised knees or scraped elbows, I'd noticed the line on the bottle's label that said the product was poisonous if consumed orally. It was not that I planned on killing myself on this day – I just wanted to taste the bitter iodine to see if I could go through with drinking the entire bottle if I ever needed to. I wanted to test how foul the taste would be in case I ever needed to down it in a hurry, to know if I needed to come up with a better plan. I screwed open the black plastic top to the small, thin glass bottle and touched the opening of the bottle to my tongue, which immediately went numb from where the drop of iodine landed on it.

I was satisfied. It tasted awful but if things ever got so bad at home that I needed to kill myself, I knew that I could force myself to consume the entire bottle.

✧

I climb the last flight of stairs and ring the doorbell to the apartment. Nothing happens. Mummy continues to scream at Mehroo, who is doing her best to respond in between coughing fits. I hear Mehroo coughing from where I stand outside the front door and as always, I fight the urge to beat on my ears with the open palm of my hands so that the sound of her cough gets fragmented and chopped up. I have been doing this since I was a child, whenever the house erupted in fighting and yelling and swearing. By beating on my ears I could manipulate sound, slice up words until they sounded funny and meaningless, could drain the poison out of them. Mehroo's coughing scares me, reminds me of how terribly frail and sick she is, and produces in me a rush of protectiveness that I want to wrap like a woollen coat around her. I ring the doorbell again, more insistently this time. The indecisiveness of a few minutes ago, the desire to run away and never return, is gone now, replaced by the urge to pull Mehroo away from the fighting that is surely sapping her strength and numbering her days.

Mehroo's health has declined a lot these past few years. The treatments for TB that she received in her childhood have damaged her lungs, so that her cough has become a part of her now, a feature every bit as much her as her voice or her laugh. But no matter how much Mehroo coughs, I can't get used to it. Her painful coughing has a visceral effect on me, just as the old cowherd's wailing did when I was an infant. When Mehroo has one of her long coughing fits, I want to cover my ears, run out of the room, smash something. My violent reaction stems from my inability to see her suffer and her coughing brings me face-to-face with the realization that all the love in my heart cannot help her even the tiniest bit. Of course, I don't say any of this to Mehroo because she is already so ashamed of her coughing, haunted as she is by childhood memories of being shunned when she had TB. She will no longer kiss me and when I try to grab her face and forcibly kiss her cheek, she turns her head away so that the kiss misfires and lands on her head. She acts as if she has TB again, although she doesn't.

Mehroo has stopped going to the factory almost completely now because the sawdust makes her condition worse. She still looks over the cloth-bound business ledgers at home but dad has hired an accountant at the factory. Mostly, she is confined to the house and that means that there are more fights between mummy and her. Whereas she could once escape to the factory during the day, she is now trapped in the house with a nemesis who seems unable to go beyond a day without a fight. Between the coughing fits and the fighting, Mehroo's strength is being sapped, daily.

As soon as mummy opens the door I take in her flushed, sweaty face, the heaving of her bosom, the mad, bloodthirsty glint in her eye. I decide to go on the offensive before she tries to suck me into her world of ancient resentments and enmities. 'I could hear every word that you were screaming from two floors down,' I say. 'All the neighbours are gathered downstairs listening to your bhea-bhea-bhea. For God's sake, keep your loud voice down.'

She turns on me with the manic energy of a young bull. 'Not even home for a minute and already siding with her, are you? Only my voice you hear, is that it? Why don't you say something to your beloved Mehroo with all her screaming and shouting? This is my reward for carrying you in my stomach for nine months, feeding you, taking care of you when you are sick, so that you side with everybody except your mother. But that's what happens when you give birth to a snake instead of a daughter.'

'Toba, toba, toba,' Mehroo says, tapping her cheeks three times in the ritualistic way. 'What kind of mother talks like this to her own daughter? God forgive you.'

My opening salvo has re-energized mummy and she does not let up, directing her pent-up fury at me, following me from room to room, calling me names. I recoil from her words but I am also relieved that I am shielding Mehroo from mummy's barrage of bullets by taking them myself. I see my body as a wall that I have erected between mummy and Mehroo, to protect the latter. I figure I can take it because when mummy attacks Mehroo or my dad, her curses carry more venom than a cobra. But even though she says terrible things to me, her attacks don't devastate me as much because I tell myself that deep down she doesn't mean it, that she is posturing, that despite her mad, hateful words, she really loves me.

Still, I have had a long day at college and I am tired of her yelling. I want to end this fight right now. I raise my voice to cover up hers, like putting a lid on a pot of boiling water, but I am no match for her. Her voice gets thicker and thicker, like a soup that's been simmering on the stove for too long, and then I can't take it for another second. I rush towards her and grip her wrist in my hand and hiss at her to shut up, just shut up, to keep her damn voice down because all the neighbours have their windows open and they can all hear every word of what she is saying. I feel like a madwoman myself, completely out of control, but now she is once again turning the tables on me because she is inching towards the open window in her bedroom, dragging me along with her, and now she is screaming at the top of her lungs that I am hurting her, that I am holding her prisoner, and I am so stunned by her treachery, by the extent of her deceit, and so intent on wanting to keep her voice down that I try cupping her mouth with my other hand but now she calls forth some demon-like strength and in one swift stroke she is out of my grip and then I watch with horror as she turns her fingers into a claw and pulls them down the length of my right arm, taking with her flecks of my skin, leaving behind faint but long lines of bloody scratches.

I yelp. You're scratching me, I say, watching her handiwork in amazement. Then I look up to her face and there is such a look of controlled excitement, of deep satisfaction, of pure, unadulterated madness on her face that my heart begins to pound with fear. She is crazy. My mother is crazy. And right at this moment she looks as if she hates me even though I don't want to believe that, despite everything that has just happened.

I rush out of her room. Already, I can tell that there will be scars where her fingers have dug into my flesh and I hurry to put on a long-sleeved shirt so that none of the other adults can see what mummy has done. This will be another one of our many secrets.

I wear long sleeves for the next several weeks. But one day Jesse somehow catches a glimpse of the scratches on my forearm. 'How the hell did that happen?' she asks.

'Oh, I was just playing around with Ronnie and he scratched me a few times, that's all,' I lie.

She nods. She has no reason not to believe me.

✧

But others are less oblivious to what's going on at home.

Although it was years ago, I still smart from the memory of the conversation I'd had with Miss D'Silva, when I was in ninth-grade.

Miss D'Silva was my elementary school teacher who lived a few houses down from us and had consequently known my family all her life. I continued to see her even after I graduated from her class because often, when I missed the school-bus because I'd overslept, Mehroo would wait downstairs with me and when Miss D'Silva would walk by on her way to the taxi-stand, Mehroo would request her to give me a ride to school. She always agreed and we'd spend the time in the cab chatting about school and other matters. 'So, kiddo. Have a boyfriend yet?' she'd always tease me. 'What, no gora-gora nice Parsi young man yet?' She had grown up around enough Parsis to know how much most of them prized light skin.

'Even if I did have a boyfriend, he wouldn't be a Parsi,' I'd reply. 'And he definitely wouldn't be fair-skinned.'

Miss D'Silva, who had the burnt chocolate coloured skin of a Goanese Catholic, would smile.

But on this day, Miss D'Silva looked uncharacteristically serious. It was the first time I was visiting my old classroom and that too, because Greta Duke had sent me on an errand to pick up something from her class. Since I was now riding the B.E.S.T buses, I had not seen Miss D'Silva in a long time.

I spent a few minutes chatting aimlessly with her and was about to return to where Miss Duke was tutoring the other kids in the library, when Miss D'Silva said quietly, 'So, kiddo. How are things at home these days?'

I looked confused. 'At home? Fine,' I said.

I made to move away but Miss D'Silva put her hand on my shoulder and pulled me closer to her. 'No, I mean, really. How are things between your mom and your aunties? And between your mom and your dad?'

I suddenly knew what she meant and felt a wave of embarrassment so thick, it could've knocked me off my feet. 'Fine, everybody is fine,' I mumbled.

But to my mortification, Miss D'Silva was not done. 'Look, kiddo, you can talk to me. You think I don't know what you've been going through all these years? Wasn't that long ago when you were in this class. I remember, I used to stand at this window and look out on the playground every evening, when you were taking on – what was it?

Five? Eight? – of the girls at one time and fighting them.'

'Ten,' I murmured automatically. 'The all-time record was ten. I beat ten of them this one day.'

Miss D'Silva went on as if she hadn't heard me. 'Heck, why do you think I allowed you to fight all those girls? By the time you got on the school-bus, you'd be all banged up and bruised, looking like Muhammad Ali or something. Sometimes I wanted to intervene but I never did because you had to get rid of all that anger you had stored up inside you. I knew what kind of home life you had.'

I stood before Miss D'Silva as if before an X-ray machine, feeling totally naked and exposed. I wanted to say something light and playful, wanted to deny her charges, but nothing came to mind.

She helped me out. 'Listen, you Mad Parsi,' she said playfully. 'I know you're plenty tough. But I only wanted to say that if you ever want to talk to an adult, I'm here.'

'Okay. Thanks,' I said, my voice sounding brittle even to my own ears. 'Well, Miss Duke is waiting, so I need to get going.'

I rushed out of her class, not looking back. I was determined never to run into Miss D'Silva again. By the time I reached the library, I had worked myself up into a fury. 'What the hell is she poking her nose into my business for,' I fumed to myself. 'Nothing wrong with my home life. As for fighting with those girls, hell, I just enjoyed fighting. Just like an adult to make more out of it than what it was. Making me out like I was a charity case or something.'

But today, thinking back on the encounter with Miss D'Silva, I wish I'd known how to ask for help. It is my own special curse that I don't know how to confide in anybody about how rapidly things are going downhill between mummy and me, how she tortures me with her words and sometimes, with her hands.

For years, when mummy was saying something

particularly hurtful to me, I'd repeat to myself, 'Turn your heart into stone, turn your heart into stone.'

It occurs to me now that I have succeeded beyond my wildest imagination.

✧

Fuck.

What a dream.

I wake up from it in a sweat and my bed feels so damp that for a confused second I think I have slipped back into my old habit and wet my bed.

In the dream, I have gone to Villoo aunty's home to plead my case. Villoo is my mother's older sister, the one who used to scare me when I was little, with threats of how she would tie me up in a dark gunny sack with roaches and rats, if I didn't do everything she asked. I used to dread the times when mummy would drop me off at Villoo's home because I knew that even if I told mummy about Villoo's threats, she'd never believe me. Luckily, dad was against my spending too much time there because it was well known that the entire family yelled and screamed at each other and he wanted to protect me from this. I was the battlefield upon which my parents waged their private wars.

'I don't want you dropping her off at your family's,' he'd say. 'You can spend your whole life there, if you want. But all that screaming and fighting. I don't want any of that poison to land on my daughter's ears.'

'Yah, if you had your way, you'd never want her to see any of my family members again. First you tried keeping me away, now her. Well, I'm the one who carried her in my stomach for nine months, not you. I'll take her wherever I want.'

In the dream, I have gone to Villoo aunty's home to plead my case. My plea is simple: I want my mummy returned to me. I want to explain to Villoo and my grandmother that their neediness, their manipulative helplessness at not being able to function in the world unless my mother helps them, has done untold damage to my family. It has left my father without a wife; it has left me without the attentions of a mother. All her energy is focused away from our home; her moods rise and fall depending on what is happening in the lives of her brothers and sisters. We bear the brunt of all her frustrations. Time after time, she walks out on a fight with her younger sister and comes home and picks a fight with Mehroo. And I am tired of it all.

In the dream, Villoo opens the door with a mask on her face. 'Hello, Villoo aunty,' I say but she pretends to be someone else and says she's never met me before and could I please introduce myself. I play along for a few minutes but as the charade continues, I grow more and more frustrated. 'I know it's you, Villoo aunty,' I shout. 'Please, just listen to me for a change.'

Just then my grandmother walks in, an uncharacteristically solicitous look on her face. 'What is it, deekra?' she says in a kindly manner. 'Come here, let me console you.' She takes my head in her hand, as if she is about to hold me to her bosom but then she moves and bangs my head against the wall. I am stunned, reeling from pain. 'Breaking a coconut,' she says and the room fills with laughter. I suddenly realize there are other people in the room.

Villoo ducks into the dining room and then reappears with a bottle. 'Here,' she says. 'Here's a gift for you.' I reach out for the bottle, thinking it is iodine for my bruised head but she pulls it away from me and opens it herself. I hear a sizzling sound, like the sizzle of tandoori chicken when they serve it to you in a restaurant, and the next instant I feel something wet and hot and burning on my face. It is acid. She has flung acid in my face. I touch my hand to my face in disbelief and stare at the layer of skin that pulls away. Even in the dream, I marvel at the fact that the acid has not penetrated my eyes and that I can still see. But thankfulness is mixed with terror and I begin to scream in panic. But the more I scream, the more Villoo and my grandmother laugh, until both sounds merge into one and I can't tell if I'm laughing or screaming.

I wake up with a start, shaking in bed. To calm myself, I do what I always do after a bad dream – I try to connect the dots, think of real-life events that may have wandered their way into my dreams. The acid-throwing, I know, is probably the result of a reading about a recent incident where a group of Muslim boys threw acid on the faces of two college-going Hindu girls who had turned down their overtures. The mask imagery probably came from having read a Phantom comic strip before going to bed. But as for the rest of it ... even if I can logically trace the incidents in the dream, I can't explain away the sad, shaky, desperate residual feeling that is left over and that leaves me tossing and turning in bed.

# Twenty-two

AMERICA.
The word comes to me as I am dozing off to sleep, comes accompanied by an electric charge that jolts me awake.

America. A way out. If I am to get away from my dead-end life, I will have to find my way to America, land of self-invention. This is the only place I know where one can start anew and I desperately need to start afresh, because my life in Bombay feels chewed up, used up and I am only twenty years old. I am close to graduating from college and even my lifelong dream of getting a job at *The Times of India*, has suddenly lost its sheen. As long as I am unmarried, I know that economics and social convention will dictate that I continue to live at home and that if I do that much longer, I will end up in a crazy asylum. Because I just can't deal with the shit at home any more. My nerves are shot; each time there's a fight at home, I begin to drop things, like I'm in a fucking Groucho Marx movie.

I'm twenty years old and I'm tired. All the things that I thought would save me – music, books, politics – have befriended me for a while but ultimately, I've had to come back and face myself. After years of looking forward to a job and the independence it would give me, I'm facing up to the facts: I do not feel prepared to enter the work world and as long as I'm living at home, I will never be truly free. Dad will continue setting curfews for me, Mehroo and Freny will continue cooking and cleaning for me, Kamala will wait on me, mummy will alternate between pulling me towards her and pushing me away. Nothing will change. I will never find out who I am, who I could be without all these people around me.

It is not in my nature to flee into the dark night, to slip out without leaving a forwarding address the way Amy has done. Nor will I be able to settle in nearby Pune or in New Delhi without embarrassing my family, without setting the neighbours' tongues wagging. There will be rumours that I have fled home because I am pregnant or because of a falling out with my family. After all, Bombay is the glittering jewel in India's crown, Bombay is the place where the rest of India migrates towards. To leave the city and settle in one of the lesser places would be a slap in my father's face, a repudiation of the life that I have here.

No, if I want to get away I will have to move to the Big Enchilada, I will have to seek out a life that is so clearly superior and dazzling compared to what I have here, that it will arouse no suspicions. I have to run away to America.

One thing I am sure of: I do not want to take the route that Amy chose. Like Amy, I want to run away from home but I want to do it legitimately and not under the cover of anonymity. Nor do I want to leave a trail of unanswered questions in my wake, like Amy has.

Amy is a distant cousin who lived two buildings down from us. Despite the differences in our age – she was almost eleven years older than me – we were close. She was a shy, soft-spoken, highly sensitive young woman, with a mind as sharp as a knife. As far as I knew, she never had a boyfriend. Our bond was our love of stories – I loved listening to them and Amy was a born storyteller. In fact, I fancy that it is storytelling that helped Amy get away, that she learned how to escape by becoming a character in one of her own stories.

From the time that I was a kid, Amy would spend every evening at our home, not returning to her parents' home until it was night-time. Each evening we had to beg her to eat dinner with us because she would protest and lie and say she'd already eaten. 'Come on, Amy, be sporting, please,' dad would insist and she would demur and finally consent.

But before we'd sit down for dinner, Amy and I would spend an hour or so together, with me sitting on her lap in the wooden rocking-chair on the balcony. 'Hey, Amy, tell me about Kirin,' I'd say and she would launch into a story about the little boy that she used to tutor who lived half-way across the city from us but whose life came alive for me because of Amy's stories. It took me years to figure out that Kirin always seemed to be facing the same dilemmas and struggles that I was facing at any given moment. Like many shy people, Amy was a good observer; like many masterful storytellers, Amy knew how to weave the strings of my life into whatever tale she was spinning that day.

Those sessions on the balcony, when it was just the two of us, were different from the stories Amy would tell the adults. With me, she was vulnerable, intuitive, unfailingly kind. But when she entertained the adults with her hilarious descriptions of her job at the bank and how she was forever making a fool out of her dim-witted branch manager, Amy was cutting, biting, sarcastic, outrageous. Babu, dad, and the rest of them would roar with laughter at some of her tales and gasp with disbelief when she went too far at spinning circles around her clueless boss. 'Careful, Amy,' dad would sometimes feel compelled to say. 'It's not good to make fools of people all the time. Sometimes one gets caught in one's own web.'

So in retrospect, there was plenty of warning about how secretive and manipulative Amy could be. Still, the whole family was in shock when Amy simply disappeared one day. She called one of her relatives a few days later to say that she was okay but it was useless looking for her, as she was going far away. She did not explain her reasons for leaving as stealthily as she had. Occasionally, she would phone our house and ask to speak with dad or Mehroo but when they asked for her whereabouts, she would get evasive although she once said she was in an ashram in the Himalayas. Sometimes when she called, she spoke in different accents. One time she told Mehroo to please only speak with her in English because she had forgotten Gujarati.

Amy has become an enigma, a puzzle, a gaping wound in all of our lives. She has walked away from us without an explanation and we don't know why. Although I'd already outgrown our evening storytelling sessions by the time she ran away, I still miss her. I see how the adults miss her on special occasions, how someone mentions her name during a Navroze dinner and how Freny still sends over a gift to Amy's parents on her birthday. I resolve that when I run away from home I will do it in broad daylight and with the blessings of my elders.

Before this minute, I have never entertained the idea of going to America. The few times someone has suggested it to me, I have laughed because my odds of getting there are about as great as my odds of walking on the moon. But then again, I have never before experienced a surge of desire and longing as strong as I am experiencing right this minute. I have never wanted something so badly that it could make the sweat pour down my face, have never had my very eyelids forced back open with ambition and hunger. My heart has never whimpered the way it is doing now, my brain has never before wound itself around the maze of my life and figured a way out. Every cell of my body has never tilted in one direction before, every throb of my blood has never beat in unison, and my body has never tingled with fear and excitement the way it does now. In the middle of a hot Bombay night, surrounded by the snores and breathing of those I love most in the world, I have allowed my treacherous heart to dream of abandoning them all. I have allowed myself to wish for the impossible. And therefore, I must now make it possible.

Dawn approaches and I'm still awake. I know this will not be easy. Even if I manage to convince my family to let me go, even if I can thrust the knife deep into their hearts, there are still a million obstacles – getting an American university to accept me despite my so-so grades, figuring out how to jump through a hundred bureaucratic hoops, filling out countless forms, going around to the various Parsi trusts trying to raise the thousands of dollars to pay for my education.

It is too early in the morning to wake dad up and besides, I need to think about this for a few days before I breathe a word to anybody. But despite all the fears and doubts that are already beginning to settle on me like soot, I remind myself of one truth: When I went to bed last night, I was bitter, washed up, directionless and at the end of my rope – a basket case at twenty. This morning, I have woken up a new person – energetic, purposeful, ambitious. Someone who is looking forward to her life. Someone who cannot be counted out yet.

And only one thing has made the difference:

America.

❖

I'm sorry, Mehroo, for what I'm about to do, for the dagger I will be thrusting into your heart. I have always wanted to protect you but I guess I can't protect you from myself, from this hot blood that flows through my veins, from this heart of desire that sings its songs of longing to me in the middle of the night. I will be your betrayer, your killer, the one whose name will be a permanent wound on your lips.

Forgive me, daddy, for plotting to abandon you, less than five years after you've lost your brother. I know now that I cannot fill his place. I know that more than any of the others, you will understand because where did I learn to dream but in your lap, from where did I learn that happiness is not a four-letter word but from your valiant, if futile, stabs at it? Forgive me, my kind, generous father, for the loneliness I will leave in my wake, like the contrails of a jet plane. I know you will understand but even understanding will not reduce the pain.

I have to turn away from you, Freny, for I cannot look you in the eye. My promise of being a son and a daughter to you, made not too long ago at Babu's funeral – what of it now? Charred it is, from the newly ignited fire of my ambition and longing.

Goodbye, Roshan, you should be pleased to see me go. All the indignities, the unfavourable comparisons that you have suffered all your life should vanish like a plane in the sky, as soon as I am gone. You can be the baby of the family again, you can be the object of all their hopes and desires, your old glory restored, untarnished. I am the thorn in your side – my going away will allow you to bloom.

Sorry, mummy, sorry for a million fights, a million words said and a million left unsaid. I guess I know now that I'll always love you and that I'll never be able to save you. I never wanted it to be this way between us but this is how it is, this is the reality and I must accept, accept, accept it.

Goodbye everybody, here's a kiss from your Judas and a thousand apologies – as Peter Sellers would say – for the confusion, the bewilderment, the hurt, the bruised pride that I will cause. I know this is useless but here's my explanation, here are my reasons why and perhaps you will understand and perhaps you will forgive . . .

Because I am restless and I have reached a dead-end and my future in Bombay seems to lead to just two hellish places: jail or the asylum, and because I want to know what one moment of perfect silence, of a perfect peace, sounds like and because I am torn by paradox – I want to reject this adult role of peacemaker, of being the carrier of other people's grief that has been my role for so long and because I want to be an adult, want to iron my own shirts and clean my own plates and make my own decisions – and because I want to know who I am away from all of you who have made me who I am and because I cannot bear the sound of Mehroo's coughing and mummy's screaming and daddy's subdued silences and because I want to see what the world has to offer before I settle down at *The Times of India* and because I yearn for privacy and freedom, for a room of one's own and I know that none of these will be possible in Bombay, my Bombay of gossip-addicted neighbours and crowded rooms and inquisitive relatives and although nothing in our culture encourages it, I want to discover who I am without the protective shell of your love, I want to taste freedom, I want to meet the Thrity who is not somebody's daughter or niece or cousin, who is not the logical inheritor of a family business, who is not a card-carrying member of the middle-class, who is not fixed in time and place by the accident of her birth. I want to be fluid, like water, like the wind, I want to belong to nobody but myself, I want to belong to no place and everyplace. In my narrow, hard bed on a sweaty, hot Bombay night, I lie with my eyes wide open and dream of inheriting the world.

Do you understand? Or are you offended? I know that by offering understanding, I must risk causing offence. But that is not my intention. I know you are not used to hearing me speak this openly, this candidly, about myself. In our house, we talk of each other – we complain about or declare our love for – each other. We do not begin too many sentences with 'I'. I guess I am breaking all the rules, all the old taboos at one time. I want perfect communication, I want to hurdle over the glassy walls of silence that I've built around myself, I want self-revelation, I want confession, I want therapeutic healing, I want absolution.

Not even a step into America yet, and already I'm sounding like an American.

# Twenty-three

THE IMMIGRATION OFFICER AT THE American Embassy is young, blond, and brash. He has cold blue eyes and sports a goatee whose yellow hairs are made invisible on a face that has been broiled pink by the hot Bombay sun. He and his fellow officers sit behind a thick glass panel that's obviously meant to protect them from the Indian hordes that stand before them, desperate for a visa to the Promised Land.

I watch him as he rejects the visa application of the man in front of him. 'Next,' he calls, already looking past the applicant.

'But, sir,' the man blubbers. 'Only a three-month visa I am wanting. Please sir, show some heart. My brother in New York is very sick and is desperately needing me.'

The American fixes him a cold, hard gaze. 'Everyday at least ten of you fellas have a brother in New York who is sick,' he says. He looks away. 'Next,' he calls impatiently.

A few more people and then it's my turn to face the immigration officer. All the folks in line ahead of me have been lower middle-class, the kind of men more likely to work at menial jobs in Dubai or Kuwait than to go to America for graduate school. Their English is not great, they have oily, badly cut hair and their polyester pants are ill-fitting and worn. They are nervous and this makes them look shifty; they do not exude the understated confidence of upper-class professionals. Instead, they cower before this young S.O.B.; it is obvious that they have never been in the company of a white man before.

I feel a rush of emotions – disgust at the servility of my compatriots; red-hot anger at the arrogance of the American. In that moment, I do not care if I don't get to go to America, do not care if this blond weasel blocks my path on the road that I have been carefully laying for almost a year. I will not be treated with the dismissive contempt with which he is treating the people ahead of me.

We have already stood in line for almost four hours. Every morning, the line for a visa begins to form on the streets outside the embassy gates at Breach Candy. The crowds begin to gather at six a.m., hours before the metal gates swing open, so that by the time we are let in, we are ready to collapse in pools of sweat and anxiety, baked by the mid-morning sun. As if the indignity of waiting on the street is not enough, the local sentries at the embassy have taken on the prejudices of their American masters, so that they talk to the visa applicants in the same disdainful, abrupt manner as the latter.

I have not waited in line as long as some of the others. Dad had sent Kishan, one of the workers from the factory, to stand in as proxy for me at six a.m. Dad, Roshan, and I arrived two hours later and I relieved Kishan while dad and Roshan went back to the car to wait. There was some half-hearted grumbling by those who had been standing in line since dawn but I could tell their heart wasn't in it. After all, they were used to a system where middle-class people like myself always managed to bend the rules enough to suit our purpose. And for all my sensitivity about middle-class privilege, I was not above asserting it when I needed to.

But although my late arrival has spared me many of the indignities that those in line with me had already been subjected to, I am still seething by the time we reach the inner sanctum of the embassy. The whole experience is clearly designed to be demeaning and humiliating, as if the simple act of applying for an American visa is a hazing ritual.

I stare at the young officer, boring holes into him with my eyes. He looks directly at me once, as if he can feel the heat from my eyes but I immediately look away. I shift impatiently from foot to foot, tired of the long wait. To hell with him, and to hell with America and to hell with Ohio State University. If this is how they treat Indians in our own country, imagine what we must face after we get there.

I manage to convince myself that I really don't care if I never reach American shores. At the same time, I am determined not to leave the embassy until I give this man a taste of his own medicine and show him that not all of us are in awe of his pink skin. I feel my face tighten in anger.

The blond man has rejected five visa applications in a row. After dismissing the last applicant, he tilts back in his chair and stretches with his hands behind his head. The middle-aged man ahead of me takes a few steps forward toward the window. Seeing this, the blond man snaps to attention.

'See that blue line?' he barks, pointing to a line painted on the floor. 'You're not to step past it until it's your turn, understand? And I haven't called for you yet.'

The middle-aged man – who is surely a bank clerk and the father of three kids who will all graduate with a commerce degree from a mediocre college – looks chastized and miserable. He smiles weakly to hide his confusion and embarrassment. 'Ah, yes, sir, yes. Right you are. Sorry, so sorry.'

I feel my body go rigid with embarrassment.

The visa officer glares at him for a full second. Then he pushes against his desk, rises from his chair and disappears. The middle-aged transgressor looks around uncertainly, trying to catch someone's eye. We all wait in a state of suspense. Finally, the officer returns, holding a mug of steaming coffee. His face is blank. There is no explanation or apology for his absence. 'Next,' he calls.

The man's application is rejected. That's six in a row. 'Please, sir, let me just explain,' he pleads. 'All my papers are here, sir, everything that you need.'

'You can try again in a few weeks.'

While they argue, I make up my mind. I'm not leaving here without a visa. But I'm doing it on my own terms. I'm going to teach this bastard a thing or two about manners.

'Next.'

I step up to the plate. 'Hi,' I say smartly. 'How are you today? Sounds like you're having a rough morning.' My face is friendly but my eyes are boring into him like bullets.

He looks up from his papers with a start. I notice with satisfaction the surprised confusion on his face. He instinctively picks up on the disconnect between my friendly demeanour and the fact that I hate him but he can't put his finger on it. Also, he is probably not used to Indian women talking to him as a peer.

'Um, I'm fine, thank you,' he says finally. 'How're you?'

'Well, that depends on you, doesn't it?' I throw in a chuckle for good effect. I am talking in my best, upper-middle-class British accent.

Again, that look of surprise. Then he smiles, a pencil-thin smile. 'Right.'

He looks over the various forms I hand him, grunting to himself at times. He is quiet as he flips through the papers, his silence a hole that I try to fill in. 'Boy, it's busy here today,' I say conversationally. 'Is it always this bad?'

I have broken his concentration. 'Yeah,' he says. 'It's a zoo in here.'

'Yeah, it's pretty bad outside, too,' I say. 'Standing in that hot sun for hours. You fellows should really consider letting these folks wait indoors, where it's a little cooler.' My tone is casual, easy, as if I'm a disinterested but genial well-wisher giving him some friendly advice.

He raises his eyebrows a bit. 'Yeah, well. The logistics

of that ... Anyway, I'm just a lowly officer. Not really my call.'

'Oh, well,' I shrug. 'Just a thought.'

He turns back to my papers. 'So your dad's a businessman, huh? What kind of business?'

I tell him. He asks a few more questions. I answer them in a casual, off-hand manner that he's unsure of whether to be offended or charmed by.

'So how'd you pick Ohio State?' he asks.

I gaze at him assessingly, wondering whether to tell him the truth or feed him some bullshit line about OSU's great journalism programme. I decide to level with him. So I tell him about the evening in my living room when I was trying to decide which three American universities to apply to. I had ticked off my first two choices – Columbia University because I knew of its journalism programme and another college in California because – well, because it was California. I had no idea what my third choice ought to be. I scanned the list of journalism programmes in front of me. A Joan Baez record was playing on the stereo. One track ended, another began. Now, Joan was singing, 'Banks of the Ohio.' Just then, my eyes fell on Ohio State University. I looked up to the heavens. It was a sign. I checked off Ohio State as my third choice.

The visa officer lets out an appreciative chuckle. But he is not done with me yet. Finally, he cuts to the chase. 'Look,' he says. 'You're young, obviously bright and well-educated. You speak fluent English. You want to be a journalist. What guarantee do I have that if you get a visa you'll ever return to India?'

This is my moment and I'm up to the challenge. I act slightly nonplussed. 'Are you telling me that people are still settling permanently in America in this day and age?' I say, incredulity dripping from my voice. 'I mean, my God, in my profession there are so many opportunities in India now. There are new magazines getting started almost daily here.'

His face flushes. 'Young lady, you'd be surprised how many people still want to settle in the US,' he says quietly.

'Not me,' I say merrily. 'My whole family's here.'

He stares at me, his blue eyes searching my face like a beam of light. 'Okay,' he says finally. 'You're in. Congratulations.'

I feel a thrill so intense, I feel my heart will burst out of my skin like buttons popping off a shirt. But I force my face to reflect none of this. 'That's great. Thanks,' I say casually.

He looks almost crestfallen, as if he had expected a greater demonstration of thanks. But then he recovers.

'Okay,' he says. 'Enjoy the US of A.' I imagine a twinge of – what? homesickness? pride? sadness? – in his voice.

'I will. Bye, now.' I gather my papers and walk past the long line of applicants, all of them dwelling in their own burrows of dreams and hopes. A few of them reach out and touch me as I walk past, mumbling their congratulations. I do not make eye contact with any of them, fearful of the desperate hope, envy or despair I may see in their faces. I feel my walk get jauntier with each step I take away from the visa official. I clench my papers tightly in my hand. I am going to America, to get a degree in journalism at Ohio State University. Thank you, God, I whisper, thank you, thank you.

I walk out of the dark, cavernous room and step into blinding mid-morning light. The sun falls on me in a warm embrace. Today, it shines only for me. I feel golden.

❖

Dad and Roshan are waiting for me in his car. As they see me approach, dad leaves the car and hurries over to me, with Roshan right at his heels. 'Yes?' he says.

I look serious for a half-second but then my smile burns as bright as the sun. 'I got it,' I say. 'I got the visa.'

The world stops spinning for a moment. The two of them simply look at me, the three of us frozen in space on a busy Bombay street, as cars whiz past us. None of us say a word. They look at me as if they're seeing me for the first time. As if they're seeing me for the last time.

Dad's face has a look I've never seen before. Half of his face is pride, a heaving, chest-bursting pride. The other half reflects the deepest, starkest sorrow I have ever seen. His eyes fill with tears. 'So it's happening,' he whispers almost to himself. 'You're really going to America.'

He smiles and his smile is like the rest of his face – selfless joy battles mightily with a cold loneliness that is already settling in him like snow. His smile is kind, sad, compassionate and stoic.

It dawns on me for the first time that despite his heroic efforts to get me to this point, dad was secretly expecting – hoping? – that this day would never really dawn. From the moment I had told him about my hopes to study in America, he has been my greatest ally – comforting and convincing Mehroo that this was in my best interest; swallowing his wounded pride and letting me apply to the Parsi Panchayat for scholarships; paying for the foreign exchange I need to apply to various American universities; helping me clear every last bureaucratic hurdle. Still, he had not seen this final moment of triumph coming. Or, he had not realized how dreadful this moment that he had wanted so badly for my sake, would actually feel – that it would land like a blow to the stomach, taking his breath away.

In that split second I see the future as he sees it – no young spirit to lighten the gloom that so often descends at home; no daughter to crack a joke and get him out of a bad mood; no buddy with whom to spend an evening walking the sands of Chowpatty Beach; nobody with whom he can impulsively go to Hotel President at midnight to share a pizza. The future rolls out before my dad's eyes like a long, dark carpet. He is standing on that carpet all alone.

Then, he snaps out of it. 'Congratulations, sweetheart,' he says, folding me into a tight embrace. 'The second person in our family to go to the West. May God go with you on this journey.'

I glance at Roshan. Her nose is red, a sure sign of unshed tears. Her face looks small, as if the cold shot of grief has shrunk it. But she, too, takes her cue from my father. 'Best of luck, Thrity,' she says, as if we're already at the airport and I am leaving today.

Dad lets out a deep sigh. 'Let's stop at a public phone and call Mehroo,' he says. 'They must all be going crazy with worry. Then we'll stop at the Taj and take a small chocolate cake home. It's not everyday that one of my daughters,' – glancing at Roshan and me – 'goes to America.'

My moment in the sun, my cheap triumph over the immigration officer, already seems long past. There is a sharp pebble of grief lodged like a blood clot near my heart. I ride in the front seat of the old Ambassador, flanked by Roshan and dad and suddenly, I want to give it all up – those hot, feverish nights of burning ambition, those daydreams of starting afresh and anew, the desire to transform myself, to shed old skin.

Instead, I want to stay right where I am, protected by the presence of those who I love more than life itself, sandwiched between these two, beloved bodies, warm from the frequent affectionate glances they throw my away. Yes, I want to stay in this car and watch my father's beautiful hands as he grips the steering wheel – the rich blue veins, the dark hair against yellow skin, the clean fingernails; I want to sit here forever, holding Roshan's delicate white hands in my callused ones, while the crowds in front of our car part as we approach and the grey-brown Arabian sea sprays its foam on our faces and the Bombay sun bites our skin, leaving rivers of sweat in its wake.

✧

The news gets around the neighbourhood. I tell Jesse myself and watch while the familiar theatre of emotions plays out on her face – her eyes get teary, she bites her lower lip, she swallows hard and finally she grins. 'Well, hooray,' she says, thumping me hard on the back. 'This is what you wanted.'

Neighbours stop by to offer their congratulations. The older ones bring me gifts, write down names of their relatives living in the US whom I should call if I need *anything*, and give me unsolicited advice. ('Now, America is a sick society. I once saw a movie where even grandmothers were carrying big-long rifles. My cousin says that people in New York will shoot you over ten-paise, only. You're not going to New York? Okay, but Ohio is probably no better. Just be careful, hah?' and 'Stay away from those Negroes. All those darkies are liars and cheaters,' and 'Women in America smoke and drink and look and talk just like the men. But you are a nice Parsi girl from a good family. Never forget that. Just say one Ashem Vahu and you will find the strength to face all temptations.')

The younger ones whisper to me how envious they are about my good fortune, confide in me their own dreams of studying in America and ask me for advice. They have the same sad look of longing that Ronnie gets in his eyes when he's begging us to share our tandoori chicken with him. I feel embarrassed and depressed around them.

Everyone at home is treating me carefully, as if I am precious cargo, as if I am as delicate as the bone china teaset that my father had brought home from Japan in 1970. Mummy is nice to me the way she usually is only when I'm sick. A few times, her eyes brim with tears. 'Who will look after me with you gone?' she cries and I feel my heart thaw before her obvious grief.

But if everyone else is tiptoeing around me, Mehroo is more fierce than I've ever seen her. Each chance she gets, she pulls me towards her and hugs me. Everyday she extracts a new promise from me – that I will write to her at least once a week, that I will return home as soon as I receive my degree and that if, God forbid, there should be a war or something while I am away, I will return home immediately. I agree to all her requests because I am in an expansive, generous mood these days and I feel softer and more solicitous towards everybody. Also, I am honestly not sure what my intentions are, whether I myself believe what I'm telling everyone – that I'm going to America to earn a degree that will improve my prospects of getting a good journalism job in India. I think this is what I want but sometimes I ask myself whether an absence of two years will be long enough to accomplish all my other goals, the ones I do not speak out loud to anyone else. Occasionally a thought flits through my mind that says, 'Look at all this clearly, take it all in because you will never return home again,' and then I feel a sadness that is so sharp, that I immediately turn my mind to other, more pleasant things.

Two weeks before I am to set off for America, Jesse puts a copy of Salman Rushdie's *Midnight's Children* into my hands. There is so much to do, so many people to visit and say goodbye to, so much last-minute shopping to do, that I'm not sure I'll have time to read the book before I leave. But I open it to the first page later that evening and read the first intoxicatingly manic opening paragraph and that is my mistake. The children of midnight sing their crazy, seductive hymns, they tug at me with their thousand and one sets of hands, they pull me into their subterranean world. I fall upon the book like a hungry wild beast, unable to tear my eyes away from it.

And while I'm reading, the city that I'm about to leave comes to life before my eyes. But this isn't the filthy, paan-and-piss-covered, inefficient, corrupt city that I have always been taught to be ashamed of. Rushdie's Bombay is grand, operatic, melodramatic, multi-coloured and tethering between magic and madness. It is a mythic city, no less mythic than the places in the Mahabharata but somehow it convinces me that it is through this mythic lens that one sees the real Bombay. How else to explain a city where an old woman earns a living selling four sorry-looking heads of cauliflower a day, than through the lens of surrealism? How else to describe a place where a man makes his living squatting on the sidewalk and removing wax from the ears of his customers? Could even Chagal have painted a street scene where a brown cow leans against a milk booth selling pasteurized milk from the Aaray Milk Colony? Can even Dylan's madcap lyrics capture the bewildering dance of skyscraper and slum, of BMWs and bullock carts, of discos and VD clinics?

*Midnight's Children* introduces me to a Bombay that I grew up in but never lived in. By the simple act of naming the names of familiar streets – Warden Road, Marine Drive – Rushdie rescues me from a lifetime of reading about streets in cities I have never visited and presents to me, like a bouquet of fresh flowers, the city of my birth. And the inexpressible joy of reading a novel full of characters with Indian names liberates me from the dilemma I have unconsciously struggled with ever since that cataclysmic day in fourth grade. And what lovely names they are. Mary Pereria. Saleem Sinai. Homi Catarak. In one glorious moment all my questions about what constitutes an Indian name, and how to create characters without blond hair, are answered.

But the greatest part is the way Rushdie's people talk. Why, they could be any one of us on the school playground or at the market. For the first time in my life, I see myself and the people I love reflected in a book. There is nothing stiff and formal about this English. Rather, this language is as supple and flexible as the cobras the local snakecharmers keep coiled in their wicker baskets. And that wonderful thing that we all do – starting a sentence in English, continuing it in Gujarati and sprinkling a few Hindi words into it – well, I never saw Ernest Hemingway pull *that* off.

*Midnight's Children* makes me want to never leave Bombay. I lament the irony that fate has waited until it is time for me to leave my hometown, for me to see it with loving eyes for the first time. Like meeting your soulmate after you've been told you're only going to live for another three days. I see now that the valour that lies beneath everyday survival in this tough city is no less than the valour that took Robert Jordon to Spain. I realize that caught up as I was in the story of the Oakies' migration to the American West, I never noticed the daily migration from the surrounding villages into the city of Bombay and the millions of stories of individual hope and desperation that accompany each migrant. Caught up as I was in Gatsby's dream of America, I never stopped to ask myself if there was any such thing as an Indian Dream and if so, what it was made up of? Even my notions of India itself were framed by writers such as Foster and Kipling, I realized, and their racist, colonial attitudes infected my blood with the disease of self-hatred. How ironic that I had read Ralph Ellison and Richard Wright without understanding that their journey from out of the shadow of cultural colonialism and into an informed identity, was also my own.

I reluctantly returned Jesse's copy of *Midnight's Children*, feeling as though I was giving away a part of my body. But

I should have known better. The day before I leave for America, Jesse presents me with my own copy. Inside, she has written: 'Soar as high as you feel you can and want to.'

And so I soar. I am flying away from a city that I have recently come to love from the pages of a book. It strikes me that the country that I am about to fly to, I also love only because of what I have read in the pages of a book. Perhaps the reality will be completely different.

But at this moment, I do not care. *Midnight's Children* has heralded in a new dawn. It has given me sight, a new way of seeing an old world. A door had been pushed ajar, never to be shut again. Even as I am packing to leave for the New World, the Old World had reclaimed its place in my heart.

The days pass quickly. There is so much to do – visiting people to say goodbye, shopping for suitcases, buying new clothes, converting money for foreign exchange. A kindly family friend stops by to drop off a heavy, furry, brown winter coat that I immediately know I will never wear. She asks me to try it on for size and I do and she looks so happy when it fits me that I refrain from pointing out that I look like an oversized bear. Visitors have taken to giving me strange things that they think I may somehow put to use – key-chains, hair-bands, antique postcards, frayed woollen scarves. Some of the gifts are practical, others sentimental: Mummy gives me an old, worn British pound that she has saved for God knows how many years, Freny gives me Babu's harmonica, Mehroo hands me a faded picture of my grandfather, dressed in his customary outfit of beige pants, dark brown jacket and a bowler hat.

✧

This is the perfect time to confide in my father, to let him in on my secret. But I am too scared of his reaction.

Five days before I was to apply for my visa, I had received a letter from the chair of the journalism school at Ohio State.

It was a reply to my query of whether I could count on receiving a graduate assistantship once I got to Columbus.

The letter contained bad news. All assistantships for the year had been assigned months earlier, it said … I may qualify for one the following year but it is much too late for this year. And then, the death knell: 'Please do not arrive without securing adequate funding for the entire year.'

Adequate funding for a whole year? After adding up every last loan, scholarship, and every penny that my father can spare, I am leaving for the US with less than four thousand dollars. My out-of-country tuition for fall semester alone will eat up more than half of that amount. I have no idea how much rent, food and other expenses will cost.

So this is where it all ends – with the lack of money. Dad was right after all – within reason, money *is* important. I have been a fool to laugh at him. I remember a ditty Mehroo had made up when I was a kid: No mon, no fun, my son. My face burns with embarrassment at the thought of facing neighbours, friends, relatives, all of whom think I am to leave for America in less than a month's time. I feel bitter, as if life has played this terrible joke on me. To bring me so close to freedom and then to trap me again … I wonder if I'll ever get over this disappointment, whether I will someday rise above it or whether I will let it sour me, so that I'll end up a frustrated, bitter woman, angry at her fate, distrusting of happiness. Bombay is filled with people like this.

The worst part is knowing that this setback will crush my father because he will blame himself for it. Already, he has told me repeatedly about how bad he feels about my having to apply to strangers for loans and scholarships. 'It was always my dream that I would pay for your entire education,' he says. 'I am so sorry that I have failed you this time.' Nothing I say to the contrary makes him feel better. He will be inconsolable once I make the contents of this letter public. He will curse his misfortune, remember every failed business opportunity, apologize to me every chance he gets. He will see himself as the killer of his daughter's dreams.

To hell with it. I will go to America regardless of the letter. The alternative is much too terrible. I will arrive in Columbus and pretend that I never received Prof Decker's letter, blame the irregularities of the Indian mail system. I will go to Columbus and talk my way into an assistantship, make something out of nothing, create opportunity out of thin air. I am my father's daughter, after all. I can do this. I can do this.

I must be very careful now. If mummy comes across this letter during one of her regular snooping-around sessions, that will be the end of this. I mustn't let slip any comment that will arouse suspicion. My family is worried enough about my being this far away. All along, I have assured them that I will find my way once I get there, told them that assistantships are there for the asking at American universities. They must not sense any wavering, any doubts on my part, at this late date.

Best to destroy the letter. I read Dr Decker's brief remarks a few times, committing them to memory. Then, I tear it into tiny pieces. But I can't risk putting the pieces in the garbage. I open the window to my study. The room overlooks a courtyard which the ground floor neighbour gets swept every morning. Making sure that none of the other neighbours are looking, I throw the letter out the window.

I watch until every last piece of my secret flies down two storeys and kisses the ground.

One evening daddy comes home and asks me to go on a drive with him. We park at our usual spot at Nariman Point and then sit on the concrete wall overlooking the water. It is a cool, windy night and the place is filled with couples out on an evening stroll, infants pestering their parents to buy them a balloon from the balloonwalla and old men walking their dogs.

'I want to tell you something,' dad is saying. 'And I want you to remember what I say to you tonight.'

I brace myself for what I think is coming – another lecture about being too impulsive and trusting, the extraction of yet another promise to never drink in public.

But he is saying something quite different. 'You are travelling further than any member of our family has ever travelled,' he says. 'Even I, with all my travels have never been that far. But that is correct – each generation should go further and fly higher than the last. I am allowing you to go because you once told me that it will make you happy to study in America. You remember? Bas, in that moment I made up my mind. Many of my friends are already telling me that I'm mad to let my own child go so far away. But I have always lectured you to have dreams and then to work to realize them. So how can I stop you now? Of course, if even one baal on your head is injured, I will never forgive myself. And when you go, I will lose not only my daughter but my best friend.'

He stops and waits for the lump in his throat to dissolve. I stare wordlessly at the tossing sea, not daring to say a word until I can control my own emotions.

'There is something I want from you,' he continues. 'A promise.'

Here it is. 'Of course, daddy,' I say. 'Anything you want.'

'Okay. I want you to promise me that if you are unhappy after getting there, if someone treats you shabbily or looks at you funny – after all, darling, you know how these Westerners with their superiority complex can look down on us – but if anybody says or does anything to make you feel small, you just come right back to Bombay. Don't worry about air-fare, pride, what people will say – nothing. I will defend you against all that. There is no shame in having tried something and changing your mind. That is not failure.'

I stare at him speechlessly, awed by the fact that in the midst of his own sorrow, in the middle of all the hustle-bustle, he has found time to think about all this.

'Daddy,' I say and then I have to stop. 'Daddy, I ... love you so much. I can't even begin to ...'

He smiles and even though it is dark I see so much kindness and love in his eyes, it takes my breath away. I am not worthy of this, I think. I am not good enough for the love of this man. 'I know, sweetheart,' he says. 'I know.'

I put my arm around his neck. We sit there for the longest time, staring at the water pounding against the black rocks, feeling its spray against our faces. Don't ever let me forget this evening, I whisper to the sea. Don't ever let me forget how loved I am.

The foam on the surface of the black water hisses as it hits the rocks.

# Twenty-four

TIME TO LEAVE FOR THE airport. But how? How to take that first step out of the apartment? This, after all, is the only home I've ever known, the house where I've spent the first twenty-one years of my life. These neighbours who, with their gossip, their nosiness, and their unsolicited advice once made my life so miserable, are also the same people who have showered me with gifts and blessings the last few weeks. Now, although it's eleven p.m., the lights in almost every apartment in the building are still on. They are all staying up to see me off.

'Come on, sweetheart,' dad says for the third time. 'We are already late for the airport.'

Still, I linger. Mehroo ushers me before the small altar that has photographs of Babu and my grandparents. 'Ask them for their blessings,' she says. 'Ask them to watch over you. And come back to us soon, accha?' Overcome by her own words, she hugs me tightly and then starts sobbing softly. I hold on to her. 'It's only two years, Mehroofui,' I say, not believing my own words. 'The time will go by so quickly. And if I can finish my degree even faster than two years, I will.'

Dad walks into the kitchen. 'No tears, no tears,' he says to Mehroo. 'Today is a happy day.' But his voice is hoarse and he must suddenly blow his nose.

It was dad's idea to have a small party earlier this evening. It was a good idea. Having close relatives like Mani aunty and her family over had kept the atmosphere relatively light. As always, I played the bartender, refilling everybody's glasses, pouring myself a stiff drink when no one was looking. Dad had opened a bottle of Johnnie Walker that he had saved for 'a special occasion'. But even the alcohol is not helping me tonight, not giving me the courage to cross the threshold of the apartment and head down the stairs.

Mani aunty comes to my rescue. 'Come on,' she says, with her characteristic blend of faux sternness and humour. 'The sooner we can drop you off at the airport, the sooner we can all go home and sleep. You know me – I need my beauty sleep.'

Everybody laughs more heartily than the joke requires. But things have been set in motion. The two men from the factory who have been squatting on the landing enter the apartment and carry my two suitcases down the stairs. As if some invisible switch has gone on, doors to various apartments fling open and groggy-looking neighbours stand in their doorways. I bend down to kiss Ronnie, my thirteen-year-old golden cocker spaniel, knowing that I may never see him again. 'Bye, Ronnie,' I say. 'You be a good boy, okay? No pulling on your chain when Freny kaki walks you.' He whines and licks my face.

My family gathers around me. Although they are all coming to the airport, it is understood that this will be the only opportunity for unfettered demonstrations of love. And so it is: Long hugs, tight as a pair of jeans. Kisses the size of Kashmiri apples. Promises extracted, like teeth at a dentist's office. Promises to write daily. To call home once a week. To not marry a foreigner. To not develop an accent. To not forget them. To return immediately, by hook or by crook, if there is a war or something, God forbid. To let them know if I need anything, any time. Love pouring like sweat out of their faces. Words, sweet as chocolates, tumbling out of their mouths. What sort of fool walks away from this much love?

We start going down the stairs, dad on my right, his protective arm around my shoulder. I will my shoulders not to shake in grief. At all costs, none of them must know how deeply grief is slashing my body. They must think I am happy, excited to be going. That is the only way this night will be bearable for them.

We stop every few feet to say goodbye to the neighbours. The ones who have known me from the day of my birth, kiss me, hold me close to them, even pinch my cheeks. The newer neighbours shake my hand and say, 'Best of luck.' The older ones bless me, ask me to make my mummy-daddy proud. All of them ask me to never forget them. As if there is any danger of that.

We step into the street. My immediate family piles into the Ambassador. Mani aunty's family follows in their cream Fiat while Jesse and Dinshaw look around for a cab. As we turn the corner, I turn back for one last look at my old apartment building. Before the sun rises on this street this morning, I will be thousands of miles away.

Bombay Airport.

Horns blaring, cars parked illegally, coolies swarming around the vehicles, jostling with each other to earn the right to carry the bulging suitcases of the passengers.

And the crowds. Families of twelve to fifteen people hover round the garlanded traveller. Among the Hindu families, there is much feet touching and head bowing and many blessings conferred.

My own family has grown subdued. Even dad is exhausted from the effort of keeping everybody's spirits from flagging. There is a part of me that wants all this to be over soon because I don't know how much longer any of us can stand this combination of sleeplessness and fatigue and bone-piercing grief. I look around in desperation for

Jesse and Dinshaw. Youth requires reinforcement from other youth.

There they are. Jesse walks up to us in her usual jaunty way, her hands thrust deep into her pant pockets but when she comes closer, I notice that her eyes are red. She has been crying in the cab.

We check in my suitcases, go through the other formalities. Dinshaw suggests we all move to the nearby café and have a drink. He and dad go up to the counter and return armed with Gold Spots and Mangolas and Limcas. We sip our drinks. I can feel everybody's eyes caressing me. When I rest my hand on the Formica top of the table, Freny covers it with her own and squeezes it. 'Thank you, kaki,' I say.

She squeezes even tighter. 'You are my sunshine, my pride and joy,' she whispers. 'Always keep my collar up.'

Jesse comes up to me and hands me an envelope. It says, 'To be read only after seatbelt is safely fastened.' We exchange a glance, a million memories ping-ponging between us. I stuff the letter in my pocket.

There is an oversized clock in the café and every few minutes I glance at it. I have never been this aware of the passing of time. I want to scale the wall where the clock hangs and grab hold of its hand, wrestle with it until it stops its relentless journey forward.

An airport photographer approaches us as we leave the café. Someone decides that there should be a group picture to commemorate this occasion. I groan inwardly. But I allow myself to be gripped by multiple hands and made to stand in the centre, feel all of them shuffle and shift behind me so that we are in the photographer's frame. Everybody is trying to touch me in some way – dad puts his arm around my waist, mummy clings to one arm, Mehroo to the other, and Freny and Roshan stand behind me, a hand on each shoulder. We are a multi-limbed organism, all greedy hands and needy fingers, held together by history and memory and love.

'Say cheese,' the photographer says and half-heartedly we comply. I smile the dead smile of someone trying hard not to look grim. I look grim.

The camera flashes and its fire makes me blink. I am sure my eyes are half-closed in the picture. But perhaps that is appropriate. After all, I am trying to will away the reality of what is going on, what is about to happen.

We move like a funeral procession through the airport until we get to customs. We stop under a huge sign that says, 'Only Ticket Holders Allowed Past This Point'. So it ends here.

I want to say so much, my mouth is full of words to say, words as sweet and rich as the mangoes I used to stuff in my mouth during the summer months. And yet ... what is left to say that I haven't said before? What does it mean to say 'I love you,' to someone moments before you plunge a knife into their heart? I have wanted this moment of emancipation, fantasized about it, salivated over it, would've sold my soul for it. And here it is. All I have to do now is find the strength to walk away from this group of people whose love is the only sure thing in my life. I have chosen this path, created it out of thin air and imagination. Now, it's time to walk it.

I pull myself away from the last embrace and start walking. The airport suddenly seems as large and lonely as a city. I am a cold-blooded killer, there is blood on my hands. I have just committed parricide, destroyed the lives of those who have offered me only love. I have stayed up nights plotting against them, prayed to the gods to deliver me from their clawing needs. And the gods have listened. So why do I have this dead, empty spot inside me?

Each step I take moves me further away from them, creates an ever-expanding galaxy between me and all I know. Even now, I could turn back. It is not too late. I could stand still, not take another step. They would come get me. I have choices. Dad has already told me to rush home if the slightest thing goes wrong. We could get a refund on the tickets. I could stay here, get a job at *The Times of India*.

I keep walking.

I turn around to wave. They are getting smaller and fainter by the second, like the setting sun sinking into the ocean. I feel myself grow large and demon-like with each step. I imagine that everybody at the airport can see the monster inside me, that people will avoid me all my life because this dead spot in my heart will grow, will travel up my bloodstream until it settles in my eyes. That I will always be a half-person, living a half-life because of this unnatural act I am about to commit. I come from a people for whom geography is destiny. My family members have not moved even six blocks from where they were born. Who am I to dare to travel eight thousand miles? Immigration is an unnatural act, an act born out of frustration and yearning. Surely nothing good can come out of such an inauspicious beginning. There is a reason why, for thousands of years, people stayed put. Yes, the history of humankind is also the history of migration but that was different – people moved with their families, their tribes, their villages. This individual taking leave is a twentieth-century phenomenon. There is something non-human about this.

Oh knock it off, cut the bull crap, drop this pseudo-historic shit. The fault lies in you. You're not strong enough to see this through, admit it. Who were you kidding all this time – all the time and money and energy wasted on begging for loans and applying for a visa and getting admitted to a college stupid enough to admit you – all this effort and now, at the moment of reckoning you can't see it through.

So end this masquerade right now, run back into their waiting arms and tell them you can't do it. Slam the door shut on dreams of learning how to do your own laundry and staying out late at night and being independent. Trade in vague, abstract notions of freedom for guaranteed love. Come on, throw in the towel. You always were a quitter anyway, nobody will be too surprised.

God forgive me, I keep walking. I am approaching a corner and once I turn this corner, my people will disappear from my view. And if they disappear, they, who are all I know, will I disappear too? Will I recognize myself, without the old signposts?

✧

I look back one last time. And see my dad hurrying toward me. He has struck gold again. With his sweet, trustworthy face and quiet dignity, he has charmed the security guards into letting him accompany me as far as he can. 'I told them you had a sprained wrist and needed help with your carry-on bag,' he whispers. 'They gave me security clearance.' We share a quick chuckle. The smooth businessman with the honeyed voice has triumphed once again.

Dad takes my bag from me and puts his other arm around my shoulder. We stand side by side as I turn around and wave to the entire family. They wave back frantically. Then we're around the corner, dad and I.

But not for long. 'Dad, stay here a minute,' I say. 'I have an idea. I'll be back in two minutes, tops.' Leaving my bag with him, I sprint back to where the rest of the family is waiting. Even from this distance, I can sense their amazement and delight. I feel a little embarrassed at prolonging this melodrama but I can't help myself. I run faster. 'What is it, Thritu? What did you forget?' Freny asks but I head straight for Mehroo and grab her in a hug. 'You see how quickly I came back?' I say, a little out of breath. 'Just when you thought you wouldn't see me any more, correct? See how quickly things can change? Well, that's how it's going to be. The two years will fly by and I'll be back before you can say hello-goodbye. See?' I stand beaming at her, as if I've just proven some brilliant and complex scientific experiment.

All of them chuckle. 'Correct,' says Jimmy uncle, Mani's husband. He smiles at me appreciatively. 'Cent per cent correct.'

I catch Jesse's eye. She gives me a quizzical look but I can tell that even she is pleased. When I take my leave this time, the mood seems lighter. Now that I've made this minor miracle happen, other miracles suddenly seem possible. They let me go this time as if expecting me to return to them over and over again.

Dad is waiting for me. 'For a second I thought you'd changed your mind and I'd have to get on that plane in your place,' he jokes. He, too, is pleased by my impulsive sprint halfway across the airport.

But my job is not over. 'Daddy, listen,' I say urgently. 'Don't let the mood at home get too sad, okay? In fact, tomorrow morning when you all wake up, take everybody out for a morning drive or something. Just get through the first few days. After that...'

'Thrituma, it is my responsibility to take care of all of them,' he interrupts. 'Your job is to go to America with a free and open mind, study hard, shine in your studies and make a name for yourself. Now promise me, no thoughts of home at all. I will manage everything at this end.'

We smile at each other.

As we walk toward the boarding lounge, I catch a glimpse of the two of us reflected in a glass door. We both have crooked noses and we both walk on our toes. The observation makes me unreasonably happy. I sneak a glance at my father and will myself to memorize his face – the wide forehead, the gentle, brown eyes, the big Parsi nose, the sensual lips. A friend of mine had once observed that even when dad took Ronnie for a walk, he carried himself like an admiral in a military parade and watching him now – straight backed and dignified – I smile to myself ... Good old dad.

The plane is late. 'Bombay,' dad sighs and there is a lifetime of love and hate in that one word. But we are glad about the delay because it gives us a few more minutes together.

Finally, the dreaded announcement. We linger in the lounge, allowing all the other passengers to board. Dad actually talks his way into walking me right up to the entrance of the plane. Then, he takes my hand and simply holds it to his chest for a minute. I kiss his hand. He has beautiful hands, the hands of a kindly country doctor. Mine are younger, darker, smaller versions of his. I tell him that when I miss him, I will gaze at my hands and know that he is right by my side. He smiles. I know he will remember that comment, that it will keep him warm on those silent mornings when he wakes up and realizes that I am gone. I want to say other warm and comforting things to him but a cold numbness, a hazy forgetfulness, is settling like mist on my brain. Besides, the stewardess is boring holes into us with her frosty smile.

It is time to enter the open mouth of the steel monster. We hug one last time. I slap him on the shoulder. 'See you soon,' I say.

He nods. 'Look after yourself, sweetheart,' he whispers. 'For my sake.'

❖

The cold, synthetic blast of the air-conditioner hits me immediately. Already, the air smells different – not the loamy, sweaty smell of India but the affluent, cool scent of what I imagine America will smell like. I stare out of the small aeroplane window at the lights of Bombay and begin to sob. My entire family is still in this building that I can almost touch (I know they will stay until the plane takes off) and yet they might as well be a million miles away. I keep looking out the window the whole time because I do not want the kindly middle-aged Britisher sitting next to me to see me cry. I suddenly feel terribly young and scared.

The plane is beginning to crawl down the runway. To distract myself, I lean back in the seat and start to read Jesse's letter.

It is just as well that I have my seatbelt on. It is just as well that the plane is taxiing fast and the lights of the city are beginning to seem as distant as childhood. It is just as well that the door is shut and there is a tall, sturdy Englishman in the seat next to me, blocking my way.

It is a marvellous letter – one that holds me close and yet nudges me away; that sings to me the wonders of flight as well as the importance of rootedness; that speaks of love and then defines love as the courage to let go. 'You will never be far away because you live on my skin,' Jesse has written and reading that line, I wish I could fly like dust and settle on her skin.

The plane gathers speed. I hear the whine of the engines and clench the arm-rest, preparing myself for the queasy feeling in my stomach as we take flight. In another second, I will be one of the sky people I've always dreamed of being. The lights of the runway are fading into a blur and now, I am rising – rising like hope, rising like the prayers that are undoubtedly on the lips of all the family members I have left on the ground. Bombay is underneath me, faint as a memory, distant as love.

And then, I am gone.

## About the author

## About the book

Insights,
Interviews
& More...

## Read on

# Meet Thrity Umrigar

Noshir Umrigar

THE FIRST WRITING I ever did was the anonymous poems I wrote to my parents when I was angry at them and fuming over some perceived injustice. I must've been five or six years old then. I'd wait until the coast was clear and then dart into their bedroom and stick these anonymous poems on the door of the teakwood wardrobe my dad had built. To my amazement, and despite my best attempts at concealment, my parents always figured out the identity of the author. I thought they were geniuses. To my chagrin, the poems seemed to amuse them rather than convince them of the errors of their ways.

Looking back, it seems to me that my reasons for writing have not changed since those early days. Now, like then, I write for two reasons: one, to express my deepest feelings about something, and two, to protest some outrage or injustice.

By the time I was seven, I knew I wanted to be a writer. But I didn't have the guts to say out loud—or even to myself—that I wanted to write books. A brown-skinned kid in Bombay wanting to be a writer? I may as well have said I wanted to be a Broadway actress. Then someone told me that people who wrote for newspapers such as *The Times of India* (whose stately stone building with the printing press at street level I loved driving by) were called journalists. So that's what I went around saying I wanted to be when I grew up. It seemed safer than saying I wanted to be a writer. And indeed, a journalist is what I grew up to be.

I worked as a daily reporter for seventeen years. And as I wasn't writing literature, I tried to infuse my newspaper articles with as much literary flavor as I could get away with. I gravitated toward magazine-style stories—stories about human beings, not sources; stories with complexity, with shades of gray; stories that challenged the conventional wisdom. The same ▶

> " I worked as a daily reporter for seventeen years [and] tried to infuse my newspaper articles with as much literary flavor as I could get away with. "

themes that I later explored in fiction—how power twists and corrupts human relationships, the gap between the haves and the have-nots, the transformative power of love—I tried to explore within the confines of daily journalism.

At times, I succeeded. My two favorite stories were both long-term projects that took topical issues and put a human face on them. The first story was about a single mother on welfare raising two children. I wanted to understand the nagging, demeaning aspect of poverty—how it takes all the spontaneity out of life, how it makes you agonize over the smallest decisions—and then explain this to my readers. For this, I needed to witness poverty, and the choices it forces people to make, up close. I moved in with the woman's family for a week and told their story in journal form, day by day, as it unfolded.

The second story was about a young couple who had given birth to a perilously premature baby. Technology now makes such births possible, but many moral, ethical, economic, and medical issues remain unresolved. But what fascinated me most was the grace with which this couple faced the challenges before them. Watching them come close to their breaking point and then, somehow, rise to the occasion again, sustained only by their love for each other and their belief in their baby, was an awe-inspiring experience for me. I reported that story for four months, from the moment of the baby's birth to that incredible day, four months later, when he left the hospital.

So you see why the leap from journalism to fiction doesn't seem all that huge. What matters most to me is the human heart that beats at the center of all great stories. When I look back on my writing life, I see that the vehicles may be different— poems, short stories, newspaper articles, novels—but the passengers remain the same. The passengers are always grappling with the darkness and trying to find the light; they are often inchoate and inarticulate but fumbling toward greater human communication; and they are almost always held together by that shaft of grace that we call love. ❧

66 When I look back on my writing life, I see that the vehicles may be different— poems, short stories, newspaper articles, novels— but the passengers remain the same. The passengers are always grappling with the darkness and trying to find the light. 99

# Return to Bombay

I WRITE THIS from a fourteenth-floor hospital room in Bombay, where I am nursing my father back to health. Outside the window, the city sprawls in the afternoon sunlight—the shabby, squat buildings up close, relics of the old Bombay, and in the distance, the tall, thin towers that are springing up daily, testimonials to the new, booming India, or, as the newspapers call it, India Inc.

This disparity between old and new, past and present, has followed me into my own life on this trip. Although I have frequently returned to India since moving to America twenty-five years ago, this is the longest I've been back. And some days, I feel light-years removed from the gawky, hypersensitive kid who left home all those years ago. I have never felt more American than I do on this trip, and the bewildered, puzzled looks I get from the nurses and doctors confirm to me that my accent, my manner of dress, and perhaps even the confident, assertive way in which I carry myself have made me an oddity, a stranger in the country of my birth. Just last night I was met with a blank look and dead silence when I asked a nurse

66 I have never felt more American than I do on this trip . . . a stranger in the country of my birth. 99

if my dad was still hooked up to the pain pump until an old friend intervened and "translated" for me, asking the nurse if he was *connected* to the machine. Finally, a look of understanding crossed her face.

But in other ways, I have become a child and a teenager with an alacrity that is alarming. Stepping into that old childhood apartment unleashes such a torrent of memories that to call them memories—with the word's implication of unearthing something from the past—feels inaccurate. What I feel is something so alive and active, as if the past had never really receded into the shadows but was simply waiting and was now making its presence felt again. Harsh words still have the power to destroy; a walk along the sea with "Jesse" still has the power to exhilarate. Dinners with old friends are still giddy, fun affairs even though it is sobering to realize that they now have children older than we were when we met. The nasally cry of the *bhelpuri* vendor still triggers a visceral response even though it's a new vendor and not the old Pathan who used to ring our doorbell at 4 p.m. every Sunday. The servants have changed—"Kamala" has long since ceased to work for ▶

> ❝ The servants have changed—'Kamala' has long since ceased to work for us—but the heartbreaking stories of their personal lives, filled with the premature loss of children and husbands, remain frighteningly constant. ❞

**Return to Bombay** *(continued)*

us—but the heartbreaking stories of their personal lives, filled with the premature loss of children and husbands, remain frighteningly constant. There is so much pain that the poor of this city carry in their hearts that even literature cannot do their suffering justice. And yet with what aplomb and humor and decency they live their lives! Last week, I accidentally gave a taxi driver a five hundred rupee note instead of a fifty—and he laughed at my stupidity as he pointed out my mistake to me. Such integrity from a man who probably earns roughly that much in a day. For all its corruption, bureaucracy, and insanities, Bombay is a city that can redeem your faith in human nature and human resiliency.

And yet, there's so much in this city that I wanted to escape as a child. Being here now, I remember the fervor—no, the desperation—with which I read books and listened to music. Books were more than a refuge; they were an escape from the reality of my life. As a teenager, I lived so much in the world created from my imagination that when the time came, it wasn't as much of a leap to leave the "real" city in which I was born. A few days ago, I walked to the pharmacy while listening to my iPod. Springsteen sang into my ear, and instead of seeing the shabby, rundown city around me, there I was, getting ready to meet him in Atlantic City. It struck me that this is what books had done for me a few decades earlier—changed the foreground and background scenery, transported me away from the world as it was and into the world as I'd wanted it to be.

Today, I marvel at the ingenuity— even the cunning—of the teenager who plotted her way out and her improbable journey to America. And what a richly satisfying journey that has been.

Oh, the stories I could tell you. ∽

*February 2008*

> " Today, I marvel at the ingenuity—even the cunning— of the teenager who plotted her way out and her improbable journey to America. "

# Excerpt:
# *If Today Be Sweet*

### Prologue

Already, I am not here. It is happening. Already she cannot sense my presence in the room, cannot feel the final kiss that I place on her forehead. This is how it should be. And I am not sad, I am not diminished by this. Rather, I am proud. I have done my part. After all, it was my push, my prodding, that finally got her off the fence. All the months of fussing and fretting, of torment and worry, are now behind her. I can see it in her face, the relief of resolution. It is in her walk, in her posture, in the angle of her head. Once again, she is the woman I loved, the woman whom I married. She has always looked deceptively fragile and God knows she is sensitive as a sparrow, but inside, inside, she is tough as nails. That's what I've always been in love with—that strength, that inner compass that has steered her through so many storms. After all, she took care of my cranky old mother until the day she died, didn't she? And if she could have survived dealing with mamma, why, she could survive anything. That's

> ❝ She has always looked deceptively fragile and God knows she is sensitive as a sparrow, but inside, inside, she is tough as nails. ❞

what I kept telling myself during
the first awful months. That my wife
was a survivor. That she would find
her way in the world without me.

Still, I cannot tell a lie: It is good
being here. I miss them all—my
dearest wife, my son, my daughter-
in-law, and my precious little
grandson. Even all the others
gathered here to usher in the new
year. If I could figure out how to do
it, I'd have one of them pour me a
good, stiff Scotch. And pop one of
my wife's kebabs into my mouth.
But this is not my place. I do not
belong here anymore. The new year
is not mine to celebrate, to bring in.
And just when the loneliness seems
unbearable, I look at my son's face.
At his eyes. They are searching the
room. Even while he's putting
a lamb kebab into his mouth,
even while he's sipping his wine,
whispering in his wife's ear, slapping
his best friend on the back, while
he's doing all these things, he is
searching the room. He is looking
for me. He is missing me. I have
to turn away from the grief I see
on that beloved face. I long to run
my fingers across that face one
more time. What is it about these
humans—and here I ask myself,
am I still human?—that injects
this string of sadness during the ▸

happiest of occasions? And so, despite my best intentions, I find myself interfering one more time. Slowly, gently, I turn my son's chin until his eyes come to rest upon his son. My grandson. Seven years old and as beautiful as the world itself. I see the fog of incomprehension and grief lift from my son's eyes. They become clear and focused again as they rest on what he has created. And he sees what I see— he sees some outline of my visage inn his son's face. Even though I am—was—an ugly, wrinkled son of a bitch, he sees something of me in my grandson's unblemished, unlined face. I see it, too. Not only that, I see my father's face—the pointed nose, the alert eyes—in the boy's face. Isn't that something? My old man from Udwada, dead for twenty years, playing peekaboo from behind the face of a sandy-haired, light-skinned boy in America. And then I have to wonder—how dead can I really be, as long as my son and grandson exist? I wish I had thought of saying that to my wife earlier today. It would have cheered her up, given her something to hold on to.

But this is just vanity. The

nonsensical thoughts of a self-indulgent dead man. The fact is that my beloved doesn't need me to point any such profundities to her anymore. She is the architect of her own life. An hour from now, she will approach my—our—her—son and tell him her decision. He will be surprised, shocked even, but he will accept it. And soon, he will be proud of her, proud of her independence, of her determination, of her sheer instinct for survival. He will learn, as I did, to see past her tiny, 115-pound body and notice instead the iron will, the strong moral compass, the roaring of a giant.

I am—I was—Rustom Sethna and I was married to a woman who was a fool. A woman who so adored me, who so relied on my strength that she forgot to measure her own worth, who never knew she carried the world, my world, in the palm of her hand.

But this is not my story. I am done here. This is now her tale. It is she who will carry it forward, take it into the new year.

I have done my part to help shape her story. And for that, I am proud. But it was she who crafted the final chapter and there was no ▶

66 I was married to a woman who was a fool. A woman who so adored me, who so relied on my strength that she forgot to measure her own worth. . . . 99

ghost-writer—pardon the pun, I am, after all, a Parsi gentleman and bad puns are mother's milk to us—to help her with that.

Yes, there was a time when my beloved sat dithering, unable to make up her mind, and yes, I grew impatient and gave her the bloody push that made her get off the damn fence. But the free fall, the blind drop, the beautiful flight into her new future, why, that was all her own. ∿

# Have You Read?
## More by Thrity Umrigar

Tehmina Sethna's beloved husband died this past year, and she is visiting her son, Sorab, in his suburban Ohio home. Now Tehmina is being asked to choose between her old, familiar life in India and a new one in Ohio with her son, his American wife, and their child. She must decide whether to leave the comforting landscape of her native India for the strange rituals of life in a new country.

This is a journey Tehmina, a middle-aged Parsi woman, must travel alone.

The Parsis were let into India almost a millennium ago because of their promise to "sweeten" and enrich the lives of the people in their adopted country. This is an ancient promise that Tehmina takes seriously. And so, while faced with the larger choice of whether to stay in America or not, Tehmina is also confronted with another, more urgent choice: whether to live in America as a stranger or as a citizen. Citizenship implies connection, participation, and involvement. Soon destiny beckons in the form of two young, troubled children next door. It is the plight of these two boys that forces Tehmina to choose. She will either straddle two worlds forever and live in a no-man's-land or jump into the fullness of her new life in America.

*If Today Be Sweet* is a novel that celebrates family and community. It is an honest but affectionate look at contemporary America—the sterility of its suburban life, the tinsel of its celebrity culture, but also the generosity of its people and their thirst for connection and communication. Eloquently written, evocative, and unforgettable, *If Today Be Sweet* is a poignant look at issues of immigration, identity, family life, and hope. It is a novel that shows how cultures can collide and become better for it.

"Umrigar has undertaken to show us the cultural divide between Indian and American cultures. . . . She makes an interesting point, one she's mentioned in other works: We make up our own families wherever we are; we choose our circumstances; we are capable of being heroes anywhere."
—*Washington Post*

> "A convincing testament to the enduring power of place."
> —*Kirkus Reviews*

### THE SPACE BETWEEN US

Poignant, evocative, and unforgettable, *The Space Between Us* is an intimate portrait of a distant yet familiar world. Set in modern-day India, it is the story of two compelling and achingly real women: Sera Dubash, an upper-middle-class Parsi housewife whose opulent surroundings hide the shame and disappointment of her abusive marriage, and Bhima, a stoic illiterate hardened by a life of despair and loss, who has worked in the Dubash household for more than twenty years. A powerful and perceptive literary masterwork, author Thrity Umrigar's extraordinary novel demonstrates how the lives of the rich and poor are intrinsically connected yet vastly removed from each other, and how the strong bonds of womanhood are eternally opposed by the divisions of class and culture.

> "[*The Space Between Us*] is a great book; I love it. . . . I couldn't stop reading until Bhima had her

amazing epiphany of freedom at
the edge of the sea. I am so happy
for Thrity Umrigar! And proud
of her as a woman, too. . . . It is
so precious to have a book about
a woman one rarely even 'sees'
in society, whether Indian or
American."

—Alice Walker

"Umrigar is a perceptive and often
piercing writer. . . . Her portrait
of Sera as a woman unable to
transcend her middle-class skin
feels bracingly honest."

—*New York Times Book Review*

**D**on't miss the next
book by your favorite
author. Sign up now for
AuthorTracker by visiting
www.AuthorTracker.com.